# THE CHANGING WORLD OF OIL: AN ANALYSIS OF CORPORATE CHANGE AND ADAPTATION

# The Changing World of Oil: An Analysis of Corporate Change and Adaptation

*Edited by*
**JEROME DAVIS**
*Dalhousie University, Canada*

## ASHGATE

Published by
Ashgate Publishing Limited
Gower House
Croft Road
Aldershot
Hampshire GU11 3HR
England

Ashgate Publishing Company
Suite 420
101 Cherry Street
Burlington, VT 05401-4405
USA

Ashgate website: http://www.ashgate.com

**British Library Cataloguing in Publication Data**
The changing world of oil : an analysis of corporate change
   and adaptation
   1. Petroleum industry and trade 2. Organizational change
   I. Davis, Jerome
   338.2'7282

**Library of Congress Cataloging-in-Publication Data**
The changing world of oil : an analysis of corporate change and adaptation / edited by Jerome Davis.
        p. cm.
   Includes index.
   ISBN 978-0-7546-4178-3
   1. Petroleum industry and trade. 2. Petroleum industry and trade--Management. 3. Organizational change. I. Davis, Jerome D.

   HD9560.5.C463.2005
   338.2'7282--dc22                                                    2005028888

ISBN 978-0-7546-4178-3

Reprinted 2007

Printed and bound in Great Britain by MPG Books Ltd, Bodmin, Cornwall

# Contents

# List of Figures and Tables

## Figures

## Tables

# List of Contributors

**Jerome Davis** is currently the Canadian Research Chair (Oil and Natural Gas Policy) at Dalhousie University, Halifax, Nova Scotia. He has previously been consecutively Professor of Public Economics and Policy (1984–1998) and Professor of Business Economics (2001–2004) at Roskilde University, Denmark, and Visiting Professor International Business Economics (Copenhagen Business School, 1998–2001). He was also a Visiting Scholar at the Oxford Institute for Energy Studies (1988) and has served as the outside board member of the Petro and Petropol research initiatives, the Norwegian Research Council, 1992–2000. He holds an MA and PhD both from the Johns Hopkins University SAIS.

**Magne Emhjellen** is currently a Senior Commercial Advisor in the Norwegian oil company Petoro AS. He came from the position as Associate Professor, Department of Economics and Business Administration at Stavanger University (2000–2002). In the period 1988–90 and 1992–2000 he held various commercial and management positions in Statoil AS (Norwegian oil company). In the period 1990–1992 he was a financial analyst in Orkla Finance AS. He holds a Doctor of Philosophy (PhD) degree in Economics from the University of New South Wales, Sydney, Australia (1999).

**Morten Halleraker** has a Master of Science and a Cand. Oecon degree from the Norwegian School of Economics and Business Administration. He has worked as Special Auditor and Advisor at the Norwegian Oil Taxation Office, and as Business Controller and Head of Economic Analysis in Hydro Oil and Energy. Halleraker is currently Director Strategy for Hydro Aluminium Extrusion, operating out of Lausanne, Switzerland.

**Flemming Helgeland** has a Master of Science degree from Norwegian School of Economics and Business Administration. He is Finance Director in Chevron Texaco, Brazil. Former positions are Manager of Planning, Budgets and Financial Analysis, Chevron Texaco, Southern Africa (Angola); Director of Finance, Chevron Norway; General Manager Finance, Saga Petroleum UK, and Finance Manager, Whitecliff ASA.

**Ola Kvaløy** is Associate Professor of Economics at the University of Stavanger. He has a PhD from the Norwegian School of Economics and Business Administration (NHH) in Bergen. In 2002 he was Visiting Scholar at Scancor, Stanford University.

**Klaus Mohn** is a senior adviser and head of the CEO's office at Statoil, the largest Norwegian oil and gas company. He holds a Cand. Oecon. degree (economics) from the Norwegian School of Economics and Business Administration (1991). From 1991 to 1994 he worked as a research fellow at Statistics Norway, and from 1994 to 1996, he was a senior economist with the largest Norwegian investment bank (DnB Markets). Mohn joined Statoil in 1997 as a senior economist, and joined the CEO's office in 2000.

**Øystein Noreng** is the holder of the TotalFinaElf Chair in Petroleum Economics and Management and Program Director of the MSc Program in Energy Economics and Management at the Norwegian School of Management. He has degrees in history and economics in addition to an MA in political science (University of Oslo) and PhD in political science (University of Paris-Sorbonne). In 2002 he was an Adjunct Research Fellow at the Center for Energy, Marine, Transportation, and Public Policy at Columbia University.

**Petter Osmundsen** is Professor of Petroleum Economics at Stavanger University College, where he is head of the Section of Petroleum Economics in the Department of Industrial Economics and Risk Management. He has a PhD from the Norwegian School of Economics and Business Administration (NHH) in Bergen. In 1992–93 he was a Research Fellow at the Massachusetts Institute of Technology and at Harvard University. He has previously held positions as Associate Professor at NHH and Research Manager at the NHH affiliated Institute for Research in Economics and Business Administration (SNF), and still holds a position as an Adjunct Scientific Adviser in the latter organisation.

**Charles Stabell** is Professor of Strategy at the Norwegian School of Management. He is currently on leave with GeoKnowledge. He has a PhD in Management from the Sloan School of Management, Massachusetts Institute of Technology.

**Arne Wiig** is an economist and Research Director at the Chr. Michelsen Institute, Bergen. He took his PhDat the Norwegian School of Economics and Business Administration (NHH) in Bergen, 1995. He worked as a visiting fellow at the Namibian Policy Research Unit in 1997–98.

# Preface

In 1970, the Seven Sisters and the French Compagnie Française des Petroles (CFP) accounted for about 81 percent of all crude oil produced in the world. Today, the so-called super majors, largely the reconstituted Seven Sisters and CFP, produce less than 12 percent of the total. Thus while an analysis of the world of oil in 1970 could focus on the Seven Sisters as essentially constituting the 'world of oil', an analysis of the super majors today, the primary focus of this volume, while perhaps less complete, is not less important. The changing role of the super major 'stars' in our analysis, together with their 'planets', the major 'Independents', explains how much things have changed in the past thirty-five years. This involves a somewhat different focus than is currently prevalent, a focus on the Brent and WTI futures markets, on OPEC quotas, and arbitrary producer government behaviour. Nonetheless, an understanding of what has happened to the West's oil industry is critical to an understanding of the forces shaping change in the world's oil markets.

This book, *The Changing World of Oil: An Analysis of Corporate Change and Adaptation,* is the third of three volumes based on research performed under the auspices of the Petropol Research Program, a Norwegian Research Council initiative. The two other volumes are *Oil in the Gulf* (published by Ashgate in 2004) and *Petroleum Industry Regulation within Stable States* (2005). The Petropol Research Program, a government/industry jointly funded initiative, started in 1996, is the latest in a series of Norwegian social science research efforts concerned with the policy making challenges presented to both government and industry by changes in the world of oil. The program's foci are wide ranging: internationalization and industrial restructuring, the impact of geopolitical, national and cultural factors on the industry, the impact of human rights and democratization on corporate strategy and policy are but a few of the areas of research. While the primary objective of the program is to maintain and extend the knowledge base of the Norwegian social science research community working on petroleum-related issues, many of its research findings are of interest to a wider audience; hence the publication of these volumes by Ashgate.

I thank the Norwegian Research Council for its financial support, our contributors for their unstinting efforts, and the series editor, Professor Helge Hveem and publishing coordinator, Maja Arnestad, for their efforts on our behalf. Finally I am very grateful to our Ashgate editors, Brendan George and Carolyn Court, for their patience and support in helping us to complete this volume.

*Jerome Davis*
*Halifax, Nova Scotia and Copenhagen, Denmark*

# Chapter 1

# 'And then there were four …'
# A Thumbnail History of Oil Industry
# Restructuring, 1971–2005

Jerome Davis

## Introduction

The dilemma of the global economy with regard to its most controversial (if not most important) energy source, that of oil, might be compared to that of several riparian nation states with a major river flowing through their several territories. Like the flow of oil, the flow of the river is a blessing. Without it, national economies would be deprived of water for drinking, agricultural irrigation, hydroelectric generation, industrial and recreational purposes as well as a major means of commercial transport. Like oil, the river is also a curse. Its flow is inconstant. In drought years, the supply of water falls; in other years, floods can take their toll, leaving death and destruction in their wake. It can become polluted, causing both health and economic problems for its users.

These vicissitudes lead to varying responses. The riparian states attempt to tame the river, building dams, levies, and canals to regulate or divert its flow. Utilisation of its waters leads to various pricing policies, favouring some users – often but not always farmers using river waters for irrigation – and discriminating against others. Users of the river attempt to insure themselves and their property against future flood damage. Various national policies impact on one another. Water pricing in one riparian state could affect the supply of water for other downstream states. An upriver nation will affect the welfare of the downstream nations through building a dam, for example. At its worst, interfering with river flow can be a *casus belli* leading to international conflict and even war.

Most importantly, however, the river continues its flow, day-by-day, year-by-year. River users get used to its daily flow, its annual variations. They let their insurance policies lapse, their levies fall into disrepair. The river is not a topic of conversation. Then, suddenly, things change: An upstream nation builds a dam severely reducing the value of the riparian rights of the downstream users. A severe winter causes flooding and widespread devastation – an international or regional catastrophe. Suddenly, the river is in the headlines throughout our little riparian world, with calls for political action, for economic relief, and accusations of policy failure.

The political economy of oil and gas, much like the riverine analogy above, is characterised by vicissitudes. Oil and gas are resources which one intermittently takes for granted, at other times are the focus of intense political economic controversy. As in our riparian analogy, nation states undertake policies to solve the problems of supply and demand. Rather than building dams and levies, nations acquire oil stocks to tide them over in periods of shortage, or to utilise in order to push OPEC oil prices down. They attempt to diversify away from a dependence on oil products. Often they possess privately or state-owned oil firms, 'national champions' whose existence is to 'guarantee' access to oil and gas resources; they furthermore have a wide range of policies either to diversify away from oil and gas, or to favour initiatives which reduce the impact of dislocations within the world of oil, as, for example, tax and other incentives to encourage national refinery construction or the exploration for national oil and gas resources. That these policies succeed or not is not really revealed until a crisis strikes – but when a crisis hits, be it in terms of too high (or too low) crude oil prices, in terms of an OPEC induced oil shortage, or in terms of a larger political economic conflict – much as in the case of Iraq and Iran in the late 1970s or Iraq in 1990 and 2003 – the vulnerabilities of the system come to the fore with consequent results.

Yet there is one non-obvious aspect of our riverine analogy. The river in our example is always changing, silting up in one area, carving a new channel in another. To a degree these changes may be induced by mankind – the building of a dam can alter the pattern of a river's silting. To a degree, these changes are caused by the flow of the river itself. Thus, each major flooding disaster is in some degree different from the others. Similarly, much as in the case of our river, various oil crises will also differ from each other. Here too, the crises will differ because what might be termed the 'oil system' is changing, often imperceptibly, as well. Oil provinces mature and deplete. Oil consumption rises and falls. Refineries age and are retired. Economic agents switch to other fuels. Oil markets change, often imperceptibly. Thus much as no two river flooding disasters are exactly the same, no two oil crises are identical.

This book focuses on a group of economic agents who have at the same time been affected by oil industry change and contributed themselves to that change – the oil multinationals themselves.

This book has two purposes:firstly …firstly, it analyses the nature of oil industry change. How is the modern oil company adapting to changing circumstances? What new modes of behaviour are emerging? And what do present trends portend for the future? To this end the various contributors have utilised some of the latest insights from what might be termed the new theory of the firm.

Secondly, this book attempts to address the political economic consequences of oil industry change. Given the fact that the oil industry is changing, how does that change impact on the political economic environment, both nationally and internationally?

It is perhaps equally important to state what this book is not about. The book takes its point of departure in 1971, the year of the Tehran-Tripoli agreements in which OPEC usurped oil MNE control of crude prices. Analyses of the period to 1971 are many: Adelman, 1972, Penrose, 1968, Yergin, 1992, Blair, 1976, de Chazeau and Jahn, 1959, to mention but a few of the more prominent analyses.

What is focused upon in this context is the nature of oil MNE organisational change and its consequences post 1971, a topic which is perhaps less thoroughly researched (although, see Bindeman, 1999, for a recent review of this literature).

This is the fascinating story of how large international oil companies have had to cope with a constantly changing environment, an environment characterised by wildly fluctuating crude oil prices, changing demand, and the continual encroachment of new state owned national entrants into the markets, on the one hand, and how changes in the industry present new challenges for consumers, nation states, and the international economy.

### 'And then there were four...' Causes of oil industry change – a brief introduction

Prior to 1971, the largest oil multinationals dominated the world of oil. Variously termed the 'Seven Sisters' – a list often expanded to include an eighth member, the Compagnie Francaise des Petroles – or the 'Majors', these firms topped the list of *Fortune Magazine*'s 100 largest multinationals. Much as the stars of our own galaxy, these firms seemed fixed for eternity. Men live, men die. Nations rise and fall. Big Oil was destined to live forever.

What has happened since 1971? Table 1.1 below gives a superficial impression of the changes which in fact occurred in the period between 1971 and the year 2000. A quick glance at Table 1.1 shows the reader that of the Seven Sisters which dominated the oil industry in 1970, only four remain. Gulf Oil, a mastodon based in Pittsburgh, USA, has simply disappeared from the firmament, having been acquired by Chevron in the mid 1980s. Of the other 'stars' only Royal Dutch Shell appears unaffected. All of the Seven Sisters have either merged among themselves ...

**Table 1.1    The 'Seven Sisters'? 1971 and 2000**

| 1971 | 2000 |
|---|---|
| Esso | Exxon/Mobil |
| Royal Dutch Shell | Royal Dutch Shell |
| British Petroleum | BP-Amoco-Arco* |
| Chevron | ChevronTexaco |
| Texaco | |
| Gulf Oil | |
| Mobil | |
| (CFP) | (TotalFinaElf) |

*Now renamed BP

(Exxon/Mobil, ChevronTexaco) or acquired other 'smaller' Independent oil firms – firms with annual turnovers measured in the billions of dollars. Thus, British Petroleum (renamed 'BP' in the year 2000) has acquired the American Independents Arco and Amoco. The same phenomenon has affected the 'Eighth Sister'– the Compagnie

Française des Petroles– has also disappeared to be 'reincarnated' in TotalFinaElf, a European champion.

Delving behind the official explanations behind this recent merger activity, that mergers were necessary given the heavy capital investments and high risk involved in developing fields in promising new oil provinces (the Caspian Sea, Kazakhistan, and deep water Gulf of Mexico), one finds that this merger wave reflects the latest step in a profound transformation. The oil industry has changed significantly in the last fifteen years. Here we will briefly look at the causal nature of these changes.

Firstly, there has been what might be termed the 'commodification' of oil and gas. Up until 1971–75, heavy emphasis was placed on oil company 'ownership' of crude oil reserves and the degree to which these crude reserves could be produced, refined and marketed within the same vertically integrated company. One discussed the difference between companies which were 'long on crude' (Gulf, BP) and those companies which were 'short' (Mobil and Royal Dutch Shell) – always referring to individual firm's refinery 'runs' as a basis of comparison – Gulf and BP, producing more crude than their refineries could utilise would be over 100 percent and Mobil and Royal Dutch Shell, who had to rely on outside sources of crude for some of their refinery runs, under 100 percent. (Note that this was the situation in 1972.) The OPEC nationalisation of the Seven Sisters oil producing assets in the years following 1971 'broke' the vertically integrated links between company production of crude and company refining and marketing of crude and crude products. But these nationalisations did not have an immediate impact on industrial behaviour.[1] Rather, the oil multinationals sought to retain their vertically integrated sources of supply, through contracting for long term supply contracts with the new owners of 'their' oil, through developing new oil provinces (Alaskan North Slope, North Sea, Angola) or through more intensive development of already mature oil provinces outside OPEC.

These solutions did not stand the test of time. The Majors soon found out that while long term contracts could provide them with a degree of security of supply, these contracts did not insulate them from volatile swings in the prices charged by the OPEC countries. Indeed, firms without upstream activities were often only too willing to agree to higher contractual prices in periods of crisis, thus crowding out the Majors on the margin and currying favour with this or that producer.

What revolutionised this situation, a situation characterised by a multiple of price regimes differing over time and between producers, was the emergence of markets where contracts for specific crude oils (Brent in the North Sea, West Texas Intermediate in the US) and contracts for oil products began to be traded either

---

1    Too much can be made of the immediate impact of the OPEC nationalisations in this period. OPEC accounted for around 40 percent of all crude produced in the world in 1971 (versus some 33 percent today). What has made OPEC significant is that the organisation possesses almost all the world's low cost crude oil and accounts for a far higher percentage of crude trade. These are the two factors which made the nationalisations in the 1970s of such great import.

in organised futures markets (International Petroleum Exchange in London and NYMEX in New York) or on an offshore basis (the Brent crude forward market). The advantages of such trading were obvious. Company producers could sell their crude to any purchaser rather than being confined to their own integrated markets. Company refineries could 'lock-in' their profits, acquiring future crude supplies through one set of futures-linked prices and selling their oil products at another set of predetermined prices. Futures and forward markets could also relieve the problems of oil storage, a 'paper'contract for future delivery substituting for the crude or product in tankage. These new markets also provided a higher degree of price transparency than had been the case hitherto. Such trade rapidly gained momentum in the period 1985–1991, the structure of future and forward contractual prices ultimately forming the informational basis of OPEC production policies – a relationship which continues today.

Crude oil price volatility, while commanding newspaper headlines, has also had another less well publicised effect – a massive restructuring of the refining industry. In 1971 a significant majority of Western refineries were simple distillation (crude skimming) plants, designed often with a single type of crude oil in mind, which could only produce a limited range of crude products from a barrel of oil. Thus a simple refinery processing a heavy crude oil would yield a high percentage of heavy fuel oil and a relatively low percentage of premium products (lighter 'fractions'). With a sudden price increase such a refiner would suddenly find that he was producing only a small fraction of (say) motor gasoline for which, as it was characterised by an inelastic price elasticity of demand, he could charge a markedly higher price, and a high fraction of heavy fuel oil. As the last product is in direct competition with coal, where prices remained flat, the refiner could not increase the prices of heavy fuel oil without losing market share. And if the refiner did not increase heavy fuel oil prices he could not cover the costs of the higher priced crude oil. Caught in this dilemma, the Majors literally spent billions of dollars upgrading many of their refineries, installing thermal and/or catalytic cracking units so these refineries could take different grades of crude and process these so that the premium product content of crude being processed was maximised. Simultaneously other refineries were ruthlessly shut down and abandoned. (In the United States alone, over 100 refineries were shut down in the period 1979–1995).

The changes in refining technology also reinforced the trend towards commodification of oil. Rather than relying solely on an input of relatively 'heavy' Kuwaiti crude provided by an integrated company's Kuwaiti affiliate, for example, the manager of the upgraded ('complex') refinery could purchase crude oil from any source, often with reference to quoted futures market prices, and process this 'foreign' crude to fit the peculiarities of local market demand. Theoretically, a single employee with a fax machine could assure that such a refinery would get its optimum mix of crudes from a variety of sources, thus freeing the refinery manager from the obligations to purchase crude from another company affiliate. The same freedom also accrued the manager of a producing affiliate. Rather than be tied to delivering to other downstream subsidiaries of the parent company, (s)he could sell the crude concerned to a third party on the best available terms available. This vertical de-integration was first introduced by Royal Dutch Shell in 1982–83, and adopted widely throughout the industry in subsequent years.

The nature of oil industry change can perhaps be best expressed by two simple models, one which we will term a 'control of crude model' that roughly approximates the situation confronting the oil companies in the period 1928 through 1984, and the other which we will term a 'core competence competition model' characterising the situation since 1984.

The nature of oligopoly rent in the two models is markedly different. In the…In the case of the 'control of crude' model,

$$\Pi_{AP} = I(EP)$$

where $\Pi_{AP}$, the oligopoly rent of from all phases of oil company operations is seen as a function, $I$, of the rate of return to, $EP$, upstream exploration and production. Note that this model appears to ignore the impact of other stages of the integrated company. Here we assume that these activities are undertaken at cost and thus have little to do with the source of oligopoly rents, although the existence of integrated operations ensured control of oil and oil products from wellhead to fuel pump. (In fact as long as tanker, refinery and marketing functions were undertaken at cost the company was doing well. Quite often rents from the production and sale of crude could cover inefficient operations elsewhere in the company.)

As the rate of return on exploration and production was ultimately dependent on the control of price and supply of crude oil on world markets, oligopoly rents were a function of joint oil MNC control of the price and supply of crude. This control, essentially in the hands of the Seven Sisters in the period 1950–61, was gradually eroded by the entrance of the Independents into North Africa and the Middle East in the period 1961–71, before being terminated by the 1971 OPEC seizure of crude oil pricing control. Nevertheless, in the decade or so which followed 1971, oil companies persistently looked to rents from their 'upstream' activities to provide the basis of their oligopoly rents (rents which were now shared with the OPEC producers).

With the 1984–86 collapse in crude oil prices, the emergence of the various forward and futures markets, and the volatility in crude prices, this situation changed. This new situation can be expressed by our 'core competence competition' model as follows:

$$\Pi_{AP} = S(EP, R, T, M, D)$$

where oligopoly rents for the individual integrated company, $\Pi_{AP}$, were now a function, $S$ of that company's competence in acquiring a maximum synergy effect from exploration and production activities, $EP$; refining, $R$; transport, $T$; marketing, $M$; and other diversified activities, $D$. It is important to note that these activities are often hard to synergise as they are quite diverse. A skill in marketing petroleum products is essentially unrelated to a skill at finding and exploiting oil reserves.

Neither of these skills may have overly much to do with upgrading refinery capacity. Thus, almost by necessity oil companies have had to focus on the synergies from no more than two or three of the above activities for their source of oligopoly rents.

It is this search for 'fit', for defining and redefining corporate core competencies in hitherto unexplored business areas which has characterised the industry up to the merger wave of the 1990s and continues to do so today. These competencies, as reported by Cibin and Grant (1996, p. 176), ranged from 'financial management' (Exxon), 'enhanced [crude oil] recovery techniques' and 'marketing capability' (Texaco), 'efficiency and flexibility in refinery operation' and 'lubricant technology' (Mobil), to 'expertise in deep sea drilling and offshore recovery' and 'mangagement of external activities' (Royal Dutch Shell). Note that these are the competencies as defined in 1996. They have certainly changed in today's mega-major world.

In this context, it must be emphasised that the two models present an over-simplified view of a transition between two archetypes. For example, those crude short multinationals in the period to 1971 often developed core competencies outside the exploration and production of crude. Thus Mobil was known for many years prior to 1971 as an extremely efficient marketer. Similarly, a focus on core competencies today should not detract from the fact that these core competencies can be defined in terms of vertical integration where this is seen as important. Thus Arco's pre-merger (with BP) strategy, for example, called for 'cost leadership' in its West Coast (US) operations, a leadership to be obtained through integrating its 'heavy upstream emphasis' in Alaska with West Coast refining and marketing (Cibin and Grant, 1996, p 170).

The transition between our two simplified representative models has been accompanied by change in the nature of oil major corporate governance, a shift from stakeholder to shareholder governance. Thirty years ago, an oil major more or less thought that replacing the crude that it used every year with newly found sources of oil or gas, was not only a source of oligopoly rents, it was also a form of 'civic duty'. While oil companies may disagree with this emphasis, there is considerable evidence today that this is less so (Cibin and Grant, 1996, pp. 176–85). Figures from the United States Energy Information Agency confirm that the task of finding new sources of oil and gas in North America are becoming more and more that of the smaller American oil companies. The larger companies, for their part, are increasingly shifting their sights to much larger but less secure prospects outside North America (and often abandoning these after spending billions). Hierarchic organisations have been replaced with 'flat' organisation, often resulting in the elimination of several administrative layers, and entire national offices. Companies have ruthlessly thinned their management staffs, most recently as the results of the merger activity discussed at the commencement of this chapter. Companies are more responsive to market signals. Assets which are seen as being a burden on the firm are rapidly disposed of, being bought and sold among companies much as schoolboys trade cards of their favourite baseball or football stars during primary school recesses in the US and Europe. And these 'assets' are not small.

## The analysis of industry change

The third volume in a series summarising the results of a Norwegian Research Council initiative, Petropol, this book is divided into three parts. The first part focuses on the nature of industrial change within the oil industry, the second, on the political economic challenges faced by today's industry, and the third, the conclusion, on future trends within the industry.

Given the nature of change in the industry, one could ask such questions as: What are the boundaries of the reconstructed majors? How should companies be structured in the future? How can one interpret the changes of the past seven years? Are the reconstructed majors (the new super majors) the right size for improved corporate performance? Part 1, 'The Boundaries of the Firm: Mega-Mergers, Transaction Costs, and Value Chains', answers these question from various perspectives. Chapter 2 (Osmundsen *et al*) looks at the issues of post merger corporate performance. Using several financial indicators and econometric model, the authors find that generally the newly merged firms outperform their competitors. Chapter 3 looks more particularly at firm boundary issues. Here Davis's analysis of the oil refining sector attempts to make sense of oil super major ongoing purchase, divestiture, restructuring, and abandonment of refining assets, assets which are key to their vertical integration. He finds that the oil super majors are 'tapering' their refinery ownership, fitting them more precisely to their strategic profiles, but that this is an ongoing, perhaps never ending, process. Chapters 3 and 4 look at the alternatives to vertical integration in the offshore upstream exploration and production. In Chapter 4, Kvaløy finds that integration in these stages is not needed as companies can use alternative disciplinary devices to counter the problems of specific assets, opportunism and appropriability. Working largely off the same framework as Kvaløy, Wiig contrasts offshore contractual practices in two different offshore oil provinces, those of West Africa (Angola) and the North Sea (Norway). Wiig finds a 'tighter' form of firm integration in offshore West African projects, a finding which he ascribes to the impact external factors have on contractual practices. Finally, working off value chain theory (Porter, 1985; 1990; 1991) Stabell (Chapter 6) argues that the value chain is an insufficient instrument for analysing comparative advantage in the offshore exploration and production sector. Stabell argues for the use of value configuration theory (Stabell and Fjeldstad, 1998) as a means to get a better appreciation of competitive advantage in this sector.

Part 2, 'Present and Future Challenges', explores how the industry is reacting to the changes occurring around it. There is evidence of an increasing oil industry concentration on finding larger giant fields, a tendency which discriminates against those nations possessing smaller structures. The rationale behind this behaviour is discussed in a second chapter by Osmundsen *et al* (Chapter 7). In Chapter 8, Noreng looks at the various regulatory modes developing in Europe and the impact of these on industry restructuring. He develops this theme by examining the impact of differing licensing practices in the Norwegian and British North Sea sectors on exploration activities in the two sectors. A chapter by Davis looks at the vitriolic controversy as to whether the rate of finding/replacement of global oil reserves is gong to remain relatively constant, increase or 'peak' and fall in the future. More important than the controversy over whether oil production has 'peaked' or not is the discussion as to the calculation of future 'reserve growth,' a topic which is further explored in an appendix to Chapter 9. The section concludes with yet another question: given the massive restructuring of the industry, why is there such a modest investment in alternative green energy technologies? The answer to this question, it is suggested, is that in fact, given management problems of coordination, of defining core competencies, and of satisfying shareholders, oil industry activities in this area are greater than is generally realised.

Finally, in Part 3, 'Conclusion', Chapter 11 defines future trends. The super majors are entering a period of falling super major market shares in world crude markets. Increasingly produced crude will be higher cost and will entail substantial investment commitments. Future crude will also tend to come from politically unstable areas where securing a satisfactory return on major investments may prove very difficult. New major consuming powers, here most notably China, are also entering world crude and product markets. Together these developments will entail increased state activism in procuring sufficient nationally 'secure' future sources of crude oil. These developments will demand increased political skills on the part of super major managers. And, even if future political developments are positive, it is likely that the world is entering a period of capacity constraints, constraints which not only could significantly affect the future prices of crude and crude oil products, but also the very nature of the industry.

## References

Adelman, M.A. (1974), *The World Petroleum Market,* Washington D.C.: Resources for the Future.

Bindeman, K. (1999), 'Vertical Integration in the Oil Industry: A Review of the Literature', *Journal of Energy Literature*, **5**(1), pp. 3-26.

Blair J.M. (1976), *The Control of Oil,* New York:Pantheon.

Chazeau, M.G. de and A.E. Jahn (1959), *Integration and Competition in the Petroleum Industry,* New Haven: Yale University Press.

Grant, R.M. and R. Cibin (1996), 'Strategy, Structure and Market Turbulence: The International Oil Majors', *Scandinavian Management Journal*, **12**(2) pp. 165-188.

Grossman, S. and O. Hart (1986), 'The Costs and Benefits of Ownership: A Theory of Vertical and Lateral Integration', *Journal of Political Economy*, August, **94**(4), pp. 691-719.

Hart, O. (1995), *Firms, Contracts, and Financial Structure,* Oxford:Clarendon.

Klein, B., R. Crawford and A. Alchian (1978), 'Vertical Integration, Appropriable Rents, and the Competitive Contracting Process', *Journal of Law and Economics*,

October, **21**(2), pp. 297-326.
Penrose, E. (1968). *The Large International Firm in Developing Countries: The International Petroleum Industry* (London: George Allen and Unwin).
Porter, M. (1985), *Competitive Advantage. Creating and Sustaining Superior Performance*, New York: Free Press.
_____(1990), *The Competitive Advantage of Nations*, New York: Free Press.
_____(1991), 'Towards a Dynamic Theory of Strategy', *Strategic Management Journal*, Winter Special Issue, **12**, pp. 95-117.
Stabell, C.B. and Ø. Fjeldstad (1998), 'Configuring Value for Competitive Advantage: On chains, shops and networks', *Strategic Management Journal*, **19**(5), pp. 413-437.
Williamson, O.E. (1979), 'Transaction-Cost Economics: The Governance of Contractual Relations', *Journal of Law and Economics*, October, **22**(2), pp. 233-261.
_____(1985), *The Economic Institutions of Capitalism*, New York: Free Press.
Yergin, D. (1992), *The Prize: The Epic Quest for Oil, Money and Power*, New York: Simon and Schuster.

# PART 1
# The Boundaries of the Firm:
# Mega-Mergers, Transaction Costs
# and Value Chains

# Chapter 2

# Size and Profitability in the International Oil and Gas Industry[1]

Petter Osmundsen, Klaus Mohn,
Magne Emhjellen and Flemming Helgeland

## Introduction

The largest vertically integrated oil companies, the so called *super majors*, show better results than smaller oil companies on core financial indicators and market metrics. Some central target figures that financial analysts use are returns on the capital employed, P/E ratios and EV/EBITDA. The different measures are presented and explained and how they vary according to a company's size is illustrated. Thereafter, the reasons for this variation in financial indicators is discussed and connected to the consolidation process occurring in the oil business.

## Profitability

Profitability shows the return on capital that is put into a company. One of the main terms used to measure results is defined as follows:[2]

RoACE = *Return on average capital employed* = (Net income + after tax net interest costs) / (Total capital − interest-free debt).

Capital employed is part of the denominator while income on the same capital is found in the numerator. The return above the fraction line must be the return on the capital entered below the fraction line. Thus, it is the result before interest costs that is part of the numerator when calculating total profitability (RoACE). Operating costs and financial costs often get mixed together; see Gjesdal and Johnsen

1   We would like to thank Trond Bjørnenak, Kjell Agnar Dragvik, Arnold Drange, Harald Espedal, Kristian Falnes, Frøystein Gjesdal, Morten Halleraker, Odd Rune Heggheim, Atle Johnsen, Morten Lindbäck, Kjell Løvås, and Arnstein Wigestrand for their constructive comments and suggestions. Correspondence: Petter Osmundsen, Stavanger University College, Department of Industrial Economics, Section for Petroleum Economics, Post Box 8002, 4068 Stavanger, Norway. Ph.: (47) 51 83 15 68, Fax: (47) 51 83 17 50, E-mail: Petter. Osmundsen@tn.his.no, Internet: http://www.snf.no/Ansatt/Osmundsen.htm
2   For the sake of simplicity, minority interests are not included in the formulas.

(1999). Suppliers often give, for example, credit to the company. This is often not included in interest costs, but is rather put in with the purchasing costs from suppliers (operation costs then become financial costs instead). The result is that interest income is underestimated and, with that, value creation of the total capital, because some of the creditors will already have received their share. In other words, there is not congruence between the return and the size of the capital in the profitability term. This is corrected by taking the part of the debt that has already been paid ('interest-free debt') and subtracting it from the numerator when making calculations. Interest-free debt includes supplier debt, public tax credits and duty credits, deferred taxes, debt to employees, advances from costumers and pension obligations. The capital terminology used is 'capital employed'.[3] In the oil and gas industry one must be especially aware of deferred taxes.

Figure 2.1 shows return on capital employed (RoACE) from a selection of core oil companies. Note that measured with this indicator, the largest companies show the best profitability.

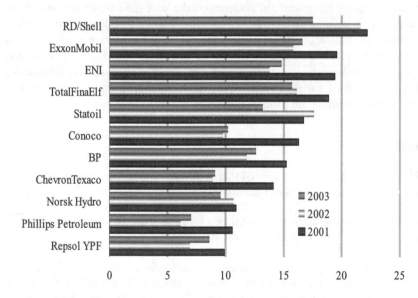

**Figure 2.1     RoACE for oil companies, 2001–2003**
*Source*: UBS Warburg, Global Integrated Oils Analyser, April 2002

***

3    According to Gjesdal and Johnsen (1999) the term capital employed is not quite as comprehensive; interest-free capital is also employed in the enterprise. Interest-free credit is not free either (this is only true for public tax credits and deferred tax), but this does not cause financial costs from a bookkeeping perspective. Implicit interest costs, on the other hand, are often accounted for in operations results, for example, in the form of higher purchasing costs from supplier credits and lower sales prices from advance payments from customers.

**Market metrics**

Central to valuating stocks is the term price-earnings ratio, or the P/E ratio. P/E measures the relationship between a company's market value and its yearly earnings. A high P/E ratio indicates 1) that the stock market believes that the company has good growth potential, 2) that the stock has less risky earnings, i.e. shareholders' return requirements are low, or 3) a combination of 1) and 2). The largest international oil companies operate with a P/E ratio with a magnitude of 15 to 20; see Figure 2.2.

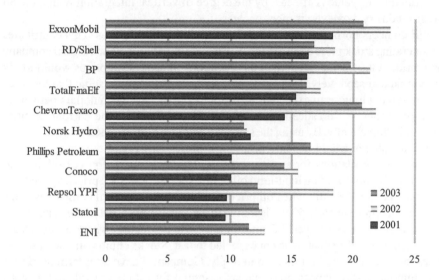

**Figure 2.2    P/E-number for different oil companies, result figures for 2001–2003**

*Source:* UBS Warburg, Global Integrated Oils Analyser, April 2002

UBS Warburg (2002) operated with a P/E ratio of 12.6 for Statoil in 2002. For Norsk Hydro the corresponding P/E ratio was 11.3 and ExxonMobil's was 23.0, thus demonstrating that the difference between Norwegian and international oil companies is, in other words, very large. The differences reflect the stock market's expectations regarding returns for different companies. A simple way in which to calculate this is to convert the P/E ratio into the implicit expectations regarding the growth of earnings per share (EPS) that these correspond to in an eternal growth price model. According to Nunn (2001), the negative growth expectations for Norsk Hydro correspond to –1, 1 per cent per year and a positive growth estimation of 3.5 per cent for RD Shell and 4.2 per cent for ExxonMobil.[4] Comparable numbers for

---

4    Calculated based on consensus estimates for 2001-2005.

Statoil are not available, but the implicit prerequisites for growth would presumably be higher than for Norsk Hydro.

By comparing the estimations of value for Statoil and Norsk Hydro, relevant structural differences exist on (at least) two levels. First, Norsk Hydro cannot be considered purely an international oil and gas company. Second, Norsk Hydro oil (and energy) operations are less focused than Statoil's overall activities. Both of these conditions can be the cause of different estimations of value. Most claim that the first item works to Norsk Hydro's disadvantage (conglomerate discount). How the estimation of value is affected by the degree of vertical integration within the oil and gas industry, however, is more unclear.

P/E numbers normally have a negative correlation to oil prices. This contributes to moderating stock price adjustments in response to varying oil prices. Oil company share prices thus fluctuate less than the variations in current oil prices would imply when looked at separately. This has a reasonable explanation. Assume that the price level involving long-term expectations is, for example, seventeen dollars per barrel. If the price then fell drastically – to ten dollars per barrel – the current earnings would fall dramatically. By using the same P/E ratio for both seventeen and ten-dollar shares, the shares would become nearly worthless. This is not the case, however, as there are expectations for a price increase. The stock market prices oil and gas companies mainly based on long-term oil price expectations. Such price expectations demand a higher P/E ratio when oil prices are low. The largest oil companies had a P/E ratio of approximately 50 the last time there was a drastic fall in the price of oil. Comparably, there is a lower P/E ratio in the current situation where oil prices are high inasmuch as the situation is not expected to last. Stocks climb with increased oil prices, but it is not usual for them to multiply. Companies have long-term portfolios with long-term price expectations that are essential for estimating value. The stock market also prices oil companies based heavily on long-term expectations for oil prices. When working out estimated value for oil companies, analysts most often use mid-cycle oil prices as their point of departure.

Objections against the P/E ratio are not just that it is a simple rule-of-thumb, but also that the metric is based on accounting data. In order to avoid disruptive elements from imputed costs, many analysts instead choose a comparable cash-flow based metric, namely EV/DACF, where:

EV=*Enterprise Value*= market capitalization plus net interest bearing debt and
DACF =*debt-adjusted cash flow* = *post-tax cash flow* + *post-tax interest charge*,
where
Post-tax cash flow=net income+depreciation+exploration charge+other non-cash items.

EV is used instead of a market capital evaluation inasmuch as EV measures a company's aggregate market value independent of the capital structure. The cash flow, DACF, replaces the accounting based result measurements of EPS. This amount is also debt corrected such that the numerators and denominators are consistent.

UBS Warburg (2001) comments explicitly on their use of metrics: 'While we consider a wide range of ratios in evaluating companies, our key valuation metric is enterprise value to debt-adjusted cash flow (EV/DACF).' They also say that while the before tax size EBITDA (*earnings before interest, tax, depreciation and amortisation*) is often used in other sectors, it offers little guidance in relation to the relative evaluation of oil companies because of great differences in tax rates: 'We are less interested in how wealthy a company may make various governments.'

## Causality

UBS Warburg (2001) calls attention to a clear positive relationship between EV/ DACF and RoACE, that is companies that have high returns on their capital employed are rewarded with a higher market metric. It is perhaps not unreasonable that a high RoACE results in a high EV/DACF metric even though the accounting goals have definite limitations as comparative indicators of profitability. Accounting adjustments can, to some degree, bias the presentation of the financial reality for several quarters, but over time the actual profitability will be reflected in the accounting data. On the other hand, valuation of an oil company is not only contingent upon short-time accounting return, but also upon reserve replacement. To the extent that a strong focus on RoACE harms reserve generation, returns are not sustainable, and the perceived connection between EV/DACF and RoACE is no longer obvious.

The relationship between a company's size and its profitability is even more controversial when it comes to causality. What comes first? The analytical reports from the investment banks – for example, UBS Warburg – often include a diagram showing a positive relationship between a company's size and its profitability.[5] The diagram cross plots profitability with a company's size for companies in a diagram in a given year. Based on the diagrams – which show the relationship between the market value and RoACE of different companies – the connection is not unequivocal. Thus it is not obvious as to whether a positive correlation exists between profitability and the company's size. Even though the correlation might be true for one year, it does not mean that it would be stable over time. HSBC (2001) criticises the customary notion of causality between size and profitability. With investment banks' own projections, see Figure 2.3, there is not a clear correlation between market value (size) and profitability (RoACE).

---

5 Strictly speaking, analysts nevertheless do not establish with this a statistically significant connection between a company's size and its profitability. They simply show indications of a positive correlation in a diagram. Correlation is a symmetrical term and cannot as a matter of course explain the actual connection. In addition, other underlying variables can possibly explain the connection. In other words, a model with only one explanatory factor could possibly be specified incorrectly, showing the need for more realistic models.

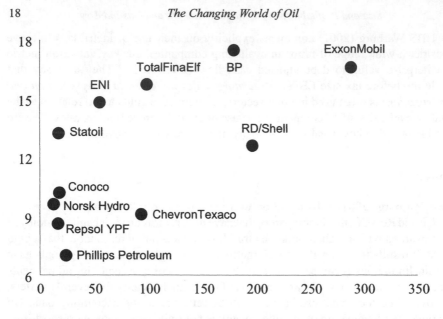

**Figure 2.3    Size and Profitability, Market Value (billion USD) and RoACE (average 2001–2003)**

*Source*: UBS Warburg, Global Integrated Oils Analyser, April 2002

Many reasons exist as to why large oil companies are more profitable than smaller ones and can thus explain the significant price differences. Current explanatory factors are greater portfolio growth potential and greater confidence that the management and the organisation will be able to convert reserves into profitability. The size of a company can also influence the allocation of petroleum licences. Size and reputation, for example, have caused operatorships in the most promising West African and Caspian Sea areas to go to the larger oil companies.  The operatorships involve extensive developments of large fields in areas where vital infrastructure is lacking. This works in favour of the companies with significant technical and commercial capacities.[6] Size makes it possible to have a greater breadth of technological and financial expertise. Size also makes it possible to be heavily involved in individual projects and areas; thus receiving the advantages of large-scale operations on projects – and area levels – without being exposed greatly to risk. Large international companies also have greater possibilities for tax planning. Profits can be moved to countries where taxation is more favourable. Furthermore, vertical integration and global risk spreading often yield low capital costs. Downstream market dominance

---

6    There are, however, many uncertain factors, for example, when it comes to taxation, regulations (the regulation of resources in Angola has delayed expansion), and transportation and marketing solutions (the Caspian Sea and Central Asia). Thus the final profitability of these fields remains very uncertain.

can also be beneficial for profitability. High confidence and good allocation of the licence area, a global presence, patience and high capital discipline can give certain opportunities for selecting the best prospects (cream-skimming); in other words, the largest companies attempt to select and bet on the best fields and geological locations in individual countries. Moreover, it is possible that in many instances, size is advantageous regarding political influence when it comes to both licence allocation and fiscal conditions.

However, it is useful to remember that size – at least in other businesses – can also have disadvantages. A lack of focus and specialisation are obvious examples. Co-ordination costs also normally grow with a company's size and geographic expansion. Large enterprises can easily become bureaucratised, possibly leading to considerable amounts of relevant information not reaching the decision makers, which can weaken the ability to react quickly to new business opportunities. Such disadvantages are perhaps less severe in the oil industry than in other businesses. Because it is a long-term industry and because the projects often are large, being dynamic and flexible are not as important as in other businesses. However, it is somewhat surprising that assets in oil companies that are taken over, which may be priced at a P/E of 8, can jump to the same P/E as the buyer, for example, 18. This deep trust in the large companies' ability to manage resources has up until now given certain opportunities for financial engineering via converting companies.

UBS Warburg (February 2001) assumes that oil prices at that time could not be maintained in the long run, but that it would take at least 12 months for oil prices to return to their 'mid-cycle level' of 17 dollars per barrel. (Other investment banks at the time had similar long-term price forecasts – which coincided with long-term forward pricing – but had different qualifications with regard to recovery time.) This is the price level that lays the groundwork for the prognoses for 2003–05. They also calculated sensitivity into the results for different oil companies with regard to oil price changes. The large integrated oil companies are less exposed to oil price volatility due to a high level of vertical integration (downstream business which has oil and gas as input) and high solidity (low level of debt). It is, however, the level of vertical integration that is decisive regarding exposure to risk, and not size as such. With regard to financial theory (CAPM), it means that vertical integration gives a lower systematic risk (lower beta), reflected by a lower required return on capital, which thus gives greater value for the companies. Nevertheless, these factors are always connected. On average, the largest companies have relatively more downstream business than small companies do. The main focus for smaller companies is usually the upstream side. Limited financial capital may make it beneficial to focus the main activity on particular parts of the value chain. Financial theory argues that investors, via stock portfolios, can diversify more cheaply than companies (lower transaction costs). If one were to focus only on transaction costs, this would probably true both for horizontal and vertical integration as well. For vertical integration, however, diversification can, on the other hand, create synergies that shareholders may be unable to duplicate (such synergy is less likely with horizontal integration). The aggregate effect can result in an increase in cash flow expectations for integrated vertical companies relative to the total cash flow from a comparable portfolio based on individual companies.

HSBC, which believes that size will be less significant in the years to come, is carrying out a critical review of traditional arguments. Even though the analysis could have been more thorough, they show determination and the ability to question commonly held truths. The greatest advantage of the analysis is the systematic decomposition of different supposed advantages of large-scale oil companies. According to HSBC, a quickly dispersing knowledge among consultants would, for example, reduce competitive advantages. Exploration and development costs do not vary systematically according to a company's size. They are not convinced either that BP and Exxon, after merging, will be able to accomplish upstream projects that would be too encompassing for them to accomplish alone. They also point out that they cannot see a growth in activity in the wake of a merger. Moreover, they emphasise that Total, *before* merging with Fina and Elf, would have staked 10 billion USD on a difficult project in Saudi Arabia even though the company was significantly smaller than the biggest ones. Under-investment and lack of self-generated (organic) growth in reserves and production caused HSBC to doubt whether the largest oil companies would be able to deliver the promised growth. They show that, among other things, the yearly growth in employed capital has been less than 1 per cent for the last 10 years. According to HSBC, downstream profitability is connected to regional concentration, and not a company's global size. They also question whether BP and Exxon have lower capital costs than before the mergers and they show than Repsol YPF has lower capital costs due to a higher level of debt. Norsk Hydro has also been shown to have the same capital costs as the largest companies because of tax deductions designed to counterbalance the special Norwegian taxation for the petroleum industry.

The HSBC analysis raises many interesting questions and it is healthy to shake up familiar ideas. Nevertheless, it can also be necessary to have a few simple opposing ideas. The project in Saudi Arabia could possibly be characterised by significant lower risk (and with lower upside potential) – technically and contractually – than projects in Angola and the Caspian Sea area. True growth in employed capital has presumably been higher than the recorded growth of 1 per cent per year considering that companies have attempted to reduce the accounted employed capital in order to improve its RoACE. Comparing capital costs must, in order to be of any significance, be done based on the same level of debt and the same tax system. For example, foreign companies on Norwegian soil have, over time, compared to Norwegian companies, been better at taking advantage of interest deductions designed to counterbalance special taxes in Norway, depending on whether the company on Norwegian soil has been organised as a subsidiary, where one is more flexible with regard to establishing the level of debt. Downstream regional concentration is also more difficult to achieve for a smaller company than for a large one because the risk could possibly be too great due to less diversification.

Within this area, it would seem that there is room for empirical research. In order to establish a causal relationship, it is not sufficient to show a positive correlation because it can be a result of other underlying variables (in such a case, there are specification errors in the estimation model). The correlation does not show causality; we do not know what the reason is or what the effect is. Is it size that gives profitability or is it profitability that makes companies big? The number of observations that are typically used are notwithstanding too low to do an econometric analysis. With regard to pricing, on the other hand, it is sufficient that the main market players believe in certain causal relations.[7] The market's opinion, to a relatively high degree, is dependent on previous experiences and on whether there is a basis for intuitive reasoning.

Empirical research has limited the power of prediction in a volatile stock market. Analysing the past, however, can nevertheless be an important source of knowledge and for establishing general causal relationships. What is it that made the stock market believe, for example, that the largest oil companies would deliver growth results of approximately 4 per cent in the near future while simultaneously predicting a weak fall in the results of Norsk Hydro? The existing portfolio and the ability to obtain new licences are apparently significant, and are to some degree, objective criteria. In addition, central subjective criteria, with regard to market confidence, also play a role. In this case, it could be assumed that confidence is something that is gained over time by faithfully fulfilling the promises made to the market. It is interesting in this context that companies that enjoy great confidence do not always keep their promises regarding profitability and growth. In 1996, the largest integrated oil companies, for example, promised a yearly growth in net income of 5 per cent up to the year 2000, but the reality was less than 2 per cent.

**Basis for comparison**

Valuation through the use of market metrics is obviously quite dependent upon which companies are chosen for comparison (reference group or peer group). It is clear that, based on Figure 2.4, the market metrics vary systematically within the following four categories: 1) the largest international oil companies, 2) integrated American oil companies 3) integrated European companies, and 4) emerging integrated oil companies.

Again, it is such that the largest companies have the highest market metrics. Choice of peer group is a discretionary decision, but the ideal point of departure is to find a group of companies that can form a relevant background for comparison (benchmarking). Figure 2.4 shows that the EV/DACF metrics for different oil companies vary considerably. As seen earlier, this is also true for the P/E metrics. The choice of reference group can thus have a strong effect on valuation. By comparing Statoil with large European upstream companies, Warburg Dillon Read (1999)

---

7 As a matter of course, however, it does not mean that an econometric analysis is uninteresting because opinions about the market that are not actually based on empirical evidence can easily change over time. Statistically significant relationships can provide the basis for more stable prognoses.

found, for example, that Statoil was valued at 94 billion NOK, whereas the value would have been 186 billion NOK if the basis for comparison had instead been the global majors. Based on this, there are obvious incentives for companies to influence which reference group they get in. The possibility of influencing the classification, however, is limited in practice.

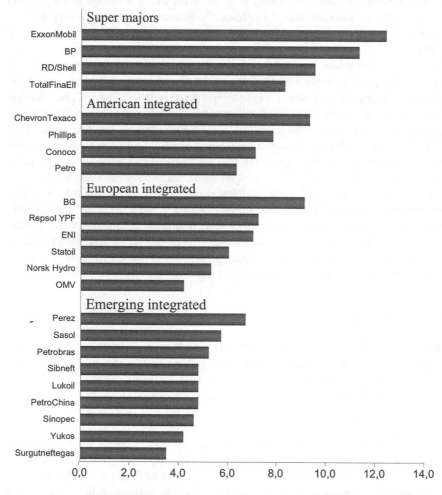

**Figure 2.4    EV/DACF (2003 estimate) for a variety of oil companies**
*Source*: UBS Warburg, Global Integrated Oils Analyser, April 2002

**Relative valuation**

There is an obvious problem connected to valuation based on comparing companies because the approach only decides relative valuation and not the absolute level.

Thus, it is necessary to have supplementary criteria. By using additional criteria, it is possible to avoid making errors at the industry level. A sure blunder – or bubble – was seen in the telecom industry. When pricing a company, the point of departure was the price/sell relationship to the company in the industry that had the highest price. Because almost everyone could always come up with a company that had a higher price, prices began to spiral.

Would this also be possible in the more established oil industry? Enron is of course a recent example of how the financial market can allow itself to be taken in, also within the energy sector. The product spectrum for Enron, however, is not representative for the oil industry. In general, there are many who believe that the oil industry has a far better basis for being able to determine value because of its access to data regarding production, reserves, price estimates, and so on. Oil and gas companies' stocks are also relatively conservatively priced. According to UBS Warburg (2002), the P/E ratio for Statoil in April was 9.6 (with exceptional sales profits taken out of earnings). Norsk Hydro (which of course is a conglomerate) had a similar P/E ratio of approximately 11.6. There are low expectations for growth implicit in such P/E ratios. With a P/E ratio of approximately 15 for the *super majors*, there are more substantial expectations regarding growth. As a result, for example, presuming an infinite horizon and a discounted rate of ten per cent, there is an implied *permanent* expectation for growth of 3.3 per cent per year. The realism of this estimate must be measured against expected market growth, growth in OPEC production versus non-OPEC production and an estimation of how large a share of OPEC growth the super majors can obtain. If the super majors do not acquire a significant share of OPEC's production growth and if growth in energy consumption does not increase very much, the largest companies must increase their production at the expense of their competitors. All companies cannot in this case fulfil the expected production increases. In the case that pessimistic expectations are fulfilled, a small price bubble may exist in some of the current stock prices.

## Growth expectations in the oil business

The current stock prices reflect the expectations of investors regarding future operations and investment output. Growth stocks are sold at high P/E ratios because investors are willing to pay for exceptional proceeds on investments that have not yet been undertaken.

A central question within this context is how investors perceive the petroleum industry. Is this a mature industry or a growth industry? There are many indications that the market views the oil industry as mature with limited growth potential. UBS Warburg (2001) points out that in the 1990s it was cost cutting (through restructuring and technological progress) that lay behind an average growth in net income of 8 per cent per year. Large-scale consolidation from 1998–2000 gave additional possibilities for eliminating duplicate indirect costs. The potential for cutting costs further is seen as limited ('...there has to be a point at which continued rationalisation requires companies to cut into muscle rather than fat.').

Cost increases are seen as more probable than reductions and it is expected that there will be more moderate growth in the results in the future, 5 to 6 per cent per year in the period 2000–05. UBS Warburg believes that even the companies themselves have admitted that further growth in net income cannot be based on continued cost cutting and that they instead ought to have growth in volume as their main focus, paying special attention to growth on the upstream side (It should also be noted that if all large companies were to pursue a volume strategy, it could cause negative price effects.) For integrated oil companies, a volume growth of 4.5per cent is expected per year from 2000–05, compared to a meagre 1.2per cent growth in the previous five-year period. Companies must deliver these volumes in order to maintain a growth in net income of 8 per cent. UBS Warburg points out that oil companies, based on experience, have less direct control over volume growth than cost cutting. They fear that volume measurements – just as previously – will be too ambitious and that the companies will perhaps weaken their capital discipline in order to ensure the volume figures. This fear is supported by the average level of debt falling from 25per cent to 5per cent and by the fact that companies also can be tempted to use cash surpluses to achieve their volume goals. The market can be sceptical of companies with high earnings; the danger is that investments will be made in projects with low returns (empire building), or that the companies get used to a high expenditure level (gold plating). In order to credibly signal that companies are not over-investing or becoming ineffective because they have ample access to free cash flow, the largest companies have undertaken comprehensive buy backs of their own shares. The reinvestment fraction has been relatively low in recent years; see Figure 2.5.

The most normal procedure for companies that wish to pay out funds to shareholders is to do it in the form of dividends. One alternative that is increasingly widespread – and, to a large extent, equivalent – is for companies to repurchase their own shares. Oil companies have been the ones who have undertaken the largest buy-backs in recent years (Brealey and Myers, 2001) and more of the large oil and gas companies have made specific programmes public for buying back their own stocks, also in the years to come. Investors are currently positive toward oil companies buying back shares because they are afraid that enhanced liquidity will go into new projects with low profitability.

**Conglomerate discount**

Previously, a consequence of scattered ownership and lack of control by owners has normally been that management developed conglomerates by going into business areas where their company did not have any comparative advantage. The agent theory explanation for this is that growth yields management power, status and influence. Empirical methods also show that the salaries of top management often vary more

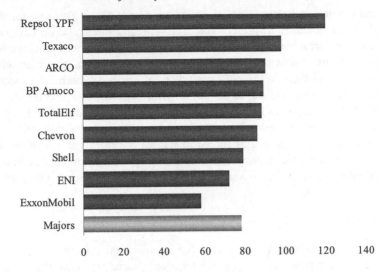

**Figure 2.5    Percentage of cash flow reinvested (*capex/cash earnings*), 1995–99**

*Source*: HSBC, Sector Report, Integrated Oil and Gas, February 2001

according to a company's size than a company's results. Shareholders, on the other hand, often look for focused companies and prefer to carry out diversification on their own by building up portfolios consisting of focused companies from different enterprises. On the other hand, conglomerate companies are usually large, and size is, in other contexts, used as an argument for a high market metric. This is true for focused, vertically integrated companies with obvious synergies. The opinion of the market regarding conglomerates is, however, that they are more difficult to manage and audit, thus resulting in lower returns.

**Vertical integration**

Shareholders' favouritism of focused companies does not seem, however, to concur with the fact that the integrated oil companies are priced much higher than specialised upstream oil companies of a similar size. As an alternative, shareholders could buy both pure upstream and downstream companies. Thus, the market seems to reward vertical integration, but not horizontal integration. There are some arguments that support a difference in pricing for focused upstream companies and fully integrated oil companies. Characteristic for such arguments is that it is difficult to verify their financial content. The market has also varied over time regarding the relative pricing of integrated and focused oil companies. One argument that is brought up in order to explain the advantages of being represented in the entire value chain for petroleum is that one is assured a share in the resource rent because experience shows that this moves up and down the value chain over time. Increased market power as a result of being represented in both upstream and downstream companies is also a reasonable consideration when it comes to market value. A vertically integrated oil company also has better opportunities for taking advantage of self-financed non-cyclical asset trading: get out of downstream activities and into upstream activities when oil prices are low, and then do the opposite when oil prices are high. The income from downstream activity – in the same way as with income from pipe tariffs – is thus valuable for oil companies because it generates a stable and somewhat hedging flow of income that can be used to invest in upstream companies. Purely upstream companies, on the other hand, will be forced to sell out of projects at low oil prices. With targeted policies for risk management, however, upstream companies could be able to reduce the risk of having to abandon projects when it is a buyer's market.

## Econometric testing

Our objective is to evaluate value drivers for international oil companies using time series data for a panel of companies. An econometric approach allows for a variety of explanatory factors in a simultaneous model. Market capitalisation, which is represented by the metric EV/DACF, is tested as to how it is affected by rentability (RoACE), company size (oil and gas production (O&G) as a proxy for size), finding and development costs (F&D), reserve replacement rates (RRR), and unit of production costs (UPC). In addition, annual dummies are used, primarily to account for changes in oil price.

The basic equation to be estimated is

$$EV/DACF = a + bROACE,$$

where $a$ and $b$ are the parameters to be estimated. To investigate the effect of additional variables the model is expanded to:

$$EV/DACF = a + bROACE + cX.$$

Here, $X$ denotes a vector of additional variables that can influence EV/DACF. The equations are estimated with OLS, where fixed effects are used to distinguish between the years when pooling the observations from different years into a panel. An error term is of course added to the specifications before estimation.

For this study, UBS Warburg have kindly provided us with panel data for the period 1997–2002, including the following companies:

- Amerada Hess
- BP
- ChevronTexaco
- Eni
- ExxonMobil
- Marathon Oil
- Norsk Hydro
- Occidental
- Petro-Canada

- Repsol YPF
- TotalFinaElf

The effect of size on oil company pricing is focused upon in our dataset, using total oil and gas production as a proxy for size. The results for this specification are reported in Table 2.1.

**Table 2.1    EV/DACF explained by RoACE, F&D, O&G, RRR, UPC and annual dummies**

| Variable | Coefficient | t-value |
|---|---|---|
| Constant | 10.183 | 3.808 |
| RoACE | -19.230 | -2.074 |
| y97 | 0.149 | 0.156 |
| y98 | 1.622 | 1.387 |
| y99 | 0.660 | 0.642 |
| y00 | -0.681 | -0.745 |
| O&G | 0.002 | 7.046 |
| F&D costs | -0.021 | -0.357 |
| RRR | 0.136 | 0.178 |
| UPC | -0.526 | -1.310 |

The explanatory power of this specification is good, as the $R^2$ is 0.72. Size is evidently a highly significant explanatory factor in the pricing of oil companies. Actually, it is the most significant explanatory factor for market capitalisation.

**Conclusion**

The largest trans-national oil companies are more profitable and are priced higher than smaller oil companies. The reasons are numerous. The size of a company, for example, may have significance for the allocation of drilling licences. Size, reputation and substantial technical and commercial capacity have, for example, caused the most promising operatorships in the West African and Caspian Sea areas to go to the largest oil companies. Size makes it possible to have a greater breadth of technological and financial expertise. Size also makes it possible to invest heavily in individual projects and areas – and thus benefit from the advantages of large-scale operations – without being heavily exposed to risk. Vertical integration and global risk spreading are often seen as giving low capital expenses. Downstream market power can also be beneficial for profitability. High confidence and good licence allocation, a global presence, patience and high capital discipline can also provide certain opportunities for cream-skimming, that is the largest companies try to choose and bet on the best fields and geological areas in individual countries.

Further consolidation in the oil industry is seen as more difficult than before due to regulations and government interference. The number of obvious take-over candidates has also been reduced. According to BP group chief executive Lord John Browne, the time for mega mergers is over in the oil business.[8] There are not many large companies left to merge with, except the super majors, and in that respect, according to Browne, there is both a regulatory and a management limit. Additional mergers and buy-outs, however, will presumably continue on a smaller scale.

## References

Brealey, R.A. and S.C. Myers (2001), *Principles of Corporate Finance*, McGraw-Hill.

Gjesdal, F. and T. Johnsen (1999), *Setting Demands, Measuring Profitability, and Estimating Value*, Cappelen Akademiske Forlag.

HSBC (1991), Sector Report, Integrated Oil and Gas, *Exploding the Myth*, February 2001.

Lehman Brothers (2001), Global Equity Research, *Oil & Gas Quarterly Scoresheet*.

Nunn (2001), 'Can We Keep the Stock Market Happy and Still Make Sensible Investment Decisions?', presentation at Seminar on Petroleum Finance, Norwegian Petroleum Union (NPF), Solstrand, October 10, 2001.

SchroderSolomonSmithBarney (2001), Oil Companies – International, 'Norsk Hydro, Worth a Look', September 11, 2001.

UBSWarburg (2001), *The Global Integrated Oils Analyser*, February 2001.

UBS Warburg (2002), *The Global Integrated Oils Analyser*, April 2002.

Warburg Dillon Read (1999), *Valuation of Statoil*.

---

8    *The Daily Business Life (Dagens Næringsliv)*, April 4, 2002.

# Chapter 3

# Vertical Integration and Industrial Restructuring: The Economic Organisation of Specific Assets in the Oil Refining Industry

Jerome Davis

## Introduction: A Tale of Two Refineries

Limetree Bay is over one thousand miles from Houston. Located on Saint Croix in the US Virgin Islands, it is home to one of the largest oil refineries in the Western Hemisphere. The 'Hovensa facility' covers an area of 1500 acres, or the equivalent of 150 football fields. It is capable of processing 495 000 bbls/day of crude oil. Neither is it dependent fully on one type of crude for its runs. In its history, it has successfully processed no fewer than 60 differing types of crude oil. On the North American continent, on the outskirts of Houston, lies another refinery, the Lyondell-Citgo refinery. This refinery, while only processing some 268 000 bbls/day, has been acclaimed 'the premier heavy crude oil processing facility in the world' (Blindview, 2004). It can process heavy low cost Venezuelan crude oil into a very desirable product mix of gasoline, jet fuel, and chemical feedstocks. It is capable of producing 100 percent distillate as low sulphur fuel oil and 70 percent of its gasoline product is in the highly desirable reformulated or oxygenated categories (Lyondell, 2004). This was the result of an upgrading which cost its owners $1.1 billion dollars, an upgrading which has yielded very acceptable returns. (The unit grossed revenues of $4.2 billions in 2003.) Both refineries are partially owned by the Venezuelan state oil company, Petroleos de Venezuela (PDV), the Hovensa unit in partnership with the American firm, Amerada-Hess, and the Lyondell-Citgo unit through its indirectly wholly owned American subsidiary, Citgo.

While academic and public focus tends towards the more sensational and visible global oil exploration and production, OPEC price setting, and fluctuations in the price of motor gasoline (mogas), refinery activities have fallen into the background. In part this neglect is said to have been a function of environmental opposition to the building of new refineries. (This is a frequently cited cause for the fact that no new refinery has been built in the United States since 1976, a period of 29 years.) In part the topic is sufficiently technical so that the issues are not clearly understood. Yet in terms of the stakes involved for the oil industry, the question of integrating refining activities into the supply chain has become crucial for oil company profitability.

The strategies followed by PDV and its American partners are a case in point here. The PDV has ample sources of heavy, sour Venezuelan crude at its disposal, but little expertise in US markets. It has acquired indirect ownership over the US refining and distribution firm, Citgo, and has purchased a share of Amerada-Hess's HOVIC facility on Saint Croix. It has thereby acquired a foothold in the US market, a natural outlet for its crude production. Similarly, Amerada-Hess and Lyondell Chemical are content: they have acquired secure sources for their refinery crude runs. Amerada-Hess, for example, markets 419 000 bbls of product a day, but produces only 259 000 bbls/day of its own equity oil. Venezuelan crude is therefore particularly welcome. But are things as simple as they appear?

## Vertical integration: a specific assets hypothesis

In fact things are not so simple. This is amply seen by the historic patterns of upstream and downstream integration within the industry. It is relatively common for upstream producers to integrate backwards downstream through refining, distribution and marketing. It is far less common for firms to integrate forward (from refining into production), the classic Rockefeller trust strategy. And, at no time, have wholesalers, jobbers, and distributors integrated forward into refining or (for that matter) into production (See Bindeman's 1999 review).

Looked at in terms of the strict specific assets argument, these trends are something of a paradox. Given that the assets in the crude oil-refining-marketing supply chain are specific assets in terms of valuation of physical assets and the degree of their specialisation to their users, why do we have this pattern of many cases of backward integration and so few of forward integration? Our answer to this question lies in the management costs of vertical integration, and in a better appreciation of human capital as a critical specific asset in the vertical integration equation.

### The Oil MNE and the costs of vertical integration

Yet what are the specific management costs involved with retaining refining operations within the vertically integrated oil firm? These are several (see Grant, 2002, pp. 396–400, in a more general context).

Matching crude production to refinery crude runs is a problem, but one with modifications. This matching not only involves differing scales of operation, but even today may involve matching particular crude types with particular refineries. This problem is somewhat less significant today, given the set of oil markets and the accessibility of different crude oil types for the individual refinery. Yet, perhaps surprisingly, there are still refineries dependent on a particular set of crude types for their feedstock.

Another problem with refining activities is that the skills which are involved in refining are substantially different from those characteristic of upstream activities. If anything, refining can probably best be seen as a manufacturing activity, an activity which not only requires skills different from those of exploration, production and transportation, but are also different from marketing skills. (Yet, as we will note, due to problems of product mix and transport differentials, refining and marketing skills have tended to overlap in the oil industry.) With management competences and skills rest a host of other problems: the necessity of following a different strategy for refining than that for exploration and production, the difficulty of developing differing (and, in many instances, conflicting) core competencies within the same over-all corporate organisation, and the need for preserving management incentives for differing activities – so that refinery or marketing managers do not feel that managers in upstream activities receive more than their fair share of any corporate incentive scheme (and vice-versa).

Finally, the question arises as to the degree of corporate flexibility and risk involved in retaining vertically integrated refining activities. It is almost a truism that the international oil industry is confronting a world of significant change. In such a world, is it wise to retain a major commitment to a sector which, in general, not only is less profitable than the other sectors, not only involves differing strategies and differing management skills, but also can hinder corporate flexibility and the accompanying vitally needed changes in corporate structure? As we shall see, differing corporations have resorted to different strategies in this regard.

*Refineries and specific assets: a reinterpretation*

Given the costs of managing the vertically integrated enterprise, any specific assets interpretation of vertical integration must complement the physical definition of specific assets with that of human capital skills as specific assets. Specific physical assets have been characterised as those assets containing one or more of the following features: site specificity, physical asset specificity, and those characteristics associated with dedicated assets (Williamson, 1983). For my purposes I shall focus on the two of these characteristics relevant for refinery restructuring.

Site specificity, the location of fixed facilities so as 'to economise on inventory or transportation expenses' (Williamson, 1983, p. 555), is relevant for our purposes in that transport, distribution, and storage differentials have always been critical to the industry: and 'dedicated assets', a specific investment by a supplier or buyer for the purpose of transacting a specific (and here a very large) amount of crude and crude products with a partner or set of partners which would otherwise not have been undertaken.

While the value of human assets was recognised as relevant twenty years ago (see Williamson, 1981; Monteverdi and Teece, 1982), academic analysis of human specific assets in an oil industry vertical integration context is non-existent. Major studies are of other industries and have tended to the analysis of sales forces as specific human assets (Anderson and Schmittlein, 1984; John and Weitz, 1988;

Anderson, 1985), or the analysis of the make-or-purchase literature (Masten, 1984; Lydon, 1995; Jensen and Rothwell, 1998; Coles and Hesterly, 1998; and Freeland, 2000). A good example of what is meant here can be seen in the various analyses of the General Motors acquisition of the Fisher Body Corporation. This is the classic example of an acquisition seen in terms of Fisher Body's specific physical assets and the problem of 'hold-up'. Freeland (2000) investigated the historical circumstances of the take-over more closely and found that

> Firstly...GM's initial investment in Fisher Body occurred primarily to gain access to the Fisher brothers' specialized human assets. Second[ly] hold-up was not the cause of GM's purchase of Fisher Body. Instead, the primary factors leading to vertical integration were GM management's fears over the Fisher brothers' impending departure, coupled with the problems of financing new body plants (Freeland, 2000, p. 33).

The literature on oil industry vertical integration and the problem of integrating refining assets in the firm misses this vital dimension, much as past studies on GM and Fisher Body have done. I feel that a purely specialised specific physical assets approach to the problem can be misleading and therefore not offer a satisfactory explanation of what has happened in the past and what may happen in the future.

*A reinterpretation: the structure of the argument*

In this reinterpretation of refineries as specific assets and oil company restructuring, I assume two sets of specific assets: a set of specific physical assets (here site specific and dedicated assets), and a set of specific human assets. I further assume that the two sets are complementary and that together they explain both the state of oil company semi-vertical integrated structure of today, and the manner in which it is likely to evolve. Fortunately evidence as to how the specific physical assets have been restructured exists in a major study by Mabro *et al* (1990) on the physical restructuring of the European refinery industry in the period 1976 through 1986. Similarly, information provided by the US Energy Information Agency provides evidence of how specific human assets may have been critical in a later restructuring wave, in the USA in the last half of the 1990s.

Accordingly, I structure the balance of this chapter in two parallel sections. I firstly review the problems of restructuring from the point of view of specific physical assets, and then discuss how the European refinery restructuring wave of 1976 through 1986 conformed to the predictions set out by that interpretation. I thereafter take a deeper look at the nature of the skills involved in refining, distributing and marketing and argue that these have the properties similar to those characteristic of specific human assets. This is followed by the changes in the US refining industry in the light of this interpretation.

This leads to the conclusions of the final section. As a consequence of the approach which I have outlined, I see the future oil company as a semi-integrated entity, one in which the boundaries of intra- and interfirm transactions are constantly moving. I see that this will be necessary for the large vertically integrated firm, if it is going to keep its costs down, its downstream markets intact, and its future secure.

### Are refineries specific assets? The specific physical assets interpretation

In this context I examine refinery asset specificity firstly, with regard to refinery location and the transport differentials (site specificity), and, secondly, in terms of refinery technology and its match to both upstream feed, and downstream market demand (dedicated assets). I will then examine the restructuring of the European refinery industry in the period 1976 through 1986, and see to what degree the pattern of restructuring might have been predicted from a specific physical assets interpretation.

*Refineries as site specific: transport differentials*

The interrelationship between transport differentials and refinery site specificity can probably best be illustrated through a much simplified figure, Figure 3.1 (below). Figure 3.1 illustrates two scenarios:

---

**(a) Three site scenario**
Producer —— $T_C$ → Export —— $T_P$ → Terminal —— $T_D$ → Consumer
                          Refinery

**(b) Two site scenario**
Producer —— $T_C$ → Refiner —— $T_D$ → Consumer
                       (Terminal)

---

**Figure 3.1    Transport differentials: two simplified scenarios**

In the first, the three site scenario includes an export refinery. The transport cost to the integrated retailer and to the non-integrated end consumer is the sum of $T_C$, $T_P$, and $T_D$, respectively the costs of crude transport, $T_C$, product transport, $T_P$ and costs associated with distribution, $T_D$. There are multiple organisational solutions here. The advantage of this scenario is that the export refinery need not be built to fit a specific regional product market, but can be built to serve several regional markets. It could be integrated into the operations of a large vertically integrated major. It could be a non-integrated 'merchant refinery' buying its crude throughput on the market and selling its product further to third parties (who then incur $T_P$ and $T_D$). If the refinery is integrated upstream, its owner transfer product to the local terminal serving the regional market concerned. In such a case, it could either sell the product through its own integrated distribution outlets, sell the product to independent distributor, or (most likely) dispose of products through a combination of integrated and non integrated outlets.

This would not be the case for the integrated refinery dedicated to the regional market (the two site scenario in Figure 3.1). Such a refinery can take crude deliveries direct from the producer, thereby saving $T_P$. But in so doing, the integrated refinery becomes a specific asset in the sense that it is tied to the specific regional market.

An export refinery (three site illustration) is not specific in this sense. Its advantage, generally, is that it can utilise scale economies where the integrated (two site) refinery might not. Generally a fall in transport differentials and an increase to economies of scale works to the disadvantage of an integrated (two site) refinery here. Much will depend on the nature of the market being served in judging the costs and benefits of this trade-off. (For example, a large export integrated refinery located close to its source of crude throughput, could reduce costs through economies of scale and of transport on the $T_C$ leg sufficiently to outweigh the costs of the $T_P$ and the $T_D$ legs and outcompete a regionally based integrated refiner competitor.) Costs of the $T_C$ legs, particularly if the $T_C$ is that of supertanker transport, however, are generally so low that savings here are sufficient to outweigh the transport differential advantage of a smaller integrated regional competitor.

What is the significance of these observations for oil company restructuring? Generally speaking, one would assume that oil multinationals when faced with a refining crisis such as that experienced in the period 1978 through 1986, would retain those refineries/specific assets (two site illustration) where final market size guarantees refining economies of scale, sell or abandon those export refineries (three site example) disadvantaged in terms of transport differentials. Such hypotheses must be advanced with caution. The increase in crude prices, for example, has reduced the transport differential advantage enjoyed by well-located smaller dedicated refineries. Similarly, improvement of refinery economics might be meaningless if corporate distribution and marketing did not become more efficient. (I shall return to these arguments later.)

### Refineries as specific (dedicated) assets: hydroskimming versus gasoline (complex) refineries

Over and above their location, refineries can be specific assets in technical terms. The range in refinery types and their matching with crude inputs and product market demand is very wide. To further analyse refineries as specific assets, therefore, we must look at the various refinery types, and thereafter first look at the consequences of these types for wholesale and retail market demand and second examine how refinery type affects the choice of crude throughputs.

*A note on refinery specificity and product demand*

Generally speaking, any refinery is a variation on three basic refinery types: simple (or 'hydroskimming'), complex (or 'gasoline') and very complex. Table 3.1 (next page) explains the differences between these types in terms of their capital plant

**Table 3.1  Refining processes simplified**

| | Unit | Purpose |
|---|---|---|
| **Hydroskimming** | Crude Distillation Unit (CDU) | Distils crude oil into product fractions: butane (+other gasses), gasoline, naphtha, kerosene, light and heavy gasoil and 'straight run residue' |
| | Naphtha Hydrotreater | Removal of impurities from naphtha runs |
| | Catalytic Reformer | Conversion of parafins + naphtha to gasoline blending (isoparafins, napthenes, aromatics) products |
| **Gasoline (complex)** | Alkylation unit | Converts propylene,butolene, isobutene into propane, butane, and alkylate (gasoline additive) |
| | Flasher | Converts residue from CDU into light flashed/heavy flashed distillates (or combined into 'flasher tops') |
| | Visbreaker | Converts 30-40 pct of flasher bottoms into gas, naphtha, and gasoil through thermal cracking (460°C) |
| | Catalytic Cracker | Through use of catalyst treats flasher tops and heavy gasoil and produces cracked gasoline, light gas oil, and heavy gasoil |
| | Hydrocracker | Catalytic cracking in presence of hydrogen converts low quality gas oil (which would otherwise become distillate) into high quality gasoline |
| **Very complex** | Coker | Severe thermal cracking. Heavy residue converted to coke, and removed (30 %). Balance cracked to gasoline ca. 8 %; naphtha 15 %; gasoil 50 %. Gasses, propanes and butanes constitute the final balance |
| | (and/or) Olefins unit | 'Cracks' refinery 'junk feed' (ethane, propane, butane, naphtha, and gas oil into ethylene (petrochemical base), more recently used to crack naphtha and gas oils into high octane gasoline blending component |

(complexity) and what that plant is designed to do. Generally speaking in interpreting the table, the following features obtain:

Crude distillation units are the core of any refinery operation. These essentially distil the various hydrocarbon 'fractions' from the raw crude fed into the distillation tower. Each fraction, for example, butane, raw gasoline, naphtha, heavy and light gas oils boil off at their evaporation ('cut off') point. All other units in a refinery exist to further refine these fractions.

Other units exist for three purposes: 'cracking', the breaking of larger molecules into smaller (generally done through catalytic agents or heat), 'reforming' creating smaller molecules into larger, and purification of the refinery throughput or products. This 'stretching' or 'squeezing' of molecules is aimed at reducing the crude oil input into as many premium products as physically and economically possible, and minimising the 'residual fraction' Some of the terms in Table 3.1 refer to intermediate products: 'flasher tops', alkylates, naphtha, for example, which are intermediate products used to increase the throughput of gasoline, ethylene, jet fuel, and lighter gas oils. Motor gasoline is the result of blending many of the more unfamiliar products mentioned in the table. 'Mogas' is really the result of a complicating blending process which I shall not go into in this context.

Note that 'topping plant', a refinery with only a crude distillation unit (CDU) is excluded from Table 3.1 as these are infrequent and often exist for other purposes than those discussed here. As could be expected, the next unit in terms of complexity, the simple, 'hydroskimming' refinery has a minimum of plant beside the crude distillation unit (CDU). The existence of a 'hydrotreater' (which gives the refinery its nickname) and a catalytic reformer aids in the preparation of gasoline blending.

The complex ('gasoline') refinery has all the equipment of a hydroskimmer but, in contrast, has many secondary processes designed to wrench as much premium product from the crude oil concerned. It converts olefins (ethylene, propylene, butylenes) into salable gases and alkylate (a valuable gasoline additive) through its alkylation unit. A flasher converts the refinery residue from the distillation unit into 'flasher tops'. These are then 'cracked' with heavy gas oil in a catalytic cracker producing additional ('cracked') gasoline, lighter (more saleable) gas oil and some heavy gas oil. The poorer quality gas oil is then 'hydrocracked' (catalytic cracking in the presence of hydrogen) into high quality gasoline. As can be seen through this description, through secondary processes, predominantly cracking, the share of motor gasoline from a crude oil run is maximised.

The very complex refinery is of two types. It has all of the units of the complex refinery but has either a 'coker' or a olefins unit. These both take refinery 'junk feed' (heavy residue in the case of the coker, and a mix of poorly refined products in that of the oliefins unit) and further process it into more valuable products. (It should be noted that we have excluded lubricant refineries from our discussion here, although they tend to be complex highly capital intensive refineries as well.)

Assuming the input of a uniform crude oil type, how do the various refinery types perform in, terms of products? An example is given in Table 3.2 (next page). As can be seen from the table, the greater the complexity, the higher the proportion of valuable products, given the same crude type. The problem remains of matching refinery throughput to regional market demand for products, and this remains in large part a function of refinery design.

**Table 3.2   Refineries as specific assets: classification and throughput (West Texas Sour Crude)**

| Refinery Classification | Simple | Complex | Very Complex |
|---|---|---|---|
| Products | ----------- Percent yield ----------- | | |
| Gasoline | 30 | 50 | 65 |
| Jet fuel | 10 | 19 | 20 |
| Distillate fuel | 20 | 17 | 25 |
| Residual fuel | 35 | 20 | 0 |
| Fuel loss (gain) | 5 | (6) | (10) |

*Source*: Leffler, 1984, p. 141

*Refinery specificity and crude throughput* Refineries, both integrated and non-integrated, must be profitable. One commonly used measure of profitability is the per barrel cash operating margin accruing to the refinery concerned. If we assume a standard barrel of crude (here we take West Texas Sour for illustration) and identical throughputs, we can observe the results in Table 3.3. As can be seen from the table, the percentage of premium products from the same crude varies considerably between the two refineries. If we include distillates, the complex refinery accounts for 80 percent of throughput as premium (commanding a price of more than 31 dollars per barrel), whereas the simple hydroskimming refinery produces only 65 percent of its throughput as premium. (The balance in both refineries, residual fuel oil ('resid') is lower priced in that it generally competes with other low priced fuels, for example coal, in markets such as that for electricity generation.) What is particularly notable, however, is in spite of per barrel operating costs three times the size of that of the hydroskimming plant ($3.00 per barrel versus $1.00 per barrel throughput), the complex (or gasoline) refinery has a positive operating margin of $1.75 per barrel while its hydroskimming counterpart has a negative margin of $0.65 per barrel.

Unnoted in Table 3.3 is the degree to which refinery profitability is a function of its capacity utilisation. If we assume that fixed costs of refinery operation are of the order 40 to 50 percent of the operating costs in Table 3.3, and that the two refineries are running at 50 or 60 percent capacity, the operating margins for the two refineries will fall from minus $0.65/bbl to between minus $1.15/bbl and $1.05/bbl for the hydroskimming plant and from plus $1.75/bbl to between plus $0.25/bbl and plus $0.35/bbl for the gasoline refinery, and this is excluding the fact that many variable costs are not manipulable in the short run. Taking these latter variable costs into account, both refineries are likely running at a loss.

*Refinery specificity and crude type* Refinery specificity is not just a matching of complexity to market demand and crude costs, as assumed above, it is also a function of crude type. To illustrate this point, we assume that both refineries are no longer processing West Texas Sour crude, but are processing lower grade Mayan crude priced at $26.00/bbl. As can be seen from comparing Table 3.3 and Table 3.4 the type of crude feed into a refinery is vital to its operating margin. Through substituting Mayan crude for West Texas Sour crude the simple hydro-skimming refinery

**Table 3.3    Refining $28/bbl West Texas Sour Crude**

|  | Hydroskimming | | | Complex Refinery | | |
|---|---|---|---|---|---|---|
|  | pct. volume | Unit cost/ price | Revenue/ Total Cost | pct. volume | Unit cost/ price | Revenue/ Total Cost |
| Mayan crude | 100 | $28 | 28.00 | 100 | $28 | 28.00 |
| Gasoline | 30 | 32 | 9.60 | 50 | 32 | 16.00 |
| Jet fuel | 10 | 32 | 3.20 | 19 | 32 | 6.08 |
| Distillate fuel | 20 | 31 | 6.20 | 17 | 31 | 5.27 |
| Residual fuel | 35 | 27 | 9.45 | 20 | 27 | 5.40 |
| Refinery fuel (gain) | 5 | -- | ---- | (6) | -- | ---- |
| Total outturn | 100 | | 28.45 | 100 | | 32.75 |
| Operating Costs | 100 | 1 | 1.00 | 100 | 3 | 3.00 |
| Operating Margin | | | (0.65) | | | 1.75 |

*Source*: W.L. Leffler, 1985, p. 139. For a similar set of calculations see also Energy Information Administration, 'Chapter 7 US Refining Cash Margin Trends: Factors Affecting the Margin Component of Price' *Petroleum 1996: Issues and Trends* (Washington, DC: US Department of Energy, 1997), pp. 121-140.

**Table 3.4    Refining $26/bbl Mayan Crude**

|  | Hydroskimming | | | Complex Refinery | | |
|---|---|---|---|---|---|---|
|  | pct. volume | Unit cost/price | Revenue/ Total Cost | pct. volume | Unit cost/ price | Revenue/ Total Cost |
| WT Sour crude | 100 | $26 | 26.00 | 100 | $26 | 26.00 |
| Gasoline | 10 | 32 | 3.20 | 25 | 32 | 8.00 |
| Jet fuel | 5 | 32 | 1.60 | 5 | 32 | 1.60 |
| Distillate fuel | 20 | 31 | 6.20 | 25 | 31 | 7.75 |
| Residual fuel | 60 | 27 | 16.20 | 50 | 27 | 12.50 |
| Refinery fuel (gain) | - | -- | ---- | (5) | -- | ---- |
| Total outturn | 100 | | 28.45 | 100 | | 29.50 |
| Operating Costs | 100 | 1 | 1.00 | 100 | 3 | 3.00 |
| Operating Margin | | | 0.20 | | | 0.50 |

*Source*: W.L. Leffler, 1985, p. 139.

is returned to profitability, and the operating margins at the complex gasoline refinery are reduced to $0.50/bbl. from $1.75 from West Texas Sour. Clearly, the refinery owners are going to specialise in the crude type which they find the most profitable. But, can the owner of the refinery refining Mayan crude find an outlet for the massive amounts of residual fuel which is a consequence of her choice? Specialising in 'resid' means competition with coal prices, and can run into environmental problems should the residual produced contain larger than permitted amounts of sulphur. Here a rapid change in either market demand or in environmental legislation can render continued operations at the simple refinery unprofitable.

What can one conclude from these interdependencies, and does this mean that refineries due to their throughputs can be said to be specific assets? While the West Texas Sour Crude example in Table 3.1 shows the advantages of complexity, this is not necessarily always the case. Generally speaking, the complex refinery is more resistant to market sensitivities, whereas the hydroskimming refinery has less latitude in its choice of crude throughput. In that a refinery is dependent on a particular set of crude grades for its profitability, it can be said to qualify for the transaction specificity condition. Should this transaction be terminated or altered considerably, the refinery must either close or be upgraded.

To look at the problem from the consumer side, is there a transaction specific character to refinery investment? This depends on the particular situation. If we assume that two refineries in competition with each other both produce residual fuel oil, but the one produces 'resid' with a higher sulphur content than allowed by the national authorities, it may be forced to sell this product to a foreign competitor at a substantial discount, or alternatively have the sulphur removed at the company's own transport and processing cost at another installation. Here the specific assets argument is 'turned on its head'. The company concerned must either abandon the refinery, and either sell its marketing facilities (or rely on product imports) or commit itself to investing in the required specific asset investments, in this example sulphur removal and treatment plants.

With regard to both crude and product type examples, it is the asset specific investment that is required to maintain vertical integration. Its role is not causal as prescribed by theory. Rather it is the reverse. Specific investments are not a cause of vertical integration; rather maintenance of vertical integration requires a specific investment. A company facing such a decision could well decide the costs of continued vertical integration in the particular case are outweighed by the benefits of corporate divestiture. Small wonder, then, that oil companies, when faced with these choices, decide to divest.

### The European restructuring 'wave' 1976–1986: redefining specific physical assets?

The aftershocks of the events of the period 1971 through 1978 were essentially two fold. Firstly, majors scrambled to assure themselves of crude for their refinery runs. By 1986 this scramble appeared to have been resolved. The world was aflood with surplus crude, and the new market mechanisms were falling into place. Secondly, however, and perhaps more importantly, the severance of vertically integrated sources of crude was coupled with price rises which significantly altered the nature of oil product markets. An illustration of this altered market situation is presented in Table 3.5. Here Dargay presents estimates of average price elasticities of demand for Western Europe calculated on historical data as of 1985. These averages, however, cover a multitude of national variations. Thus, long run price elasticities for gasoline vary from -0.20 (Greece) to -1.60 (Austria) (Dargay, 1990, p.75). Clearly refinery owners were facing extreme change in their respective domestic markets. Not only would they be forgoing anticipated increases in oil product market demand, but the nature of this demand would be significantly different from that of previous forecasts.

**Table 3.5**　　**Weighted average price elasticities for various products by end-user category: Western Europe 1965–1985**

|  | Short run | Five-year | Long-run |
| --- | --- | --- | --- |
| Gasoline | -0.25 | -0.67 | -0.91 |
| Automotive Diesel | -0.08 | -0.13 | -0.14 |
| Light Fuel Oil (Industry) | -0.18 | -0.49 | -0.72 |
| Light Fuel Oil (Other) | -0.29 | -0.74 | -0.96 |
| Heavy Fuel Oil (Industry) | -0.25 | -0.75 | -1.66 |

*Source*: Dargay, 1990, p.92

The oil MNEs would have to cut back on their refinery plant, restructure surviving plant to match changed market demand, and rationalise their downstream marketing outlets. Table 3.6 summarises the resulting refinery siting activities in the period. A total of 54 refineries closed in this period but three new refineries also came on stream).

What explanatory value have the site specific and dedicated assets characteristics here? With regard ......to site specificity, here primarily transport differentials, the following results obtained: the further the refinery from other refineries, or more particularly one of the European refinery centres, the greater the chance for survival. For those smaller refineries located inland, the number of closures was far over the average. Another locational factor of importance was the number of refineries owned by the same company in a single national market (Long, 1990, pp.100-110). The greater the number, the greater the probability that one or more of them would be closed. Finally, those large scale refineries (1) with tanker facilities suitable to supertankers, and (2) located close to large regional markets had a higher than average probability of remaining open.

**Table 3.6    European refineries 1976–1986: the pattern of closures**

|  | Wholly owned | Shared ownership | Total |
|---|---|---|---|
| Open 1976 | 133 | 41 | 174 |
| Changed hands (1976–1986) | 30 | 32 | 62 |
| [then closed] | [7] | [8] | [15] |
| Other closed | 36 | 3 | 39 |
| Survivors 1984 | 90 | 30 | 120 |

*Source*: Long, 1990, p. 111

With regard to the dedicated assets argument, here refinery complexity, the picture was equally clear. There were 34 topping refineries in operation in 1976, 14 in 1986. There were 68 hydroskimming refineries in 1976, and only 14 in 1986. Thus at the topping/hydroskimming end of the complexity scale, the number of such refineries fell over-all from 102 to 28 (Chadwick, 1990, p.166). Clearly not all of these refineries were closed; many were upgraded. In 1976 67.7 percent of all crude runs, 13 900 600 bbls/day by volume went to hydroskimming plants. By 1986 this figure had fallen, 29.4 percent of such runs, 4 290 400 bbls/day, were going to such plants. Table 3.7 gives a further impression as to how refineries have been restructured in the period 1976 to 2002. As can be seen from the table, in the period 1986 to 2002 only an additional 17 refineries have been closed, while catalytic cracking facilities have continued to increase.

There would appear to be a pattern here that more or less conforms to our analysis. Refineries as specific physical assets vary predictably with regard to their value for the firm, and vary in accordance with our measures of specificity: transport differentials, and the overall matching of refinery throughput with demand (here the complexity factor is of importance). But, is this explanation sufficient? A major statistical analysis measuring variables such as those posited here, attempted in retrospect to predict which refineries in 1976 would be closed in 1986 was conducted by Bacon (1990). Using both linear probability and probit models, his predictions erred by a factor of 14 percent vis-a-vis the total population (174) or 45 percent in regards to the actual identity of those refineries closing (54). Thirteen refineries which Bacon's models predicted would stay open in fact shut down, and eleven refineries they had predicted would shut down in fact stayed open. While there are some statistical explanations as to why this should be the case, Bacon mentions 'special features, unaccounted for in the model, or management aims' (Bacon, 1990, pp. 157-158) as accounting for the deviances from accurate prediction. Could specific human capital also have played a role here?

**Table 3.7       Refinery plant: restructuring in Western Europe**

| Refinery Classification | 1976 | 1986 | 2002 |
|---|---|---|---|
| Nr. of Refineries | 174 | 123 | 106 |
| | -------------------- 1000 bbl/day --------------------- | | |
| Crude Distillation | 20,527 | 14,496 | 14,531 |
| Cat Cracking | 986 | 1,643 | 2,143 |
| Thermal Cracking | 500 | 1,528 | 1,559 |

*Sources*: Long, 1990, p. 101. 2002 figures from Energy Information Agency, *International Energy Annual, 2001*, pp.62-64. 1976 and 1986 figures from Long, 1990, p. 101. Note that in Europe hydrocracking often substitutes for catalytic cracking. Thus catalytic cracking figures thus understate the true capacity by 60 000 bbls/day (1976) and 247 000 bbls/day (1986).

## Are refineries specific assets? II. The specific human assets interpretation

In this context, specific human assets are defined as human assets characterised by 'knowledge occurring via education, skills acquired by training, experience gained during employment, ideas and inventions developed in research, [even] personal networks established in the workplace' (Tang and Tseng, 2004, p. 2). As noted in the introduction, the idea of specific human assets was early seen as critical to corporate organisation in the early specific assets interpretation. Yet the question remains, does the maintenance of valuable firm specific human assets lead to vertical integration?

The problem here is that the implications of specific human assets are somewhat different from those of specific physical assets. Given that vertical integration typically involves several very different sets of activities, one could make the argument that specific human assets can have a negative effect on vertical integration. This would particularly be the case where specialisation in one set of activities precludes its effective integration into other activity sets. The refining industry may be a case in point here.

*Are specific human assets an incentive to vertical integration?*

In fact, the efficient running of a refinery requires skills and know how which are high specialised to the refinery concerned, in terms of its upstream supply, the balancing of its 'runs' with demand, and its management of relations with an often very complex transportation, distribution and marketing downstream network.

Selecting crude for refinery runs is a highly complex task. Refineries, particularly complex refineries, will take a multiple of crude types and grades. (The Hovensa example in the introduction had utilised no fewer than 60 differing crude types). Generally speaking, refineries classify crudes into three basic categories, depending on the conditions of their supply. There are crudes which are used for 'balancing' refinery runs. These are crudes which have 'marginal values which equal their prices' and are 'neither upwardly or downwardly limited' (Hartmann, 2003). Then there are crudes which are supplied within defined maximum/minimum quantities with marginal values higher/lower than their prices. And finally there are crudes which are not being processed but, given the supply/price of competing crudes, (and the result of the relevant linear programming model) might qualify as a 'balancing crude' in the future (Hartmann, 2003). Adequate supplies of all three basic types of crude must be assured. Tankage for the various grades must be made available. Supplementary refinery feedstocks (natural gas liquids, for example) might be available, and the 'feed' of all these grades into various refining units must be carefully monitored so that the product blends maximise returns and are appropriate to the specific markets.

Crude valuation and scheduling, a process which requires coordination of pipeline and marine terminals, crude tanks and input to the basis crude units (CDU), is followed by an additional series of specialised tasks. Crude scheduling is complemented by unit scheduling and blend scheduling. After distillation, semi-finished products and 'junk' is fed into secondary units (catalytic cracker, alkylation plant, hydrotreater and the like). This all has to be done in a coordinated manner:

> Refinery operations scheduling is one of the most challenging activities, where the technologies and the tools have not been successful across the board. The reason for this is COMPLEXITY, covering the crude system logistics, process units, blending, offsites, and shipping each with vastly different time constants, economic models, procedures, and constraints. In addition the scheduler has to react to daily process and business variability, human interaction unpredictability, and time consuming integration of data (Barsamien, 2001, pp. 9-10, emphasis is Barsamien's).

Not only do units and throughput have to be coordinated, but many refinery products are the result of blending. Batches of multiple components have to be blended in the specified manner and stored for sale. Scheduling of throughput is dependent on the planned recipes for the final products. New environmental rules and regulations now require that products must 'meet 20 to 30 property specs simultaneously' (Barsamien, 2001, p12). Today, for example, it is not unusual for a merchant refinery to prepare no fewer than 60 different blends of gasoline (ibid).

Specific human assets here are invaluable. An efficiently run refinery where the problems discussed above have been solved in a satisfactory manner, can earn $0.50 to $1.00 per barrel more than a less well managed refinery. This translates into 40 to 80 million dollars per year for a 200 000 bbl/day refinery. Yet as Barsamien notes of the newest refinery programming technology: '[E]xperienced people are the key to success; software and computers, no matter how powerful and glitzy, are not substitutes for understanding the refining business and processes' (ibid, p.17).

To be successfully integrated downstream furthermore involves even further complexity. There are two types of refinery: merchant refineries which refine products which are then sold from its 'rack' to a network of wholesalers, jobbers, dealers, distributors each with his own particular demands for product, and a refinery which is either partially or wholly integrated downstream into its own transportation, storage, distribution, retailing network. And each of these downstream agents is highly professional. Gasoline wholesalers, for example, purchase the product, transport it, pay direct and indirect terminal expenses, add additives, blend on their own account, and provide hedging services for their customers (Spletter and Star, 2001, pp. 46–7). Their product is generally held in a terminal which may or may not be owned by the wholesaler. (Many terminals are independently owned and operate as a service to the industry.) A similar degree of complexity and fierce competition characterises the other segments of the downstream gasoline industry.

Whereas many vertically integrated oil companies may have partially integrated to the gasoline pump, independent marketers provide the gateway to other distillate products. Here too, competition is fierce, with oil companies disengaging from those markets where they do not have strategic advantage.

Taking the pattern that emerges in terms of human specific assets, it would appear that integration in the oil industry is breaking into two core activity sets, both of which are characterised by highly specific human assets: upstream through the refinery gate (crude production and refining), and downstream from the refinery reception terminal through final product marketing. How does this putative pattern look? To answer this question, I will look briefly at the restructuring evidence from the North American refining industry.

*Are specific human assets an incentive to vertical integration? Evidence from North America*

If the implications of the discussion about refinery processes and their up- and downstream integration 'hold water', one should expect to see oil firms breaking into two differing integrated groupings: an upstream grouping – only minimally, if at all, engaged in downstream product distribution and marketing; and a downstream grouping – minimally engaged, if at all, in upstream activities, but actively involved in refining, distribution and marketing. In fact, the picture is both more complex and more interesting than I have implied.

This can be seen in Table 3.8 – a listing of the top US refiners between 1982 (when restructuring in the US really began) and 2002 is organised by company refinery capacity, and ranking in 1982 (columns to the left). To the right are the same firms (often renamed, reorganised or both), in the same order (but not the same ranking) as on the left. In that the 1982 column includes firms which have risen to the top ten in 2002, there are 15 firms listed with their rankings in 1982. One additional firm is included in the 2002 column, PDV America (the PDV Venezuelan joint venture with refiners Citgo, and Lyondell-Citgo, and (through Hovensa) with Amerada-Hess, both discussed in the introduction to this chapter).

Some of the changes in rankings are predictable, given the mergers discussed in the first chapter of this book. Thus BP (ranked number 13 in 1982) through its acquisition of Amoco (number 4 in 1982) and Atlantic Richfield (number 8 in 1982) is ranked number 3 in 2002. Exxon/Mobil have risen from rankings as number 2 and 7 in 1982 to number 1 in 2002. Other changes are more surprising.

Table 3.8    Patterns of ownership: US refining industry 1982–2002

| Name (1982) | 1982 | | | Name (2002) | 2002 | | |
|---|---|---|---|---|---|---|---|
| | Rank | No of refineries | Capacity (1000 bbl/d) | | Rank | No of refineries | Capacity (1000 bbl/d) |
| Chevron | 1 | 12 | 1469.7 | Chevron/Texaco | 7 | 12 | 1049.0 |
| Exxon | 2 | 5 | 1200.0 | Exxon/Mobil | 1 | 6.5 | 1863.5 |
| Shell | 3 | 7 | 1092.0 | Shell Oil[a] | 4 | 8.5 | 1157.7 |
| Amoco | 4 | 7 | 1011.0 | -- | -- | -- | -- |
| Texaco | 5 | 9 | 937.0 | -- | -- | -- | -- |
| Gulf Oil | 6 | 5 | 881.1 | -- | -- | -- | -- |
| Mobil | 7 | 6 | 859.7 | -- | -- | -- | -- |
| ARCO | 8 | 5 | 708.0 | -- | -- | -- | -- |
| Amerada-Hess | 9 | 3 | 612.0 | Amerada-Hess[b] | 16 | 2.5 | 354.5 |
| Marathon | 10 | 4 | 588.0 | USX/Marathon[c] | 9 | 2.5 | 597.7 |
| Sun | 15 | 3 | 358.0 | Sunoco | 8 | 4.0 | 724.0 |
| BP | 13 | 3 | 456.0 | BP(Amoco) | 3 | 8.0 | 1662.4 |
| Phillips | 18 | 3 | 295.0 | Phillips[d] | 2 | 13.0 | 1699.3 |
| Saber Energy | 79 | 1 | 19.0 | Valero[e] | 5 | 13.0 | 1083.9 |
| | -- | -- | -- | PDV America[f] | 6 | 6.0 | 1075.3 |
| Apex Oil | 31 | 2 | 104.5 | Premcor | 10 | 4.0 | 561.0 |

[a]Includes former Equilon, 50% of Motiva and 50% of Deer Park
[b]Includes 50% of Hovensa
[c]Includes 38% of Marathon Ashland Petroleum
[d]Result of 2000 purchase of Tosco (which owned 10 refineries 1813.3 bbls/day capacity at that time)
[e]Acquired Shamrock Diamond Ultramar (UDS) (2001); UDS, a merger between Diamond Shamrock and Ultramar (1997), acquired Total Petroleum (1998). Valero acquired in addition to UDS, Solomon (1997)
[f]Includes Citgo, 50% of Lyondell-Citgo and 50 % of Hovensa

Chevron (number 1 in 1982) despite its acquisition of Gulf Oil (number 6 in 1982) and merger with Texaco (number 4 in 1982), falls in rankings from its 1982 number 1 position to number 7 in 2002. It should be noted in this context that many of the refinery asset sales in this period were required by regulatory authorities as a precondition for oil company merger. This in turn aided the non-integrated refiners in their acquisition strategies.

Equally interesting is the fact that the top ten ranked refiners in 1982 were all vertically integrated into exploration and production. In 2002, only seven of the top ten firms were vertically integrated; six, if one disallows the 1999 acquisition by Phillips of the then second ranked refiner Tosco. Of the top ten refiners in 2002, 50 percent were not among the top ten in 1982: Sunoco, BP (Amoco), Philip, Valero, PDV America, and Premcor.

There is a marked rise in the size of downstream refiners. Tosco, ranked number 21 in 1982, with four refineries and 258 800 bbls/day capacity through astute acquisition of refinery plant (much of it from the majors), merger, and innovative downstream marketing, rose to the number 2 ranking in 1999 with 10 refineries and1 813 000 bbls/day capacity, to be bought out by Phillips, until then a minor refiner (three refineries with 355 000 bbls/day capacity in 1999). Saber Energy, another minor refiner ranked 79 in 1982 with 19 000 bbls/day capacity, emerges as Valero, fifth ranked in 2002 as a result of an active mergers and acquisitions strategy whereby it had acquired other non-integrated refiners, themselves a product of merging activity (Ultramar Diamond Shamrock). Finally, Apex Oil, ranked 31st in 1982 with two refineries (104 500 bbls/day capacity) redubbed Premcor, comes in as the number ten ranked refiner in 2002 (four refineries and 561 000 bbls/day capacity.

What is interesting here is how merger and joint venturing has substituted for firm exit from the refining sector. This is clearest in the mergers of Exxon and Mobil, Chevron and Texaco, and BP (with Arco and Amoco).

Interestingly, the most significant joint ventures are with upstream suppliers. This can most easily be seen in the footnote entries to Table 3.8. The Shell ownership of 100 percent of Equilon (formerly 50 percent Shell and 50 percent Texaco venture) and its acquisition of 50 percent of Motiva (a 35 percent Shell, 32.5 percent Texaco and 32.5 percent Saudi Refining Inc. venture) is a result of a liquidation of Texaco refining assets upon the latter's merger with Chevron. (Aramco supplies 550 000 bbls/day to Motiva which has four refineries with a total production capacity of 800 000 bbls/day and a network of 13 000 branded gasoline stations.) Similarly, Shell's ownership of Deer Park is shared with Pemex, the national Mexican oil company and primarily utilises Mexican crudes in its refinery runs. And Hovensa and the Lyondell-Citgo refinery efforts and how these fit with Amerada-Hess, Citgo and PDV was discussed in the introduction to this chapter. Joint ventures have been one way for companies to share costs, thereby reducing per-unit costs for each. They have also been useful in setting up long-term crude supply arrangements, thereby enabling stability.

Yet merger and joint venture have not been sufficient strategies in themselves. Where these corporate strategies have occurred, they have been accompanied by a form of 'tapering integration', the JV or merger would rid itself of many of its less economic downstream outlets. Here there was a tendency to rely on wholesalers to sell motor gasoline, the most profitable premium product, while relying more on wholesale and direct sales and bypassing their company-operated and dealer outlets. What is interesting here is that this pattern has not be followed by the non-integrated refiners, In 1990 US independent refiners had retail operations in an average of ten states (13 117 retail outlets). Ten years later the average number of states had risen to 22 (21 970 retail outlets). Figures for outlets for integrated refiners fell overall, from 51 085 outlets in 1990 to 33 753 in 1997 (US Energy Information Agency, 2001b, p. 63), and was continuing its decline in 2001. The average number of states where integrated refiners had a marketing presence fell from 28 to 25 in the same period.

The simultaneous coincidence of two patterns of refining-marketing strategies, the strategy of consolidation along the lines dictated by transport differentials followed by the integrated refiners, and that of expanding both through acquiring and opening new marketing outlets, increasing economies of scale and scope, followed by their non-integrated competitors poses a puzzle. It might appear that the one grouping is restructuring its activities along the specific physical assets attributes possessed by refineries and their marketing outlets respectively while the other is relying more on the specific human assets involved in the refining-marketing relationship. At issue as well has been the revolution in gasoline marketing, the main downstream money maker. Introduction of such technologies as pay-at-the-pump, point of sales payment systems, in-store teller machines have been revolutionising outlet costs. The introduction of the convenience store concept to gas stations diversified their sources of income. Not content with this, oil firms introduced branded fast food outlets, and finally hypermarkets to their retain chains. Non-integrated independents such as Tosco led the way in this restructuring wave. (Others, however, followed somewhat different strategies. Premcor for example has decided to focus on refining only, and is alone among the top ten refiners of being purely a non-integrated merchant refinery firm.) For the industry as a whole, the effects were remarkable. Gasoline sales which averaged around 32 000 gallons per station month in 1982, passed the 100 000 level in 1999 and have kept rising ever since (US Energy Agency Information Administration, 2001a, p. 3).

## Conclusion

In the introduction to this chapter, I suggested the following themes: firstly, that physical specificity, especially in terms of site specificity and dedicated assets was of importance to oil company integration of refining activities; and, secondly, the role of specific human assets tended to be overlooked as an explanatory factor in this regard. I also suggested that differing companies would have differing strategies with regard to their refining activities. Finally, I argued that during the post 1976 period, specific investments tended to be aimed at preserving a degree of vertical integration, rather than being a cause of vertical integration.

With regard to the first argument, that specific physical assets were critical to oil company restructuring in the period 1986 to today, I found general (admittedly somewhat weak) confirmation through examining the Western European restructuring efforts during this period. Phenomena associated with site specificity were critical in the major European restructuring efforts in the period 1976 through 1986. Similarly, the upgrading of capital plant matched the changing nature of demand, a weak confirmation of the dedicated assets argument. Particularly notable here is the fact that refinery upgrading was limited to the nature of the changing European markets of the time. (Fully complex refineries are relatively fewer in Europe when compared to those in the North American market; European refinery upgrading normally occurred to the semi-complex level, the minimum needed to continue to match market demand.)

Evidence regarding the second argument, that specific human assets are an important cause of integrating refinery activities into corporate structures, is perhaps even sketchier. Here I turned to the US market for evidence, finding it in the diverging strategies followed by fully vertically integrated majors and by their non integrated competitors with regard to downstream marketing. The problem with this evidence is that it is not fully conclusive. Vertically integrated majors, for example, were also innovative in their downstream marketing investments. Similarly, the ability of the non-integrated refiners to expand in terms of both scope and scale, in part, was due to the sell-off of refining assets by the majors, some of which was dictated by lack of downstream profitability, and some, the regulatory considerations stemming from industry consolidation among the majors.

The problem with explaining oil industry refinery strategies solely from a specific assets point of view is essentially two-fold: the existence of intervening variables, and the multiple reasons for desiring vertical integration.

Intervening variables here are numerous, although there are fewer than would be the case should I have excluded human specific assets in my explanation. A major variable, here must be the regulatory systems within which refinery operations are conducted. We have looked at two patterns of behaviour: one characteristic of Western Europe, 1976–86, and one of refiner behaviour in the US market from around the mid 1980s to 2003. The patterns here have many characteristics which may not apply to other regions, other national markets. Refiner-owner behaviour will vary between regions and between countries, depending on the regulatory environment within which refiners find themselves. (For a further discussion of this point note the contribution by Oystein Noreng in the second section of this book.)

Then too, there are multiple reasons for desiring vertical integration. As I have remarked earlier, during the past 20 years, vertical integration was not the logical result of the construction of sets of mutually dependent specific assets; rather, firms committed resources to better design their specific assets to changing market and technological environments. Where firms have remained committed to vertical integration, this commitment may not have been due the existence of specific assets. Other reasons are likely many: a form of path dependency, the perception that one might take advantage of market imperfections to increase profitability, the perceived benefits accruing from ownership of multiple interlinking assets, to name but a few.

Where are oil companies going in terms of integrating their downstream activities? The evidence here indicates that the preferred emerging form of organisation is that of 'tapered integration' – a form of incomplete vertical integration which is supplemented by market exchange for many of the inputs and products at each stage of the corporate value chain. There are advantages to this structure. An oil firm can increase its throughputs without overly increasing its capital outlays. It can use its information about internal costs, technology and human skills in negotiating with external input suppliers or with non-integrated downstream marketers. Simultaneously, an oil firm can utilise the information provided by its arms length relationships to economise on its own internal operations. It must be stressed that this is only one set of options among many, joint ventures, alliances, informal inter-company networks, and the like. Still, tapered integration would allow future oil companies the means to remain flexible and competitive as they confront an uncertain future.

## References

Anderson, E. (1985), 'The Salesperson as Outside Agent or Employee: A transaction cost analysis', *Marketing Science*, **4**(3), Summer, pp. 235-254.

_____ and D.C. Schmittlein (1984), 'Integration of the Sales Force: An empirical examination', *Rand Journal of Economics*, **15**(3), Autumn, pp. 385-395.

Bacon, R. (1990), 'The Propensity of European Refineries to Shut between 1976 and 1986', in R. Mabro et al, *Demand, Prices and the Refining Industry,* Oxford: Oxford University Press for the Oxford Institute for Energy Studies, pp. 135-158.

Barsamien, A. (2001), 'Fundamentals of Supply Chain Management for Refining', *Refinery Technology Online*, December (Petroleum Institute for Continuing Education), 18pp.
www.r-t-o-l.com?modules.php?name=News&fil=News&file=art&sid=168. Accessed December 22, 2003.

Bindeman, K. (1999), 'Vertical Integration in the Oil Industry: A Review of the Literature', *Journal of Energy Literature*, **5**(1), pp. 3-26.

Bindview Corporation (2004), 'Lyondell-Citgo Refining LP', www.bindview.com/ Resources/CaseStudies/LyondellCitgo.cfm. Accessed November 21, 2004.

Blair, J.M. (1976), *The Control of Oil,* New York: Pantheon.

Chadwick, M. (1990), 'Refinery Yield, Capacity, and Output', in R. Mabro, et al, *Demand, Prices and the Refining Industry* (Oxford: Oxford University Press for the Oxford Institute for Energy Studies), pp. 163-192.

Dargay, J. (1990), 'Trends in the Demand for Petroleum Products', in R. Mabro et al, *Demand, Prices and the Refining Industry,* Oxford: Oxford University Press for the Oxford Institute for Energy Studies, pp. 39-65.

Davis, J. D. (1990), 'How Secure International Oil? Organisational Instability and Change within the Oil Industry', *International Interactions*, **16**(1), pp. 19-32.

Energy Information Administration (1997), *Petroleum 1996: Issues and Trends,* Washington, DC: US Department of Energy.

Freeland, R.F. (2000), 'Creating Hold-up Through Vertical Integration: Fisher Body Revisited', *Journal of Law and Economics*, **18**(1) April, pp. 33-66.

Hartmann, H. (2003), 'Crude Valuation for Crude Selection', *Refinery Technology Online*, May (Petroleum Institute for Continuing Education) 14pp. www.r-t-o-l.com?modules.php?name=News&file=article&sid=275.    Accessed November 25, 2004.

Leffler, W.L. (1985), *Petroleum Refining for the Non-Technical Person,* Tulsa, Oklahoma, Pennwell 2nd ed.

Long, D. (1990), 'The European Refining Industry: Structure and Changes, 1976-1986', in R. Mabro et al, *Demand, Prices and the Refining Industry,* Oxford: Oxford University Press for the Oxford Institute for Energy Studies, pp. 99-124.

Lyondell Chemical Company (2004), 'Enterprise: Refining: LYONDELL-CITGO Refining LP', http://wwww.lyondell.com/html/lyondell/enterprise_33.shtml. Accessed April 4, 2004.

Spletter, K.G. and S.L. Starr (2001), 'US Gasoline-marketing Margins Statistics Begin in this Issue', *Oil and Gas Journal* (October 15), pp. 46-55.

Tang, K-K, and Y-P Tseng (2004), 'Constructing a Measure of Industry Specific Human Capital using Tobin's q Theory', *Economics Bulletin*, **10**, www. economicsbulletin.uiuc.edu/2004/volume10/EB-03J40002A.pdf. Accessed April 4, 2004.

US Energy Agency Information Administration (2001a), *Restructuring: The Changing Face of Motor Gasoline Marketing,* November 30.        h t t p : / / www.eia.doe.gov/emeu/finance/usi&to/downstream/index.html. Accessed July 3, 2003.

_____(2001b), *Performance Profiles of Major Energy Producers 1997,* September 21, http://www.eia.doe.gov/emeu/finance/sptopics/ downstrm00/ index.html. Accessed March 16, 2003.

US Environmental Protection Agency 'Hovensa LLC' (2004), www.epa.gov/region02/ waste/fshovens.htm. Accessed November 25, 2004.

Williamson, O.E. (1983), 'The Economics of Organization: The Transaction Cost Approach', *American Journal of Sociology*, **87**(3), pp. 548-581.

# Chapter 4

# Economic Organization of Specific Assets in the Offshore Industry

Ola Kvaløy

## Introduction

A considerable amount of inputs are required to extract oil and gas offshore. One has to explore the petroleum deposits. One has to design and build equipment to extract the oil from the seabed. And, finally, one has to extract the oil. It is a great logistic challenge to organize all the involved activities in an effective way. In order to study the overall economic organization of these activities, it is useful to identify a few aggregate and strategic inputs. Two important inputs then emerge as natural choices within this framework: 1) the engineering of the oil platform and 2) the oil platform. With 'oil platform' I mean 'all type of installations that are built with the purpose of offshore oil extraction'. The engineering includes 'all activities involved in the planning and designing of the construction'.

We then have three products in what we can call a vertical supply chain: engineering of the oil platform, oil platform, oil. What is the economic organization of these products? This question can be divided into the two following: a) Under which ownership structure are the products organized? b) What are the contractual relationships between and within the ownership entities?

To take the latter first: the contractual relationships between the parties in the supply chain vary, but they always contain elements that are difficult to treat legally. For instance, the quality of an engineering service may be possible to observe for the parties involved, but difficult to asses by a third party. But even if it is difficult, or impossible, to formulate legally enforceable contracts, effecient incentive contracts are still necessary both to reduce costs and promote quality. The solution to this problem is to develop contracts that are enforced through reputational motivations. In the economics literature, a contract that cannot be legally enforced is most often referred to as a 'relational contract'. A relational contract must be self-enforcing: the present value of honouring the contract must be greater than the present value of reneging. Important economics papers on relational contracting includes Klein and Leffler (1981), Bull (1987), Macleod and Malcomson (1989), Baker, Gibbons and Murphy (1994, 2002) and Levin (2002, 2003).

Under which ownership structure are the products organized? We can identify six archetypes of ownership structures in the oil industry:

<u>Alternative A</u>: Total integration. The oil company (O) undertakes the engineering (E) and construction (C) of the oil platform.

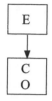

<u>Alternative B</u>: An independent engineering company designs the platform and delivers the service to an integrated oil company, which both builds the oil platform and extracts the oil.

<u>Alternative C</u>: An integrated supplier both designs and builds the platform, and sells it to the oil company.

<u>Alternative D:</u> An independent engineering company delivers project services to the main contractor that builds the platform and sells it to the oil company.

<u>Alternative E:</u> The engineers work in the oil company. They supply their services to the main contractor that builds and delivers the platform to the oil company.

<u>Alternative F</u>: An independent engineering company supplies drawings/solutions to the oil company, who passes these on to the main contractor. The main contractor then constructs a platform for the oil company.

**Figure 4.1    Organizational forms**

Alternative A and B are not observed in the offshore industry. The oil companies and the construction companies always enjoy seperate ownership. The main engineering company does seldom operate as an independent company. Alternative D and F are therefore seldom observed. Today alternative C best illustrates the economic organization of the three activities. The oil company and the main contractor agree on a so-called EPCI-contract, in which the main contractor gets the responsibility of Engineering, Procurement, Construction and Installation (for more details, see Osmundsen, 1999).

There may exist a number of explanations on why alternative C is a preferred way of organizing the oil industry. The oil companies want to focus on its core competence (defined as exploration, extraction, refinement and distribution of oil and gas) and therefore find it optimal to outsource the development projects. This focus may give them flexibility in adjusting the labor force, which again reduces costs. Strategic focus may also generate economies of scale in organization and production. The main contractors often find it optimal to integrate the engineers into their organization to better manage the requirements in the EPCI-contracts. Engineering has become a part of the main contractors' core competence.

However, within the traditional theory of the firm, this organizational solution emerges as a puzzle. In short, the theory states that specific assets are best managed when organized under the same ownership. Klein, Crawford and Alchian (1978) emphasize the problem of 'hold-up'. A party that has invested in specific assets may be forced to accept a worsening of the terms of the relationship after the investment is sunk. Hence, asset specificity creates appropriable specialized quasi rents. Klein et al. claim that 'integration by common or joint ownership is more likely the higher the appropriable specialized quasi rents of the assets involved'. Williamson (1985, 1991) emphasizes the problem of maladaptation. As investments in specific assets increase, disturbances requiring coordinated responses become more numerous and consequential. The high-powered incentives of markets may impede efficient coordination, since both parties want to appropriate as much as possible of the coordination gains. Vertical integration is a way of reducing this kind of maladaptation. The 'property rights approach', developed by Grossman, Hart and Moore (GHM) (1986, 1990), does not formulate an explicit hypothesis concerning asset specificity, but states that if assets are strictly complementary, then some form of integration is optimal. GHM show that if complementary or co-specialized assets operate under separate ownership, the parties owning the assets will underinvest in the relationship.

The assets in the oil industry must be considered as specific: the supplier's capital stock, and the inputs they produce and delivers to the oil companies, does not enjoy a significant value in any alternative use. Specific inputs may reach a certain value for a competing oil company, but the technology is often tailor made for a specific field or a specific oil company. Also, the building of the platform can be considered as intensive in physical capital while engineering is intensive in human capital. Thus we should expect to see alternative B (outsource specific human capital, employ specific physical capital) in the oil industry. But alternative B is never observed.

In recent years, more sophisticated models on economic organization have emerged (see for example Holmström and Milgrom, 1994; Rajan and Zingales 1998; Holmström, 1999, among others) where ownership has been considered as only one of many dimensions within the feasible organizational forms. Outsourcing of specific assets has partly been explained by relational contracting, but also general equilibrium models have provided explanations: Grossman and Helpman (2002) show that outsourcing may consitute a unique industry equilibrium for moderatly specific assets.

In this chapter I show how increased specificity level may induce outsourcing. The following model is an extension of a model developed by Baker, Gibbons and Murphy (BGM) (2002). The main difference is in terms of the punishment strategies. In the model presented here, the players' strategy is not one in which deviation results in an eternal non-cooperative mode. Instead the players use the more realistic carrot and stick strategy in which cooperation can exist also after deviation. This difference gives us interesting implications on the nature of specific assets. These implications also help us understand the oil industry's preference for alternative C.

The rest of the chapter is organized as follows: first I present an extension of the Baker, Gibbons and Murphy model. Then I discuss the theoretical and economic implications of the model. After that I apply these theoretical implications on the oil industry. Finally I conclude.

## The model[1]

Baker, Gibbons and Murphy analyse an economic environment consisting of an upstream party (U), a downstream party (D) and an asset, where both parties and the asset live forever or cease to exist simultaneously at a random date. The parties are risk neutral and share the discount factor $\delta$ per period. The upstream party uses the asset to produce a good that could either be used in the downstream party's production process, or put to an alternative use. In each period the upstream party chooses a vector of n actions (or investments) $\mathbf{a} = (a_1, a_2, ..., a_n)$ at a cost $c(\mathbf{a})$ which affects the value of the product both for the downstream party ($Q$) and for the alternative market ($P$). The downstream value is either high or low, where $q(\mathbf{a})$ is the probability that a high value $Q_H$ will be realised and $1 - q(\mathbf{a})$ is the probability that a low value $Q_L$ will be realized. The alternative-use value can also be either high or low, where $p(\mathbf{a})$ is the probability that a high value, $P_H$, will be realized and $1 - p(\mathbf{a})$ is the probability that a low value $P_L$ will be realized. Given the upstream party's actions, the downstream and the alternative-use values are conditionally independent. It is assumed that $c(0) = q(0) = p(0) = 0$, so when the upstream party decides not to take actions, he bears no costs but also has no chance of realizing the high values. It is further assumed that $P_L < P_H < Q_L < Q_H$ so that the value to the downstream party always exceeds its value in the alternative use. In other words,

---

1    The following section is a revised version of Kvaløy (2003), 'Asset Specificity and Vertical Integration'.

the asset is relationship specific. The first-best actions, $\mathbf{a}^*$, maximizes the expected value of the good in its efficient use minus the cost of action, hence the total surplus from the transaction is given by:

$$S^* = \underset{a}{Max} \left[ Q_L + q(\mathbf{a}^*)\Delta Q - c(\mathbf{a}^*) \right] \text{ where } \Delta Q = Q_H - Q_L$$

The actions are unobservable to anyone but the upstream party, so contracts contingent on actions cannot be enforced. It is assumed that Q and P are observable, but not verifiable, so it is possible to design self-enforceable contracts, but not to contract on Q or P in a way that a third party can enforce.

The parties can organize their transactions through different choices of contract governance and ownership structure. With respect to ownership structure, it is assumed that asset ownership conveys ownership of the good produced, so if the upstream party owns the asset (non-integration), the downstream party cannot use the good without buying it from the upstream party, whereas if the downstream party owns the asset (integration), then he already owns the good. With respect to contract governance, the parties can agree on either a spot contract or a relational contract. In a spot contract, a spot price is negotiated for each period and is determined by ownership structure and bargaining positions. If the upstream party owns the asset, 50:50 Nash bargaining over the surplus from trade decides the spot price. If the downstream party owns the asset, he can just take the realised output without paying, so the upstream party will refuse to take costly actions. In a relational contract, the parties agree on a compensation contract $(s, b_L, b_H, \beta_L, \beta_H)$ where salary $s$ is paid by downstream to upstream at the beginning of each period, and $b_i$ is supposed to be paid when $Q_i$ is realized, $(i = H, L)$ and $\beta_j$ when $P_j$ is realized, $(j = H, L)$. For example: If the upstream party produces a good which yields a high value in the specific relation, $Q_H$, and a low value in the alternative market, $P_L$, the downstream party should, according to the contract, pay the bonuses $b_H + \beta_L$ to the upstream party. Such a contract induces the upstream party to yield effort even if he does not own the asset. Since the contract cannot be enforced by a third party, the parties will honour the contract only if the present value of honouring is greater than the present value of reneging.

BGM's taxonomy of organizational design is summarized as follows (see BGM, *QJE* pp. 46 ):

|  | Non-integration | Integration |
|---|---|---|
| **Spot contract** | Spot outsourcing (SO) | Spot employment (SE) |
| **Relational contract** | Relational outsourcing (RO) | Relational employment (RE) |

So far, I follow BGM's set-up. Here, I will compare relational outsourcing with relational employment using other player strategies than the grim trigger strategies analysed by BGM. In BGM, if a party reneges on a contract, the other party refuses to enter into a new relational contract with that party. Instead, they agree to trade in spot governance forever after. In this chapter, however, if one of the parties reneges, they first agree on a spot price (as in BGM). In the next period, the party who did not renege punishes the other party by refusing to enter into any agreement (including a spot agreement) and instead chooses to trade in the alternative market. After this 'punishment phase' the parties return to a relational contract (see strategy specifications below). These kinds of trigger strategies are in the literature referred to as mutual punishment strategies, carrot and stick strategies, or two-phase punishment strategies (see Gibbons, 1992).

BGM's strategy specifications have the advantage of both being simple to analyse and making it possible to compare all four organizational forms within the same framework. In the modification studied here, it is simply assumed that specificity deters spot contracting from being a long-term option. Still, there are several reasons for making for this modification. First, it can be argued that the carrot and stick strategy is more realistic than the grim strategy, especially in buyer/supplier relationships with high levels of asset or investment specificity. It is difficult to understand why the parties would stick to spot governance forever after a contract breach when specificity makes relational contracting significantly more efficient than spot contracting. Second, analysing carrot and stick strategy equilibria is more appropriate if asset specificity is regarded as a significant explanatory variable. In order to analyse the effect of asset specificity in long-term contracts, the alternative market must be modelled as a real threat point, not merely a reference point for spot negotiations.

The strategy for U (D) is here specified as follows:

1. In period $t$, honour the terms of the relational contract $(s, b_L, b_H, \beta_L, \beta_H)$ if D (U) honoured in period $t-1$.
2. In period $t$, honour the terms of the relational contract $(s, b_L, b_H, \beta_L, \beta_H)$ if there was no trade with D (U) in period $t-1$.
3. In period $t$, refuse to trade with D (U) if the trade between the parties in period $t-1$ was accomplished by spot contracting.

To 'honour the terms of the relational contract' means for the upstream party to accept the bonuses offered and for the downstream party to pay the promised bonuses. We enter this game ex post quality realizations in period $t$. When the parties are to decide whether to honour or renege on the contract, they know the quality realizations of period $t$, but can only have expectations regarding the remaining periods. The parties honour the contract if the present value of honouring exceeds the present value of reneging. A relational contract is self-enforcing if both parties choose to honour the contract $(s, b_L, b_H, \beta_L, \beta_H)$ for all possible realizations of $Q_i$ and $P_j$. The critical part of the analysis is to deduce the conditions for when the relational employment contract and the relational outsourcing contract are self-enforcing. Technically, these are conditions for when the strategies specified above constitute subgame perfect Nash equilibria of relational contracts.

I assume that both parties incur a switching cost $s$ by trading in the alternative market when the product has already been produced for the purpose of trading in the specific relation. We can view these costs as time costs or extra transport costs associated with the unexpected move from relational trade to alternative market trade. They avoid this cost if they know ex ante that no trade will occur between the parties.

I will now in brief deduce the model's main expressions. For more details, see Kvaløy (2003).

### Relational employment

If the upstream party honors the relational employment contract, he will earn $b_i + \beta_j - c$ **(a)** in each period. If he reneges on the contract he will not receive bonuses in any of the first two periods, but in the second period he will bear no investment costs.

If the downstream party honors the contract, he will earn $Q_i - b_i - \beta_j$ in each period. If he reneges on the contract, he will in the first period not pay the promised bonus and instead take the good and pay nothing. In the second period the upstream party will punish by refusing to produce the good, so the downstream party has to buy the good in the alternative market. The good he buys in the alternative market is not specific to his needs; both the value he sets and the price of the good is $P$, so he does not earn a specific surplus from this trade. Hence, the profit from trade is zero in the second period. In the third period the relational contract will again be established provided that they follow their initial strategies.

There are eight constraints that have to hold if the relational employment contract shall be self-enforcing. Combining these restrictions yields (see appendix):

$$(1) \quad |\Delta b| + |\Delta \beta| \le \delta \left( Q_L + \Delta Q q(\mathbf{a}^{RE}) - c(\mathbf{a}^{RE}) \right)$$

where $\Delta b = b_H - b_L$, $\Delta \beta = \beta_H - \beta_L$, $\delta =$ discount factor, and where the superscript (RE) denotes relational employment. The effecient relational employment contract maximizes total surplus, subject to (1).

### Relational outsourcing

If the upstream party honors the relational outsourcing contract he will, as in the relational employment contract, receive $b_i + \beta_j - c$ **(a)** in each period. If he reneges on the contract by refusing to accept the bonuses, he can, since he owns the asset, renegotiate a new price. We assume that the parties by 50:50 Nash negotiations agree on a price $\frac{1}{2}(Q_i + P_j - s)$ in the first period.[2] In the second period the downstream party will punish the upstream party by refusing to trade with him and instead buy

---

2   The downstream party will pay the upstream party the alternative value $P_j - s$ plus half the surplus from trade with the downstream party: $\frac{1}{2}(Q_i - (P_j - s))$, that is $\frac{1}{2}(Q_i + P_j - s)$.

the product in the alternative market at a price $P$. In the third period the parties reestablish their relational contract. The strategy, in which the downstream party waits to the second period to start the punishment, coincides with subgame perfect equilibrium for $s$ exceeding a critical level (see appendix 2). In the second period, the parties know that no trade will occur between them, so they avoid the switching cost $s$. In the third period the parties reestablish the relational contract provided that they follow their initial strategies.

If the downstream party honors the contract he will, as in the relational employment contract, earn $Q_i - b_i - \beta_j$ in each period. If he reneges by refusing to pay the bonuses, the upstream party can, as distinct from the relational employment contract, refuse to deliver the product. The parties will agree on the 50:50 Nash price so that the downstream party earns $Q_i - \frac{1}{2}(Q_i + P_j - s)$. In the second period the upstream party will punish the downstream party by refusing to trade with him and instead sell the product in the alternative market at a price $P_j$. The downstream party then has to buy the product in the alternative market at a price $P$, earning nothing.

There are eight constraints that have to hold if the relational outsourcing contract shall be self-enforcing. Combining these restrictions yields (see appendix 1)

$$(2) \quad \left|\Delta b - \tfrac{1}{2}\Delta Q\right| + \left|\Delta \beta - \tfrac{1}{2}\Delta P\right| \le \delta\left(Q_L + \Delta Q q(\mathbf{a}^{RO}) - c(\mathbf{a}^{RO}) - P_L - \Delta P p(\mathbf{a}^{ROd}) + c(\mathbf{a}^{ROd})\right)$$

where RO denotes relational outsourcing, and ROd denotes the deviation period of the relational outsourcing contract. The effecient relational outsourcing contract maximizes total surplus, subject to (2).

Since $Q_L$ denotes the assets' specific value before any investments are made, and $P_L$ denotes the assets' value in the alternative market before any investments are made, $Q_L - P_L$ can be interpreted as the level of asset specificity. Since $\Delta Q$ denotes the possible return from investments in the specific relation, and $\Delta P$ denotes the possible return from investments in the alternative market, $\Delta Q - \Delta P$ can be interpreted as the level of investment specificity. We see that the relational contract is stronger the more specific the asset and/or the investment are.

## Implications of the model

As opposed to Baker, Gibbons and Murphy's model, the stability of the contract depends on the level of asset specificity. Technically, this means that the organizational solution depends on the difference, $Q_i - P_j$. This happens because of the presence of a valid alternative market. In BGM, the alternative market is merely a point of reference for the negotiating parties. In the present model, the carrot-stick strategy turns the alternative market into a valid alternative that actually is traded if the parties deviate. A high degree of specificity makes the alternative market less attractive compared to a stable relation with the specific trading partner.

If we now compare the right side of the outsourcing restriction (2) with the right side of the employment restriction (1), we see that the employment restriction does not depend on the level of asset specificity in the same way as the outsourcing restriction. We then have that the organizational structure may depend on the asset's specificity, and more importantly: if the asset contains a high level of specificity, outsourcing may prove a better alternative than integration. Why? In the outsourcing contract, both parties have to take into account what the alternative market actually offers. In the employment contract, the value of the alternative market does not make any difference for the upstream party. As long as the product he produces is not his property, he cannot carry through a hold-up strategy or sell the product on the alternative market.

In both the outsourcing restriction and the employment restriction, the strength of the incentives affects the stability of the contract. The incentives to exert effort are measured by $\Delta b$ and $\Delta \beta$. If there is a strong relationship between effort and quality realization, the downstream party may find it profitable to design strong incentives. But the stronger the incentives, that is the larger the difference between high and low bonuses, the larger is the temptation to renege on the contract. Low bonuses may induce the upstream party to renege, while high bonuses may induce the downstream party to renege on the contract. In the outsourcing contract, a high degree of asset specificity can function as a buffer against this kind of opportunistic behaviour. If high-powered incentives are desirable, asset specificity can thus ease the implementation of these incentives.

It is important to notice that in the model the investments are made in physical capital.[3] Once the investments are sunk, the specific surplus can be realized without the upstream party's participation. In the relational employment contract, the downstream party had the opportunity to just take the good and realize the surplus without any further participation from the downstream party. If the the investments are made in human capital, in the sense that the upstream party's human capital is essential in ex post realization of values, the upstream party can still hold-up the product, even if he is employed by the downstream party. Thus, if the upstream party has essentiel human capital, the relational employment analysis above would be identical to the relational outsourcing analysis. So the outsourcing arguments presented here is not relevant in the case of ex post essential human capital. In the case of physical capital, the fear from trading in the alternative market disciplines both parties only if they are non-integrated. In the case of human capital the fear from trading in the alternative market disciplines both parties without regards to their choice of ownerhip structure.

Can we say anything meaningful about the position of human-capital-intensive activities in a vertical supply chain? Notice that we are not looking for obvious 'business arguments' of the kind: 'It is important for a firm to attract clever people, thus it is important for a firm to attract valuable human capital.' We are looking for economics-arguments that say something about the strategic behaviour of this capital. Klein, Crawford and Alchian (1978) advocate outsourcing of human capital: Human capital can always be managed strategically; independent of the ownership structure, and integration is therefore not perceived to reduce the problem of opportunistic behaviour.

---

3   I apply Hart's (1995) distinction between physical and human capital investments.

I will here briefly present an argument for integration of human capital: in an integrated solution where the investments are made in human capital, the upstream party knows that the surplus realization depends on his participation even after the product is made, and this motivates him to exert effort. If we assume that the downstream party must also make an investment ex ante the product realization, it would be reasonable to believe that he would not exert maximum effort since he has to share the surplus with the upstream party (as in Hart, 1995). If it is not possible for the upstream party to holdup values ex post, as typical for investments in physical assets, the downstream party would exert higher effort, while the upstream party would exert lower effort. It is in general assumed that investments over a certain level is a positive, but decreasing (decreasing return to scale). It then follows that the return from two 'medium sized' investments are greater than one small and one big. This implies that integration is a more valuable solution if the specific investments are made in essential human capital.

*Conclusion*: A high level of asset specificity can actually be an argument for outsourcing. The fact that this argument only applies in the case of physical assets, and the assumption that the return from specific investments in general is assumed to be positive but decreasing, implies that there may exist a reason to suggest: 'Outsource specific physical capital. Employ specific human capital.' Interestingly it is what we observe in the oil industry.

## Application to the oil industry

The model presented above can easily be applied to the oil industry. The downstream party can be interpreted as the oil company, while the main contractor can be interpreted as the upstream party. If we look at the relationship between the engineering activities and the main contractors, it is reasonable to interpret the engineers as the upstream party, and the main contractor as the downstream party.

If we look at the dynamics of the model, it has several similarities to the dynamics in the oil industry. First the parties agree on a relational contract that specifies quality and bonuses. These specifications are, both in the model and in the real world, difficult to verify. If mistrust arises, the parties agree on a spot contract where costs and benefits are renegotiated. When mistrust arises in the real world, the parties typically renegotiate a contract that is more explicit and has fewer bonuses and other incentive instruments than the relational contract. The contract is more like a spot contract which specifies 'who's going to pay how much for what went wrong'. After the spot contract the model leads us to the punishment period where the parties trade in the alternative market. This can be interpreted as a period where new contracts are about to be made. In the mean time, they have to seek alternative revenues. If the specificity-level is high, the alternative revenues are low. Finally comes the period where the parties reestablish their relational contract. 'Reestablishing' does not have to be interpreted as 'the parties have again found each other'. 'Reestablishing' can also mean that the parties have agreed on relational contracts with other partners.

Following the arguments in the previous section, one should expect that the oil company and the main contractor enjoy separate ownership. The main contractor (the upstream party) manages a capital stock that is highly specific to the oil company (the downstream party). The oil platform (or any other kind of installations made by the purpose of oil extraction) and its many components do not enjoy a significant value in any alternative use. The installation can, of course, have a certain value for another oil company. But the installations are often field specific: they are built with the purpose of oil extraction in a specific field and for a specific operator. Also, strong incentives are desirable as long as there is a lot to gain in promoting quality and reducing costs. Finally, the inputs produced by the contractor are physical. A contractor working as an employee would not own the platform. These factors make us expect non-integration, and non-integration is what we see. The engineers do also manage a capital stock and produce inputs that are specific to the oil industry, and strong incentives are desirable to reduce costs and promote quality. But their assets and the inputs they produce are non-physical. Education and experience are their main assets and technical solutions are their products. Their assets and their input production exist in their minds. An oil company or a main contractor (which here represents the downstream party) would not attain a complete possession of the engineer's product even if he was employed by the downstream party. Following the arguments above, he can be given strong incentives even if he is employed, and low values in the alternative market would still discipline him as long as he controls what he produces and consequently can sell it. In other words: there does not exist a strong outsourcing argument. The engineer also produces physical write-downs of his thinking. These write-downs can be valuable in an alternative market. Concept evaluations or pre-engineering services may be valuable for some of the oil company's or the main contractor's rivals. This may be an argument for the downstream party to employ, rather than outsource the engineers.

In real life we see that the engineers usually are employed in the oil company or at the main contractor. In the EPCI contracts the main contractor is given, to a certain extent, the right to decide who shall produce the main engineering services. Contractors, such as Aker-Kværner, have their own engineering units that usually are awarded these engineering contracts.

From the archetypes introduced in the first section, alternative C seems to be the best description of the basic economic organization of the oil industry. And alternative C fits with the implications of the model presented: 'Outsource specific physical capital. Employ specific human capital.'

## Conclusion

I have shown that a high degree of asset specificity can induce outsourcing of physical capital. Outsourcing increases the feasibility for the supplier to behave opportunistically, since he can 'hold up' his product. But hold-up strategies are less profitable if the assets are specific. A high degree of specificity implies that the alternative market offers significantly lower values than the specific business relation does. If the alternative market offers significantly low values, it can function as a buffer against opportunistic behaviour. But this buffer does not work if the parties are integrated. An integrated supplier does not care about the alternative market as long as what he produces is not his property. Hence, if the assets are sufficiently relationship-specific, the temptation to behave opportunistically is smaller if the parties are non-integrated, and they are therefore able to design more efficient incentive schemes.

I have argued that this reasoning only prevails in the case of physical capital. If a supplier delivers human-capital intensive services that are essential in the ex post realization of values, the alternative market matters even if the buyer owns him. Thus, the outsourcing argument presented above does not prevail in the case of human capital.

I have introduced six archetypes of ownership structures feasible in the oil industry. The archetype that best fits with the world is the one where an independent supplier both designs and builds the oil platform before it delivers it to the oil company. This archetype is consistent with the analysis presented here: outsource specific physical capital, employ specific human capital.

## Appendix

*1. The conditions for honouring the relational employment contract*

The upstream party will honour rather than renege on the relational emplyment contract if:

$$b_i + \beta_j + \delta\big(b_L + \Delta bq(\mathbf{a}^{RE}) + \beta_L + \Delta\beta p(\mathbf{a}^{RE})\big) \geq \delta c \ (\mathbf{a}^{RE})$$

The downstream party will honour rather than renege on the relational employment contract if:

$$b_i + \beta_j + \delta\big(b_L + \Delta bq(\mathbf{a}^{RE}) + \beta_L + \Delta\beta p(\mathbf{a}^{RE})\big) \leq \delta\big(Q_L + \Delta Qq(\mathbf{a}^{RE})\big)$$

Since *i=H,L* and *j= H,L,* each of these two conditions contains four constraints. We see that the high quality realization always gives the binding constraint for the downstream party, while low quality realization gives the relevant constraint for the upstream party. The relevant constraints are then:

$$(b_L + \beta_L) + \delta\big(b_L + \Delta bq(\mathbf{a}^{RE}) + \beta_L + \Delta\beta p(\mathbf{a}^{RE})\big) \geq \delta c \ (\mathbf{a}^{RE})$$
$$(b_L + \Delta b + \beta_L + \Delta\beta) + \delta\big(b_L + \Delta bq(\mathbf{a}^{RE}) + \beta_L + \Delta\beta p(\mathbf{a}^{RE})\big) \leq \delta\big(Q_L + \Delta Qq(\mathbf{a}^{RE})\big)$$

Multiplying the upstream constraint by (-1) and adding the downstream constraint yields the following necessary condition for honoring the relational employment contract:

$$(1) \quad |\Delta b| + |\Delta\beta| \leq \delta\big(Q_L + \Delta Qq(\mathbf{a}^{RE}) - c(\mathbf{a}^{RE})\big)$$

*2. The conditions for honouring the relational outsourcing contract*

The upstream party will honour rather than renege on the relational outsourcing contract if:

$$b_i + \beta_j + \delta\big(b_L + \Delta bq(\mathbf{a}^{RO}) + \beta_L + \Delta\beta p(\mathbf{a}^{RO}) - c(\mathbf{a}^{RO})\big)$$
$$\geq \tfrac{1}{2}(Q_i + P_j - s) + \delta\big(P_L + \Delta Pp(\mathbf{a}^{ROd}) - c(\mathbf{a}^{ROd})\big)$$

The downstream party will honour rather than renege on the relational outsourcing contract if:

$$\tfrac{1}{2}(Q_i + P_j - s) + \delta\big(Q_L + \Delta Qq(\mathbf{a}^{RO})\big) \geq b_i + \beta_j + \delta\big(b_L + \Delta bq(\mathbf{a}^{RO}) + \beta_j + \Delta\beta p(\mathbf{a}^{RO})\big)$$

It is now less obvious which constraints that bind. But it is always at most two constraints that will be binding. We see that it depends on the differences: $\tfrac{1}{2}\Delta Q - \Delta b$ and $\tfrac{1}{2}\Delta P - \Delta\beta$.

When $\frac{1}{2}\Delta Q > \Delta b$ and $\frac{1}{2}\Delta P > \Delta\beta$, the relevant constraints are:

$$\frac{1}{2}(Q_L + \Delta Q + P_L + \Delta P - s) + \delta\left(P_L + \Delta P p(\mathbf{a}^{ROd}) - c(\mathbf{a}^{ROd})\right)$$

$$\leq b_L + \Delta b + \beta_L + \Delta\beta + \delta\left(b_L + \Delta b q(\mathbf{a}^{RO}) + \beta_L + \Delta\beta\, p(\mathbf{a}^{RO}) - c(\mathbf{a}^{RO})\right)$$

$$\frac{1}{2}(Q_L + P_L - s) + \delta\left(Q_L + \Delta Q q(\mathbf{a}^{RO})\right) \geq b_L + \beta_L + \delta\left(b_L + \Delta b q(\mathbf{a}^{RO}) + \beta_L + \Delta\beta\, p(\mathbf{a}^{RO})\right)$$

When $\frac{1}{2}\Delta Q > \Delta b$ and $\frac{1}{2}\Delta P < \Delta\beta$, the relevant constraints are:

$$\frac{1}{2}(Q_L + \Delta Q + P_L - s) + \delta\left(P_L + \Delta P p(\mathbf{a}^{ROd}) - c(\mathbf{a}^{ROd})\right) \leq b_L + \Delta b + \beta_L$$

$$+\delta\left(b_L + \Delta b q(\mathbf{a}^{RO}) + \beta_L + \Delta\beta\, p(\mathbf{a}^{RO}) - c(\mathbf{a}^{RO})\right)$$

$$\frac{1}{2}(Q_L + P_L + \Delta P - s) + \delta\left(Q_L + \Delta Q q(\mathbf{a}^{RO})\right) \geq b_L + \beta_L + \Delta\beta + \delta\left(b_L + \Delta b q(\mathbf{a}^{RO}) + \beta_L + \Delta\beta\, p(\mathbf{a}^{RO})\right)$$

When $\frac{1}{2}\Delta Q < \Delta b$ and $\frac{1}{2}\Delta P > \Delta\beta$, the relevant constraints are:

$$\frac{1}{2}(Q_L + P_L + \Delta P - s) + \delta\left(P_L + \Delta P p(\mathbf{a}^{ROd}) - c(\mathbf{a}^{ROd})\right) \leq b_L + \beta_L + \Delta\beta$$

$$+\delta\left(b_L + \Delta b q(\mathbf{a}^{RO}) + \beta_L + \Delta\beta\, p(\mathbf{a}^{RO}) - c(\mathbf{a}^{RO})\right)$$

$$\frac{1}{2}(Q_L + \Delta Q + P_L - s) + \delta\left(Q_L + \Delta Q q(\mathbf{a}^{RO})\right) \geq b_L + \Delta b + \beta_L + \delta\left(b_L + \Delta b q(\mathbf{a}^{RO}) + \beta_L + \Delta\beta\, p(\mathbf{a}^{RO})\right)$$

When $\frac{1}{2}\Delta Q < \Delta b$ and $\frac{1}{2}\Delta P < \Delta\beta$, the relevant constraints are:

$$\frac{1}{2}(Q_L + P_L - s) + \delta\left(P_L + \Delta P p(\mathbf{a}^{ROd}) - c(\mathbf{a}^{ROd})\right) \leq b_L + \beta_L$$

$$+\delta\left(b_L + \Delta b q(\mathbf{a}^{RO}) + \beta_L + \Delta\beta\, p(\mathbf{a}^{RO}) - c(\mathbf{a}^{RO})\right)$$

$$\frac{1}{2}(Q_L + \Delta Q + P_L + \Delta P - s) + \delta\left(Q_L + \Delta Q q(\mathbf{a}^{RO})\right) \geq (b_L + \Delta b + \beta_L + \Delta\beta) + \delta\left(b_L + \Delta b q(\mathbf{a}^{RO}) + \beta_L + \Delta\beta\, p(\mathbf{a}^{RO})\right)$$

Multiplying the downstream party's constraints by (-1) and adding the upstream party's constraints yields an identical necessary condition for each pair of constraints:

$$(2)\quad \left|\Delta b - \tfrac{1}{2}\Delta Q\right| + \left|\Delta\beta - \tfrac{1}{2}\Delta P\right| \leq \delta\left(Q_L + \Delta Q q(\mathbf{a}^{RO}) - c(\mathbf{a}^{RO}) - P_L - \Delta P p(\mathbf{a}^{ROd}) + c(\mathbf{a}^{ROd})\right)$$

If we assume that the parties have the opportunity to agree on a fixed payment prior to the quality realizations, this payment can always be chosen in a way that (1) and (2) are not only necessary but also sufficient conditions.

# References

Baker, George, Robert Gibbons and Kevin J. Murphy (1994), 'Subjective Performance Measures in Optimal Incentive Contracts', *Quarterly Journal of Economics*, **109**, pp. 1125-56.

Baker, George, Robert Gibbons and Kevin J. Murphy (2002), 'Relational Contracts and the Theory of the Firm', *Quaterly Journal of Economics*, **117** pp. 39-94.

Bull, Clive (1987), 'The Existence of Self-Enforcing Implicit Contracts', *Quarterly Journal of Economics*, **102**, pp. 147-59.

Gibbons, Robert (1992), *A Primer in Game Theory*, London: Harvester/ Wheatsheaf.

Grossman, Gene and Elhanan Helpman (2002), 'Integration Versus Outsourcing in Industry Equilibrium', *Quarterly Journal of Economics*, **117**, pp. 85-120.

Grossman, Sanford and Oliver Hart (1986), 'The Costs and Benefits of Ownership: A Theory of Lateral and Vertical Integration', *Journal of Political Economy*, **94**, pp. 691-719.

Hanisch, Tore Jørgen and Gunnar Nerheim (1992), *Norsk oljehistorie, bind 1: Fra vantro til overmot?* Norsk Petroleumsforening, Leseselskapet.

Hart, Oliver (1995), *Firm, Contracts and Financial Structure,* Oxford: Clarendon Press.

Hart, Oliver and John Moore (1990), 'Property Rights and the Nature of the Firm', *Journal of Political Economy*, **98**, pp. 1119-58.

Holmström, Bengt R. (1999), 'The Firm as a Subeconomy', *The Journal of Law, Economics & Organization*, **15**, pp. 74-102.

Holmström, Bengt R. and Paul Milgrom (1994), 'The Firm as an Incentive System', *American Economic Review*, **84**, pp. 972-991.

Holmström, Bengt and John Roberts (1999), 'The Boundaries of the Firm Revisited', *Journal of Economic Perspectives*, **12**, pp. 73-94.

Klein, Benjamin, Robert G. Crawford and Armen A. Alchian (1978), 'Vertical Integration, Appropriable Rents, and the Competitive Contracting Process', *Journal of Law and Economics*, **21**, pp. 297-326.

Klein, Benjamin and Keith Leffler (1981), 'The Role of Market Forces in Assuring Contractual Performance', *Journal of Political Economy*, **89**, pp. 615-641.

Kreps, David M. (1990), 'Corporate Culture and Economic Theory', in J. Alt and K. Shepsle (eds), *Perspectives on Positive Political Economy*, 90-143, (town ref.): Cambridge University Press.

Kvaløy, Ola (2003), 'Asset Specificity and Vertical Integration', *Discussion Paper 07/2003,* Norwegian School of Economics and Business Administration.

Levin, Jonathan (2002), 'Multilateral Contracting and the Employment Relationship', *The Quarterly Journal of Economics*, **117**, pp. 1075-1103.

Levin, Jonathan (2003), 'Relational Incentive Contracts', *American Economic Review*, **93**, pp. 835-57.

MacLeod, Bentley and James Malcolmson (1989), 'Implicit Contracts, Incentive Compatibility, and Involuntary Unemployment', *Econometrica*, **57**, pp. 447-80.

Nordås, Hildegunn K. (2000), 'Libralization of Trade in Services and Choice of Technology in the Norwegian Petroleum Sector', *Working Paper 2000:1*, Christian Michelsen's Institute.

Norsok (1995), *Samarbeid operatør og leverandør*, Norsok report 3, Utbyggings og Driftsforum for Petroleumssektoren.

Norsok (1996), *Integrerte samarbeidsformer og incentivkontrakter*, www.norsok. olf.no/rapporter.html

Osmundsen, Petter (1999), 'Cost Overruns from the Perspective of Contract and Incentive Theory', *Attachment to Norwegian Government Report*, **11**, pp. 113-131.

Rajan, Raghuram and Luigi Zingales (1998), 'Power in a Theory of the Firm', *Quarterly Journal of Economics*, **113**, pp. 387-432.

Tronslien, Peter J. (1998), 'The Importance of the Procurement Process to Statoil, and the Development within Statoil's Supply Chain', *Statoil Forum*.

Williamson, Oliver E. (1985), *The Economic Institutions of Capitalism*, New York: The Free Press.

Chapter 5

# Supply Chain Management in the Offshore Oil Industry: The Angolan and Norwegian Cases Compared

Arne Wiig

## Introduction[1]

Different external environments lead to differences in supply chain management. This chapter focuses on the organisation of the supply chain in the offshore oil industry, examining the Angolan and the Norwegian case, primarily the level of integration and contractual obligations between oilcompanies and their main suppliers.[2] Variations in technology and trust are used as explanatory variables for the supply chain management in the two markets.

While focusing on supply chain management I follow the transaction-cost tradition, as I am particularly interested in how the organisation of a supply chain depends on the complexity of the technology applied (Williamson, 1985; Coase, 1960 Grossman and Hart, 1986). These theories claim that more complex tasks are undertaken in-house (by integrated units) while simpler tasks are outsourced. I will also analyse how factors in informal relationships such as trust, influence the organisation of the supply chain when contracts are incomplete (Sako, 1992; Baker et al, 2002). Trust reduces the importance of integration since it makes relational contracts easier to sustain.

1   I would like to thank Hildegunn Kyvik Nordaas, Line Tøndel, Tako Koning, Inge Tvedten, Øystein Kristiansen, Henri de Groot and Per Heum for helpful comments on an earlier draft. Financial support from the Norwegian Research Council 'Petropol' is gratefully appreciated.

2   By supply chain, I mean all the activities and information associated with the flow of goods and services from the raw material stage until the final product reaches the consumer. Offshore oil industry represents one part of a broader supply chain (or value chain) of oil and gas. I will look only at the extraction and development phases in this chain. The oil company is, thus, our final consumer while oil service firms are the main subcontractors (see Table 5.1). A supply chain is defined independent of the ownership structure among the firms in the chain. Some tasks in the chain are undertaken by vertically integrated firms while other parts may be undertaken by individual firms.

Production in deepwater (more than 3000 metre water depth) represents one of the fastest growing oil markets in the world. While subsea and deepwater wells constitute approximately one third of the global market for offshore engineering and construction services in 2000, they will increase to nearly 50 per cent of the market or approximately USD 30 billion in 2004.[3] In order to highlight the importance of the complexity of technology, I have compared the Angolan and Norwegian cases. Angola is currently considered the most promising oil market in the world, with significantly increased production from deepwater wells. As a contrast to the Angolan case, I will use the Norwegian market. In the North Sea, oil is produced from shallow water, which needs less technically advanced solutions than production from deep water.

The Angolan case is important for several reasons. First, Angola gives information on the organisation of the supply chain in a new, *technologically advanced* segment of the oil market, namely deepwater exploration. According to the transaction cost perspective, one should expect more integrated supply chain solutions in Angola than in Norway. By contrasting two different geographical markets, I find some support for the transaction costs analysis, a result that differs from Hallwood (1992) who contrasts different markets in the British part of the North Sea. I argue that the supply chain in Angola is more integrated than in Norway in the sense that integrated oil service companies play a more significant role in supply chain management. Integrated oil service firms have through their governance and contractual relationships substituted the operator in determining the trade-off between specialisation and integration. Dealing with this trade-off is one of the core questions in supply chain management. Second, deepwater exploration is an increasingly important segment of the oil market. The structure of the supply chain in Angola will therefore most likely be mirrored elsewhere. The supply industry consists of multinationals and I see a rising international trend in acquisitions and integration of tasks among service providers that early was noticeable in Angola. Third, Angola sheds lights on how differences in cultural factors such as trust, influence the structure of the supply chain. I argue that in Angola contracts between the supply industry and the oil companies are based on market transactions rather than on the relational contracts (between the operator and a large number of independent contractors) more common in Norway.[4] Trust is key to both the NorSok initiative in Norway and the CRINE

---

3    Estimate by Coflexip Stena Offshore.

4    See for instance Trondslien, P., *The Importance of the Procurement Process to Statoil, and the Development within Statoil's Supply Chain.* http://www. Statoil com. He claims that supply chain development is characterised by a focus on maximising the joint profit of the supply *chain* – not on individual gain. From such a perspective, the competition arena is supposedly among *'integrated chains'* (where a company is only one of many links in a supply chain). As oil companies and oil service companies mainly are independent firms, I find it difficult to understand what mechanisms would explain a focus on joint gain without some sort of trust or long term relationship between the firms.

initiative in the UK (NorSok, 1996; Crabtree, 1997).[5] Both initiatives were taken to reduce costs in the North Sea through partnering and standardisation of products and documents. There are not any corresponding initiatives in the Angolan case, making relational contracts harder to sustain. Finally, the structure of the supply chain has implications for the internationalisation strategies of the supply industry. Penetrating the Norwegian market may require other assets than penetrating the Angolan one.

This chapter is organised as follows: first, a brief overview of the oil industry in Angola and Norway is given. While the structure of the Norwegian supply chain in the North Sea is presented in several publications (Heum, 1999; Greve, Haugland and Walderhaug, 1996; Nordaas, 2000a and b), hardly any comprehensive analysis has been done of supply chains in Angola, and our focus is therefore on this. Based on transaction cost-inspired theories of supply chain management, I generate some hypotheses regarding the organisation of the supply chain in Angola. By presenting two case studies from Angola, I proceed by analysing this supply chain, particularly in terms of contracts awarded, ownership structure and informal networks among the parties. The two case studies chosen, Kuito and Girassol, have recently started production in deepwater fields. The concluding section emphasises the way in which the organisation of the supply chain influences strategies for penetrating this type of market.

### Supply chains in the offshore oil industry

This section gives an overview of the offshore oil industry in Angola and Norway, the types of firms involved in the supply chain, their core activities, and factors determining their choice of market segments. It should be noted in this context that unless otherwise specified 'upstream' and 'downstream' refer to activities within the offshore supply industry. 'Upstream' firms having the option of integrating forward (downward the value chain towards the consumer), 'downstream' firms that of integrating backward (upward the value chain), both within the confines of the offshore offshore industry, here defined as all activities from initial exploration to the final transport of oil or natural gas from the production platform or like installations.

*The offshore supply chain*

This sub-section provides an overview of the main tasks in the oil sector. Table 5.1 classifies tasks or markets in the offshore oil sector. Firms specialising in more than one task integrate or *bundle* their activities; that is, the firm seeks to be an integrated provider of oil or gas. Normally the supply industry (the oil service companies) deals with tasks 1-5 in Table 5.1, while the core activity of the oil company is the production of oil (task 6 in Table 5.1).

---

5 See also Department of Trade and Industry, UK, *How Supply Chain Management Works* http://www.og.dti.gov.uk/sponsorship/docs/study.pdf.

The supply chain is characterised by two physical assets: production facilities (for example platform and subsea equipment) and the fluid and reservoir characteristics (for example the oil); and the *human* asset, namely knowledge (for example engineering services). All assets are essential in order to produce oil. In addition to the market potential in the different market segments, the key determining factor in the choice of market is the *assets of the firm*, particularly its knowledge and capabilities.

**Table 5.1    Key tasks in the offshore oil sector**

1. Exploration (including seismic) and drilling (which in deepwater is undertaken by drill ships or drilling platforms)
2. Engineering and project management
3. Construction of production facilities e.g., platforms
4. Subsea construction, pipelay and fabrication of subsea equipment
5. Installation (platform and subsea)
6. Operations (production of oil)[6]

Since refining and marketing competition is fierce, an oil company may increase its profits either by increasing the scale of its downstream production (to achieve economics of scale), by differentiating its products (through branding) or by undertaking lifecycling cost savings in its offshore activities. Regarding the last option, the most important criteria are the success rate in exploration and the reduction in development or production costs. Procurement of goods and services constitute more than 50 per cent of an oil company's cost. For the oil company, this means that a considerable part of its gross output is created outside the company. Since even a small change in the organisation of the supply chain may lead to a significant change in profits for the oil company, providing the supply industry with incentives for cost reduction is important.

From the operator's point of view, there are different ways of organising the supply chain. Two extremes are the vertical integrated supply chain, in which all tasks are undertaken by one firm and specialisation, in which all market transactions are based on arm's length trade. Normally, there is *a trade off between specialisation and integration*; integration reduces the transaction costs of using the market at the expense of scale economies and specialisation. The integration of tasks represents one way of increasing the information flow between firms and reduces the transaction costs in the supply chain. The importance of efficient information flow between the agents involved in a project increases with the technological complexity of the projects. Smooth information flow is therefore particularly important in the oil industry. Producer services such as engineering act as intermediate goods at every step in the supply chain and play a significant role in the co-ordination of the

---

6    There is also a separate market focused on well maintenance. The importance of this market increases during the production phase.

whole process from field development to shipment of crude oil. That oil companies increasingly prefer to deal with a limited number of suppliers gives additional support to the integration of tasks. The other side of the coin is that integration may lead to inefficiencies, since markets generally provide more high power incentives than firms. Supply chain management deals with mechanisms for solving this trade-off.

There are also hybrid institutions in between markets and hierarchies. *Business groups* vary not only by degree of *ownership*, but also according to *authority structure, trust* and *solidarity* (Granovetter, 1995; Feenstra, Huang and Hamilton, 1996). With independent service providers, forming partnerships based on mutual trust is one mechanism for improving the incentives to reduce costs – not only the service providers' costs, but the total costs in the value chain. In many cases ex ante uncertainty related to technical specification leads the oil company to specify functional requirements to a product or technology. This gives the contractor some degree of flexibility to develop a particular piece of goods or services. At the same time, unforeseen contingencies frequently arise. Party appraisal of such contingencies may differ, and, since contracts are incomplete, bargaining represents one way of solving such disputes. But bargaining may fail to provide the necessary incentives for cost reductions if parties cannot trust each other. Trust enhancing mechanisms are therefore of particular importance when contracts are incomplete, the environment is uncertain, under rapid technological change and under asset specificity (assets are specific to particular fields or oil companies).

*The oil industry in Angola*

Angola started oil production in 1957 and oil has played a significant role in the Angolan economy ever since. Oil production constitutes 50 per cent of the GDP, and 90 per cent of the government's revenue and export earnings. In 2003, a Chevron-led consortium produced nearly two third out of a total Angolan production of 923 000 barrels per day (bpd).[7] Other companies – Total and the Angolan state oil company Sonangol produced the rest.

Since 1996, major oil companies have started to discover huge oil reservoirs in Angola's deep water, from depths of 300 metres to over 1200 metres. Reserves have in proportions far exceeded anything onshore. In half a decade, some eight billion barrels have been discovered. Angola's proven plus probable remaining reserves is close to ten billion barrels (as at January 1, 2005). This does not include any of the discoveries on ultra-deepwater Blocks 31 and 32. In addition to Girassol, 14 other fields have been found in Total's successful Block 17 (as of September 2004). Exxon has made huge discoveries in 17 different fields in Block 15 and Chevron has made a number of significant discoveries in Block 14. All new fields are based on production sharing agreements (PSA) with Sonangol. Sonangol plays the leading role in the oil industry as the sole concessionaire in exploration and production, as

---

7    http://www.eia.doe.gov/emeu/cabs/angola.html

licence partner, a partner in the supply of goods and services and as a regulator and implementing agency for the Angolan oil policy.

In 2000, about 200 firms offering services and goods to the oil industry were registered in Angola. There is no available information about the number of employees or the turnover in these firms. Less than 20 per cent are Angolan companies. Most of the companies have some relationship to Sonangol. The rest are local offshoots of multinationals put in place to service the Angolan market. Angola is not being used as a stepping stone to service other markets in the region such as Nigeria or Chad. In Angola, like elsewhere in the world, oil companies make most of their important logistical decisions in their headquarters in Paris, London or Houston. Angolan authorities expect annual investments in the oil sector (mainly in the exploration and development phases) to be approximately four billion USD.[8] The American oil companies ChevronTexaco and Exxon play an increasingly significant role in the production of oil in Angola while an increasing share of oil is distributed to the American and Chinese markets.

*The oil industry in Norway*

In the late 1960s, Ekofisk was the first discovered North Sea oil field, and production began in 1971. The Phillips group leads the Ekofisk operating consortium, which includes Total, Norsk Agip, Norsk Hydro, and the state owned oil company Statoil. Ekofisk was the starting point for both Norwegian oil companies Norsk Hydro and Statoils' oil activities. Ekofisk's production was about 381 000 bpd of crude oil in 2002. The Statfjord field was discovered by Mobil in 1974, and production began from Statfjord A in 1979. Statoil took over the operations from Mobil in 1987. Norway's third largest field is Gullfaks, which produced 223 000 bpd in 2002.

In 2001, Norway was the world's third largest net oil exporter. Norway's oil reserves are located exclusively offshore and mostly in the North Sea at water depth of around 150 metres, which is significantly lower than the deepwater fields in Angola. According to EIA, the proven reserves of oil in Norway is twice that of Angola. In 2001, oil production was about 3.4 millions bpd while Norwegian oil investment was about $7.5 billion.[9]

Gullfaks was the first Norwegian oil field developed and operated by Norwegian companies (Nordaas, 2000a). Statoil became the operator in 1981 and production started in 1986. The Norwegian policy of promoting the local supply industry, especially early in its oil history, made it possible for Norwegian firms to compete with multinational energy suppliers, even on specialised task. More than 600 firms service the oil market, mainly the home market (Heum and Vatne, 1999), although more attention has been devoted to servicing an international market, partly because

---

8   http://www.angola.org/referenc/reports/oil_diagnostic_eng.pdf. Capital expences for 2003 is 4.3 billion USD.

9   Facts presented in this sub-section are based on http://www.eia.doe.gov/emeu/cabs/norway.html

investments in the oil sector is now in decline. Aker Kvaerner is the leading Norwegian service provider with world-wide operations. Others in Norway include PGS, the world largest seismic acquisition and processing company.

## Theories of the firm

Scholars' knowledge of the glue in an oil supply chain are limited, both in terms of what type of factors hold the different firms together and the degree of this integration. Based on transaction-cost inspired theories and the property rights perspective, this section seeks to present hypotheses concerning the organisation of the supply chains in Angola and Norway.

### Transaction costs

According to transaction-cost analysis, governance structure is treated as a dependent variable (Klein, Crawford and Alchian, 1978; Williamson, 1985). Between the polar extreme of arm's length trade and vertical integration, the degree of integration is assumed to be increasing with *asset specificity, uncertainty and the frequency* of transactions. The degree of integration between companies in a supply chain can be analysed by a similar approach.

When transactions are characterised by asset specificity, they have a higher value between the parties than to parties outside the relationship. The outcome is that the upstream firm risks to underinvest in technology improvements. According to this theory, I would expect the supply chain in Angola to be more integrated than in Norway since the intermediate good is more differentiated and complex (making asset specificity a more likely option).

One of the weaknesses with transaction cost analysis is that it mainly focuses on the costs (transaction costs) and benefits (economics of scale) of market transactions, not on the costs of vertical integration. One of the costs of vertical integration is that it may give *lower* incentives for an upstream firm to undertake product development and *innovation* since the downstream firm (as an owner) can deny upstream firm application of the technology elsewhere.[10] Such incentives are of particular importance when the upstream firm, by its actions, has a great influence on the downstream agent's value of the product. For this reason, I supplement transaction costs analysis with that of the property rights school.

### A property right perspective

Grossman and Hart (1986) raise the question *why do we have firms?* In a world of complete contracts (which can be verified by a third party), firms are to some

---

10 But integration represents one way of acquiring firm-specific knowledge. The recent merger of Coflexip and Aker represents one example of this. One problem with such a strategy is that it gives few incentives for Aker in further improvement of its deepwater technology.

extent unnecessary. Transactions can be handled by independent agents based on arm's length trade. However, when contracts are incomplete, ownership (firms) are necessary in order to give proper investment incentives. Based on the same approach, we might ask why we have a group of firms organised as a supply chain. Similar to the tradition in transaction costs analysis, the degree of integration of the supply chain is the endogenous variable and the key issue is what type of hierarchical (governance) structure will most efficiently facilitate product innovation, quality improvement or cost reduction by the upstream firm. Ownership of assets is important because it gives the owner bargaining power under unforeseen contingencies (which require bargaining) and it confers ownership of goods. According to this theory, firms are only needed in order to deal with incomplete contracts and the focus in the analysis is therefore on the incomplete part of contracts.

It is reasonable to assume that contracts are incomplete in the sense that not all contingencies are covered. Complex technologies and uncertainties in the oil industry require extensive applications of functional contracts and change orders. The property right perspective is therefore an interesting point of departure for analysing the structure of the supply chain.

Grossman and Hart focus on formal structures (ownership) *between* firms, but do not analyse self-enforcing informal structures such as the parties' concern for their reputation. Baker, Gibbons and Murphy (2002) extend Grossman and Hart's model by analysing the interplay between formal structures and informal relationships (relational contracts such as partnership based on mutual trust), particularly how the former facilitates the feasibility of the latter. This interplay can be analysed both between firms and within a firm (for instance between different departments). In contrast to the transaction cost approach where 'relational contracts' are placed in a continuum along one dimension (degree of ownership), Baker and Gibbons distinguish between two dimensions and four prototypes of ownership/governance regimes (see Table 5.2).

**Table 5.2    Outsourcing versus integration**

| Governance Environment | Ownership Environment | |
|---|---|---|
|  | Non Integrated (Upstream owns) | Integrated (Downstream owns) |
| Spot ('arm's length') | Spot Outsourcing (1) | Spot Employment (2) |
| Relational (trust) | Relational Outsourcing (3) | Relational Employment (4) |

In line with our definitions in the previous section there are two agents, an upstream firm (with an option to integrate forward) and a downstream firm (with a backward option). The upstream agent (the sub-contractor) produces an item that can be used in a downstream agent's (main contractor) production process. The upstream firm may undertake observable but unverifiable investments in the good such as technology improvement. Let us assume that no investments are made by the downstream firm. Downstream firms want upstream firms to invest in order to improve quality or technology and thereby reduce costs. After observing the value of the good to the buyer and the seller, the parties negotiate the price and split the gain according to a Nash bargaining solution. Ownership matters because it determines the stakeholders' threat points (or outside options) under the negotiations and thereby the way in which the gain is split between the players. This split in turn influences the parties' incentives to invest. According to the theory, there are two incentive mechanisms: asset ownership and relational contracts. For spot transactions, ownership is the main incentive mechanism. Let us start by analysing such a case.

If the upstream firm owns the asset, the transaction is non-integrated and the upstream producer is an independent contractor using his own assets. I term this outsourcing (or segmented supply chain). He can then negotiate with the downstream agent about the sale price (a possibility that is unavailable if a downstream agent owns the asset). When the downstream firm owns the asset, asset ownership is integrated and I term it 'employment'. Under employment the downstream firm can renege and refuse to pay a potential bonus for technology improvement. Knowing this, without any reputation mechanism in place hindering the downstream firm from reneging, an upstream firm will not invest.

Under spot employment, the upstream firm has no incentives for cost reduction while under spot outsourcing an upstream firm does have such incentives. In cases where it is important for a company to provide incentives for investments in cost reductions and technology improvements (and explicit contracts are not attainable), it is therefore important to outsource (1 in Table 5.2) part of their activities. However, outsourcing creates a temptation ex post for the upstream party to renege by declaring the bonus too low.

When the parties have more frequent interactions, as assumed in the case of the oil market, the sales price or bonus can form the basis of a *relational contract* (cf. (3) or (4) in Table 5.2) enforced by the parties' concerns about their reputation. In contrast to spot transactions, a downstream firm, can provide incentives for technology improvements to an upstream firm even as an owner. Relational contracts between integrated parties ('relational employment') differ from those between non-integrated ('outsourcing') parties in the ways the parties attempt to renege.[11] Under relational outsourcing the upstream firm may undertake investments which improve its best alternative (threatpoint) and thereby its bargaining position. However, in the integrated case, the upstream firm has no resources if the downstream firm declares poor performance and is unwilling to pay the bonus. In a relational contract, the downstream party promises a bonus. The temptation to renege is less under non-

---

11 A key difference between outsourcing and employment with relational contracts is that the goods' value in its alternative use affects the reneging decision under relational outsourcing, but not under relational employment.

integration. This reduced temptation makes it credible to promise a larger bonus to an independent contractor. [12]

## Predictions derived from the property right approach

I will derive three predictions from the theories presented above:

First of all, one would expect assets to be more *relation-specific* and complex in Angola than in Norway, with a subsequent tendency towards *integration* ((2) or (4) in Table 5.2). I therefore predict that acquisition and mergers are of particular importance for the service providers operating in the Angolan market. Mergers represent a way of getting access to new technology (for instance, pipes in deepwater), new customers (oil companies) and a greater market (by providing integrated solutions). Mergers may also increase the financial strength of the service provider, and strength is particularly important in new markets characterised by a high degree of uncertainty.

Secondly, since the importance of ownership is inversely related to the importance of providing *incentives* for cost reduction or technological improvement (as is the case with outsourcing), one should accordingly expect *non integration* ((1) or (3) in Table 5.2) to be more common in Angola than in Norway, particularly between the oil company and the main contractors.

Thirdly, higher risk increases the discount rate and makes *relational contracts less likely*. Even if the operation risk may be similar between Norway and Angola, the country risk (the oil companies face a severe political risk in terms of civil war, unaccountable government, corruption[13] and human development) is higher in Angola. Integrated oil service firms with diverse activities around the world can better bear the risk involved in one particular oil province such as Angola. Oil companies may therefore seek to convert risk to their main contractors. There are some additional factors making relational contracts more difficult to sustain in Angola. While relational contracts have been promoted in the North Sea by the government as the NorSok and CRINE initiatives (see below), similar initiatives are lacking in the Angolan case. One also needs to recall that cultural and political differences may impede the development of trust, and is pinpointed as an explanation why the structure of supply chain differs across countries.[14] Angola is a 'new' oil-producing country, and local Angolan companies have yet not established brands for quality as has happened in Norway. Some of the majors lack experience from Angola. Kizomba A was for instance the first field where Exxon was an operating

---

12 Let B refer to the bonus under relational contracting, where B>0 if performance is good. In the non-integrated case, the upstream firm can extract some of the value of the good through bargaining (say S, where S<B). Reneging under integration saves B, but reneging under non-integration saves the difference (B-S).

13 Cf. Global Witness report on Angola where Elf in particular is blamed for its non-transparent actions (Global 1999).

14 Sako (1992) discusses the automobile case.

producer and production began in 2004. Finally, although the agents may have long lasting experience with each other from other parts of the world, deepwater fields in Angola represent new markets where the agents may lack technological experience. Since relational contracts are more difficult to sustain, accordingly, one should expect spot transactions, to be more common in Angola than in Norway (fields (1) or (2) in Table 5.2).

## Supply chain management in Angola and Norway

Guided by the discussion in the previous section, I identify four sets of indicators to help analyse the structure of the supply chain in the two markets. First of all *technology* and the degree of asset specificity matters for the way supply chain are organised. Compared to Norway, production takes place in deeper water and shallower reservoir. Two main technological challenges associated with such depths are flow assurance and riser weight. Oil occurs closer to the seabed (reducing its heat) and the risers length provide an opportunity to cool down oil and reduce its flow. Risers weight increases with depth and reduce the platform capacity. On the other hand, the climate is tougher in Norway. I therefore presume that deepwater development requires more complex technology than in shallow water and that the degree of asset specificity differs across tasks in the supply chain. I am particularly concerned about the parties' fear of imitation. Second, I emphasise how trust and the informal network between the contract partners may influence the structure of the supply chain. The *informal* network between the contract partners indicates how difficult it is to sustain relational contracts. I discuss the agents' previous experience and common culture. Finally, I apply two indicators of the governance structure of the supply chain. The way the supply chain is organised, is first of all measured by the *characteristics of the contracts* (in terms of the number of contracts, their size and the incentives provided) and by the *ownership* structure between the agents.

The *number* of contracts awarded and their size represent a measure of the degree of integration in the chain. They also provide information about the relationships between the contract partners. If one contract is awarded only, for instance, the contractor is likely either to be an integrated oil service firm providing all services from drilling to production or subcontracts some of these tasks to independent firms. The other extreme is a situation where there are numerous contracts between the oil company and its suppliers. In the first place, it is a bilateral relationship between the contract partner and the oil company, but in the second place, these relations are fragmented. The incentives provided also give a measure of the degree of integration. Providing high-powered incentives to contractors indicates that the transactions between the partners are characterised by market transactions. *Ownership* is a direct measure of integration, and I will emphasise how contract partners through acquisitions and joint ventures (JVs) have integrated different tasks or market segments (cf. Table 5.1).

I structure the following analysis along the four factors mentioned above. First, I present the Norwegian benchmark case. I focus on the Angolan cases, and I restrict the analysis to two deepwater fields, namely Girassol and Kuito.

*Norway*

As a benchmark for the subsequent analysis, a brief overview of the supply chain in the Norwegian part of the North Sea is presented with a particular focus on the variables discussed above. As far as technology is concerned, I presume that it is less complex than in Angola since the oil is found in shallow water.

The most common way of organising the supply chain in the North Sea is increasingly that of the independent and integrated supplier (contractor) that undertakes engineering (designing the platform), procurement, construction (build the platform), and installation (EPCI contract), and delivers the platform to the oil company. At the same time, the number of awarded contracts is high. As the Gullfaks field example shows, more than 1700 contracts were awarded and there are a number of additional suppliers involved. The oil company plays an important co-ordination role towards these suppliers (Nordaas, 2000a).

In the EPCI contracts applied in the North Sea, the potential gain from a reduction in the field development cost is split between the contractor and the operator, and there is a downside amount for the contractor's potential loss. Partnering is a key to understand the reduction of field development costs. According to (Crabtree, Bower and Keogh, 1997), the outcome of the CRINE initiative for the oil companies, are 30 per cent saving on capital expenditure. The use of partnership and teamwork has played a significant role in this process. Similar reductions of costs have been achieved in Norway, even though this has led many suppliers into financial distress.[15]

Trust is a keyword in both the NorSok and the CRINE initiatives in the Norwegian and British parts of the North Sea respectively. Both initiatives were initiated by the oil industry and the governments in the respective countries in order to increase *co-operation* between contractors and operators. By providing larger incentives for cost reduction in field development, service providers were accordingly exposed to more uncertainty. These initiatives focus on how the stakeholders in a supply chain through *informal* mechanisms and institutional *relationships* may minimise joint costs in the whole value chain in uncertain environments. Both initiatives try to build up new business groups independent of how the individual actors perceive ownership integration. Close co-operation between the customer and the contractors

is a precondition if projects are to be completed in a faster and less costly way... Mutual trust between the parties is imperative to succeed. The need for formalities is replaced by a culture of work where the contractor and the customer are expected to implicitly know what is right and what is wrong based on agreed attitudes and objectives(NorSok 1996:6).

---

15 In Njord in the Norwegian part of the North Sea, a 40 per cent cost reduction was achieved due to changes in project organisation.

One additional reason for the upbeat Norwegian attitude towards NorSok is that it stimulates the development of a national supply industry (at least in its home market). Trustworthy business relations facilitate the co-ordination of tasks, and are particularly important in market where service providers are small. At the same time, trust between independent actors is probably easier to establish between firms of equal origin since they share common cultural conceptions, at least a common language. The facilitating of a national industry seems to have been a successful strategy. In Norway around 60 per cent of procurement is produced by Norwegian firms (Nordaas, 2000a and b).

Statoil is particularly concerned with forming partnerships with suppliers based on interaction and mutuality. Statoil tends to look at the supply chain as a business group where the players create informal partnerships, networks and alliances. In such networks, long-term relationships, *trust and mutual dependence substitute financial integration* and lead to an integrated supply chain where the oil company largely controls the value added outside the company.[16]

NorSok does not address mechanisms that can create trust. It rather appeals to the moral obligations of the parties. Sako and Helper (1998) analysed such mechanisms and found that trust increases with the *information flow* between the parties and by the level of *technical assistance* provided by the customer. The building of trust can therefore be regarded as a relation-specific investment. Trust between an oil company and the main supplier (or between the first and second-tier suppliers) represents a sort of 'relation-specific skill' (Asanuma, 1989). This means that changing partners has switching costs, which ultimately strengthens the glue in the chain.

*Angola*[17]

At the time of my fieldwork in Luanda in March 2000, Girassol and Kuito were the only deepwater fields where contracts were public. I therefore studied these two fields in more detail (see Wiig, 2001 for an elaboration). The contracts and service providers involved in these two fields are representative for more recently awarded contracts in deepwater fields such as Dalia, Benguela, Lobito and Kizomba.[18] I undertook interviews among the main contract partners in the two fields. I also used Alexander's Gas and Oil Online (http://www.gasandoil.com/goc/company/) and the homepages of the firms involved, to collect additional information. All information about ownership structure is based on data from 2000 or at the time contracts were awarded.

---

16 Except for the integration of suppliers in the decision-making process for technical solutions, Statoil is not explicit regarding what is meant by the creation of relationships and what partnerships mean for the (independent) parties. A business partner can, for instance, be a buyer in one relationship and become a seller or a competitor in other relationships.

17 This section represents a condensed version of Wiig, 2001.

18 See Upstream 17 September 2004:24 *Angola Focus* for an overview of more recently awarded contracts.

*Girassol*

Girassol was discovered by Elf in 1996, and is located in Block 17 at 1400 metres
depth. In addition to Elf (now Total), the operator, both Statoil, Hydro and BP are
partners. Girassol involved the largest infrastructure for such depths ever installed,
as well as innovative technology. The FPSO was the largest to date and has a storage
capacity of 2 000 000 barrels and a production capacity of 200 000 bpd.

*Contracts awarded and incentives provided* The three largest contracts awarded
for the development of Girassol were i) the FPSO ((2) and (3) in Table 5.1); ii) the
FUR ((4) and part of (5)) and iii) the contract for subsea equipment (part of (5)).[19]
The total values of these contracts amount to USD 1.5 billion (or 60 per cent of total
development costs). Bouygues offshore (BOS) plays a leading role in the consortium
of contractors, particularly the FPSO and FUR contracts.[20]

Elf takes all risks above a particular downside amount for the FPSO while there is
no downside amount for the FUR contract. The subsea equipment contract is a fixed-
price contract, and gives the supplier high incentives to achieve cost reductions. At
the same time, the oil company does not achieve any rewards from it. Since strong
incentives are provided to the main contractors, this indicates that the relationship
between the main contractors and the operator is based on market transactions.
One important explanation is that the oil company seeks to reduce uncertainty.[21] In
terms of incentives, the chain is more fragmented in Angola than in Norway, at least
between the oil company and the main contractors.

*Ownership and acquisition* Fewer, but larger contracts are awarded at Girassol than
what normally is the case in Norway. This indicates that the contractors in the chain
are more integrated than in Norway. Main contractors are integrated oil service firms
providing a bundle of goods and services and acquisition of important technology
providers have been a common integration strategy of the main contract partners.

BOS specialises in providing integrated solutions for the design, construction,
installation and management of offshore and onshore oil and gas production-related
turnkey projects. BOS formed the construction firm Petromar Uem Angola in 1984,
a 70/30 joint venture between BOS and Sonangol.[22] With the acquisition of Doris
Engineering, BOS covers the entire value chain from basic engineering to maintenance,
including detail engineering, procurement, construction and installation (but not
operation and subsea equipment). The other contract partner, the French firm ETPM,
owned by Stolt Offshore specialises in turnkey projects and deepsea work. With
the acquisition of ETPM, Stolt complements its activities and competence with i)

---

19  FPSO refers to floating production storage and offloading barge and offloading buoy.
FUR refers to flowlines, umbicals and risers.

20  BOS has recently been bought by the Italian firm Saipem.

21  Given the high degree of uncertainty in Angola and the strong incentives provided, the
main contractors operating in Angola need significant financial strength.

22  Petromar owns the Soyo Kwanda Base.

competence in *engineering* of all types of platforms; ii) *fabrication* through ETPM's yards in Nigeria and in Angola; iii) *pipelay*.[23] Stolt produces flexible flowlines and dynamic flexible risers (through NKT Flexibles where Stolt Offshore holds 49 per cent stake).

None of the main contractors was afraid of hold-ups by the oil company or that their technology might be imitated by competitors, either indicating a low degree of physical asset specificity or that those asset-specific assets were already integrated. As discussed above, the contractors merged with upstream firms to get hold of new technologies and know-how and thereby cover a larger part of the value chain. Not all tasks were integrated, the production, but not the engineering of the FPSO is outsourced. Construction activities are fragmented. When applying the theories discussed above within tasks in a sector, both results fit: more advanced technology is produced in-house while general-purpose technology (such as construction) is outsourced.

*Informal partnerships* BOS has been dealing with a number of oil companies, but Elf predominates. In fact, in 1981, Elf acquired a 34 per cent stake in the equity capital of BOS which it sold back in 1990.[24] BOS has considerable experience of Western Africa, including Angola.

The following table summarises the relationship between the main contract partners at Girassol according to the typologies applied in Table 5.2 (where (3) indicates non-integration, but relational contract, and (3-) indicates that the contract is relationally biased but also include elements of spot transactions).

**Table 5.3     Typologies of contracts at Girassol: a wrapping up**

|  | Operator/Contractor | Contractor/sub-contractors |
| --- | --- | --- |
| FPSO | (3-) | (1) |
| FUR | (3) | (4) |
| Subsea | (1) | - |

*Kuito*

Kuito is located in Block 14, which is operated by Chevron (holding of 31 per cent).[25] Kuito is the first field that is developed in Block 14, and is located in 400 metres of water. Kuito is merely a step out of Chevron's Block 0 operations offshore Angola. It was easy to develop a facility and tie it to the inshore production. Chevron was,

---

23  Stolt Offshore and Sonangol are the main owners of Sonamet. Sonamet fabricates metallic platforms and pipes at its yard in Lobito.

24  This is one of the few examples where a constructor is owned by the oil company (Saipem is another).

25  The remaining interests are held by Sonangol (20 per cent), Agip, a subsidiary of the Italian state owned oil company ENI (20 per cent), Total (20 per cent) and Petrogal (9 per cent).

however, unsure about the real size of the field, and its connections to other sites nearby. Kuito was considerably easier to develop than Girassol. The FPSO has a production capacity of 100 000 barrels per day and a storage capacity of 1.4 million barrels.

*Contracts awarded and incentives provided*   Chevron opted for a fast but phased development of Kuito. The first phase brought together ABB and Coflexip Stena Offshore (CSO) in a consortium headed by the Monaco-registered firm SBM (Single Buoy Mooring Inc). SBM was responsible for the FPSO, the mooring system and export facilities and for the management of the consortium. SBM was chosen because it was perceived to be technologically capable (only a few energy servicing firms are able to undertake operations [cf. stage 6] and SBM already owned a vessel which could be used). As in the Girassol development, a small number of contract partners cover most of the procurement, indicating an *integrated chain*. The contract partners play a more important role in Kuito than Girassol, since they are in charge of production. Chevron therefore plays a less dominant role in supply chain management in Kuito than ELF at Girassol.

The initial development included the drilling and completion of 12 subsea production wells. The contract value for the first phase was USD 400 million. This includes the installation of the FPSO along with a calm buoy, subsea trees and manifolds, flowlines, risers and mooring systems.

In contrast to Girassol, the operator leases the platform. Chevron seems to have pressed for a leasing solution because of uncertainty related to the size of the reservoir. The FPSO is *leased* from Sonasing, a joint venture *between SBM and Sonangol*. The leasing period is five years, with the possibility of an extension of five additional years. The daily rate is fixed, but it is a small variable element based on an operating agreement giving penalties and bonuses based on a complex set of formula. The consortium takes all risks of misspecification of costs and there is no bottom line of losses. Therefore, *incentives are provided to SBM to reduce the fixed cost of the FPSO*, but few incentives to reduce variable costs (for some reason, hardly any incentives are provided to increase the production of oil).

The PSA agreement makes it possible to deduct a certain amount of capital investments. When an oil company owns the FPSO, and the field is smaller than expected ('nature is bad'), an oil company risks not recovering all of its capital costs. In contrast, by leasing, all leasing costs are recovered independently of nature's whims.[26] However, when nature is good (huge reservoir), Chevron has the *flexibility*

---

26 When nature is bad (good), the host government therefore receives more (less) income compared to a leasing situation. If prospects are good, it therefore makes sense for a government like the Angolan to require a more common use of leasing contracts or to prefer contractors that are able to control production (which is a requirement for leasing). In fact, this is also what happens. Foreign operators are under pressure to lease, not buy, FPSO vessels in order to reduce initial investment costs and increase early revenue flow for Angola. *Financial Times* November 15, 2000, 'Angola to firm grip on foreign oil companies'.

to get a bigger ship while the Angolan authorities receive earlier revenue flows. Under bargaining arrangements, integrated firms like SBM that are able to handle the production are fundamental for proper supply chain management. There are no reasons to believe that SBM had more information about the reservoir than Chevron has. However, SBM has the advantage of dealing with *asymmetric asset specificity* as regards the FPSO. Even though the technology of the FPSO is general, its alternative value is higher for a firm specialising in providing FPSOs for a number of firms than for an oil company with the primary objective of exploring oil. Partly for this reason, SBM takes the risk of high residual value and relocation risk.

*Ownership and acquisitions*   SBM is a wholly owned subsidiary of the Dutch public company IHC Caland. SBM is a turnkey supplier or key element supplier in more than 50 per cent of the installed floating terminals world-wide (based on the Single Point Moorings or SPM principle). In addition to being a major supplier of SPMs, the company has gained substantial experience in the conversion of trading tankers and the construction of new-built units for FSO and FPSO projects.

SBM has no world-wide alliance or frame agreement with Chevron or other contract partners, but has an agreement with the Italian contractor Saipem to cooperate on deepwater FPSO projects. Eni, a partner in the licence of Block 14 holds 45 per cent of the shares in Saipem.[27] Saipem provides subsea construction while SBM undertakes the operations. The two parties therefore *complement each other* and it gives the 'group' a position to be a global offshore service provider (covering nearly the whole value chain except for drilling).

CSO provides a wide range of services (project management, engineering design, procurement, subsea pipeline and umbilical laying, construction and maintenance work) and products (design and manufacture of flexible pipes. CSO is the biggest world-wide subsea-contracting firm. CSO has a world-wide frame agreement with Chevron for flexible flowlines.

After a sale of a 30 per cent stake in CSO by Stena to the French group Technip, a world-wide strategic alliance in offshore activities was established in April 2000 between Technip and CSO. A joint bidding strategy for integrated projects was formed. Whereas CSO has a leading position in the deep offshore market ((4) and (5) in Table 5.1), Technic brings additional competence in engineering and project management capability (2); a broad geographic presence; and a more diversified client base (national oil companies in particular). Technic is primarily involved in downstream activities (oil refining and gas processing) and has established an Angolan subsidiary seeking to establish a refinery in Angola.

---

27 Since Saipem more recently has bought BOS, it turns out to be a significant player in the deepwater fields in Angola and this firm is a more complete integrated unit than similar oil service firms since it is owned by ENI.

*Informal partnerships* Both ABB and CSO have a frame agreement with Chevron. Apart from this, I do not find indications of any informal relationship between the parties.

In sum: few, but large, contracts were rewarded at Kuito indicating integrated oil service firms. Contracts between oil companies and oil service firms were based on market transactions. As in Girassol, none of the main contract partners were afraid of imitation of their technology. Contractors were mainly integrated service providers since Chevron decided to lease the FPSO.

*Alternative explanations*

In a study of Statoil's procurement by Dir. Trondslien (www.statoil.com), the degree of integration was found to vary between different phases of production and between different tasks in each phase. The suppliers' contribution to total inputs amounted up to 95 per cent within drilling/well technology and the development projects (cf. stages 1:5 in Table 5.1), 50–70 per cent within the operation (stage 6) of on- and offshore installations, up to 70 per cent within distribution/sales and approximately 50 per cent within innovation (stage 2 in particular). It therefore seems that the oil companies are vertically linked downstream, but not upstream. Several studies confirm this results (Al Moneef, 1998; Al Obaidan and Scully, 1993; Bindemann, 1999). Hallwood (1992) found little support for the transaction costs analysis in an analysis of the organisation of the supply chain in the British part of the North Sea, while I found some evidences that service providers operating in technological advanced areas tend to be integrated energy service firms.

There are two main problems with empirical analyses based on transaction costs (Shelanski and Klein, 1999). First, there is the *measurement* problem of comparing the value of the investments inside and outside a relationship. Normally, survey methods where respondents are requested to state their opinions on a Likert scale are applied for this purpose. I reduced this problem by asking whether the supplier was afraid of imitation and hold-ups. Second, and more importantly *alternative hypotheses* could in many cases equally well confirm the data. Two such alternative hypotheses giving the same predictions as the property right approach are:

- *Market power.* Neo-classical approaches are based on market power explanations or economics of scope between successive stages in order to explain vertical integration (Stigler, 1951). The market power explanation of (vertical) integration says that gains will increase by degree of supplier market concentration (Spiller, 1985). When upstream firms have market power, vertical integration eliminates the divergence between the value of the marginal product of the input and the marginal cost. On the other hand, the downstream firm also has market power and this reduces the gains from mergers. Assuming the downstream market power is the same in Norway and Angola (most of the multinational oil companies are located in both destinations), and that the supply industry is 'thinner' in Angola than in

Norway, a more integrated supply chain is likelier in Angola than in Norway. If upstream market power stems from access to a superior technology or other physical assets, for example a yard, one should accordingly expect i) the tendency of acquisition to increase, and ii) that the main contractors tend to integrate with upstream firms. The market power explanation represents an alternative explanation, which has not been falsified by our data.

- *Domestic political reasons.* The pressure for integration can come from the state in order to create a geographically segmented chain. I do not find much evidence to confirm the latter theory, at least not in the Angolan context. The integrated solution concept chosen was requested by the oil companies and adapted to their needs. Angola has no preferences for a particular organisation of the supply chain, although, similar to most other oil producing countries, it has preferences for the use of local firms. I cannot falsify this explanation of the supply chain development in Norway (and probably not in the UK part of the North Sea), but also here one may argue that technology and partnering were two important keys to the success. In Norway, lower technical uncertainty combined with the higher likelihood of successful partnering made it possible for the government to support the development of a cost effective local supply industry.

## Conclusion

Our findings support the predictions derived from the property right perspective:

- The supply chain is more integrated in the technically advanced Angolan markets than in the North Sea. Our case studies from Angola have few, but large, contract partners. Tailor-made solutions in deepwater are generally more technically advanced or complex and require integrated solutions. The oil companies achieve such integration by using integrated oil service firms (confirm prediction one). There are some differences across markets in Angola: Technically advanced tasks are undertaken in-house while low-skill intensive tasks are fragmented (that is, construction activities and the building of ships are done by independent companies).
- Contracts between the supply industry and the oil companies are mainly based on market transactions (confirm prediction two). Since oil service firms are integrated units and relational contracts are harder to sustain in Angola, the competition occurs primarily among integrated oil service firms rather than among integrated supply chains (as claimed is the case in the North Sea; see footnote 4). However, Girassol and Kuito display slightly different patterns. At Girassol, main contracts are awarded to firms sharing the nationalities of the majority interests in the licence (French and Norwegian). I do not find similar preferences for American firms in the Chevron case (at Kuito).
- Since the supply industry is 'integrated', the importance of relational

contracts based on mutual trust is currently less important in Angola than in the North Sea. There are no initiatives in Angola similar to the Norsok and CRINE initiatives in the North Sea, and a local supply industry is lacking. Relational contracts were harder to sustain in Angola than in Norway (or in the UK), partly because of more technological and political uncertainty and less experience among business partners in deepwater development projects (confirm prediction three).

The 'glue' in the chain has an important impact on a firm's strategies regarding their choice of market segment and their formation of relationships to the main actors in the supply chain. When most transactions in the chain were based on arm's length trade, upstream firms competed with regard to costs. To the extent that the establishment of relationships to customers is important, one would expect the supplier to get in touch with the oil companies, and especially the *operator*, since they are the ultimate customer and organiser of the chain (as in the North Sea). The flip side of the coin is projects in which the oil company prefers an integrated approach (as the Angolan cases presented). There are several reasons for this choice, but in essence, the oil company prefers to deal with a limited number of suppliers in order to reduce transaction costs, spread the risk, and concentrate on core activities. In an integrated project, the main contractors are thereby more involved in the organisation and design of the project. To serve as a main contractor, one therefore needs to provide integrated solutions. Although first-tier suppliers (for example, big turnkey contractors) will never succeed without a proven record or reputation vis-à-vis the oil company, second-tier suppliers and sub-suppliers need to create relationships to first-tier suppliers (*main contractors*), not primarily to the oil companies.[28] Without previous experience with multinational contractors, this may create problems for the sub-suppliers (Crabtree, Bower and Keogh, 1997). In both cases, a supplier not only needs to be competitive in price but also needs a good business reputation. When the host government, for instance the Angolan Government, requires or prefers that foreign suppliers link up to local suppliers or oil companies, suppliers also have to establish working relationships with *local* companies in the host country.

**References**

Al Moneef, Majed A. (1998), 'Vertical Integration Strategies of the National Oil Companies', *Developing Economies* **36**(2), pp. 203-22.

Al Obaidan, Abdullah M. and G.W. Scully (1993), 'The Economic Efficiency of Backward Vertical Integration in the International Petroleum Refining Industry', *Applied Economics*, **25**(12), pp. 1529-39.

Asanuma, Banri (1989), 'Manufacturer-Supplier Relationships in Japan and the Concept of Relation-Specific Skill', *Journal-of-the-Japanese-and-International-*

---

28 There are also some opportunities for bypassing the contractors by making direct contact with the operator.

*Economy*, **3**(1), pp. 1-30.

Baker, G., R. Gibbons and K.J. Murphy (2002), 'Relational Contracts and the Theory of the Firm', *Quarterly Journal of Economics*, **117**(1), pp. 39-84.

Bindemann, K. (1999), 'Vertical Integration in the Oil Industry: A Review of the Literature', *Journal of Energy Literature*, **5**(1), pp. 3-26.

Coase, R.H. (1960), 'The Problem of Social Cost' in R.H. Coase (ed.), *The Firm, the Market, and the Law*, Chicago and London: University of Chicago Press.

Crabtree, Elisabeth D., J. Bower and W. Keogh (1997), 'Conflict or Collaboration: The Changing Nature of Inter-firm Relationships in the UK Oil and Gas Industry', *Technology Analysis and Strategic Management*, **9**(2), pp. 179-91.

Feenstra, Robert C., Deng Shing Huang and Gary G. Hamilton (1996), *Business Groups and Trade in East Asia: Part 1, Networked Equilibria*, U CA, Davis; Academia Sinica; U WA.

Global Witness (1999), *A Crude Awakening. The Role of the Oil and Banking Industries in Angola's Civil War and the Plunder of State Assets*.

Granovetter, Mark (1995), 'Coase Revisited: Business Groups in the Modern Economy', *Industrial and Corporate Change*, **4**(1), pp.93-130.

Greve H., S.A. Haugland and K. Walderhaug (1996), *Partnerskap og leverandørrelasjoner i norsk oljeindustri*, SNF (SNF report 10/96).

Grossman, Sanford J. and Oliver D. Hart (1986), 'The Costs and Benefits of Ownership: A Theory of Vertical and Lateral Integration', *Journal of Political Economy*, **94**(4), pp. 691-719.

Hallwood, C. Paul (1991), 'Perceptions of Market Efficacy, Transaction Costs, and Vertical Disintegration in Offshore Oil Gathering', *Journal of Economic Studies*, **19**(3), pp. 36-49.

Helper, Susan (1991), 'Strategy and Irreversibility in Supplier Relations: The Case of the U.S. Automobile Industry', *Business History Review*, **34**, pp. 781-824.

Heum, Per and Eirik Vatne (1999), Hjemlandseffekter av direkte utenlandsinvesteringer i norsk oljeindustri. (In Norwegian) SNF, Bergen (R25/99).

Klein, Benjamin, Robert G. Crawford and Armen A. Alchian (1978), 'Vertical Integration, Appropriable Rents, and the Competitive Contracting Process', *Journal of Law and Economics*, **21**(2), pp. 297-326.

Kvaløy, Ola (2000), *The Economic Organisation of Specific Assets*, Chr. Michelsen Institute, Bergen, (Working paper 2000: 14).

Markusen, James R., Thomas F. Rutherford and Linda Hunter (1995), 'Trade Liberalization in a Multinational-Dominated Industry, *Journal of International Economics*, **38**(1-2), pp. 95-117.

Masten, Scott E. (1986), 'Institutional Choice and the Organization of Production: The Make-or-Buy Decision', *Journal of Institutional and Theoretical Economics*, **142**(3), pp. 493-509.

Nordaas, Hildegunn Kyvik (2000a), *Gullfaks – the First Norwegian Oil Field Developed and Operated by Norwegian Companies*, Chr Michelsen Institute, Bergen (Working Paper 2000: 13).

Nordaas, Hildegunn Kyvik (2000b), *The Snorre Field and the Rise and Fall of Saga*

*Petroleum*, Chr Michelsen Institute, Bergen (Working Paper 2000:16).

NorSok (1996), *Integrated Forms of Cooperation and Incentive Contracts,* Task Force Report, March 1996.

Sako, Mari (1992), *Prices, Quality and Trust: Inter-Firm Relations in Britain and Japan*, Cambridge Studies in Management, No 18.

Sako, Mari and Susan Helper (1998), 'Determinants of Trust in Supplier Relations: Evidence from the Automotive Industry in Japan and the United States', *Journal of Economic Behavior and Organization*, **34**(3), pp.387-417.

Shelanski, Howard and Peter G. Klein (1999), 'Empirical Research in Transaction Cost Economics: A Review and Assessment', in G.R. Carroll and D.J. Teece (eds), *Firms, Markets, and Hierarchies: The Transaction Cost Economics Perspective*, New York and Oxford: Oxford University Press.

Spiller, Pablo T. (1985), 'On Vertical Mergers', *Journal of Law, Economics and Organization*, **1**(2), pp. 285-312.

Stigler, George (1951), 'The Division of Labor Is Limited by the Extent of the Market', *Journal of Political Economy*.

Trondslien, P. (no reference to year), 'The Importance of the Procurement Process to Statoil, and the Development within Statoil's Supply Chain'. www. Statoil com.

Wiig, Arne (2001), *Supply Chain Management in the Oil Industry: The Angolan Case*, Bergen: Chr. Michelsen Institute (CMI Working Paper WP 2001:6).

Williamson, Oliver E. (1985), *The Economic Institutions of Capitalism. Firms, Markets, Relational Contracting*, London: The Free Press.

Chapter 6

# Competitive Strategy and Industry Structure: A Value Configuration Interpretation

Charles Stabell

## Introduction

The petroleum industry has recently seen mega-mergers where some of the largest firms in the global economy have joined forces to become even bigger. What are the forces that lead to this behavior? What do these events tell us about the attractiveness of the petroleum industry, about competitive strategies and about how the industry might evolve?

Consider Chevron's 2000 acquisition of Texaco. In the immediate aftermath, several arguments and interpretations have been advanced (NYT, Oct 10 2000).

One argument for the Texaco-acquisition is size and competitive response: 'The last two years have produced industry mammoths such as ExxonMobil and BP Amoco, now known as BP. Smaller companies like Chevron and Texaco face the risk of losing out on oil projects and investor interest if they stay small.' Note that both Chevron and Texaco are large companies by any standard.

Another line of argument refers to the potential of complementary (read cheap) assets: 'Texaco has good assets and Chevron has the management to turn them around.' A variant of the same argument is access to particularly attractive and synergistic assets: 'The merger would give the combined company the greatest number of leases to oil reservoirs far below the waters of the Gulf of Mexico. Chevron Texaco would also become an even more powerful presence in the deep-water offshore areas of Brazil and West Africa.'

Simplifying a great deal, these interpretations suggest two basic arguments: a cost argument and a relationship argument. These are potentially interrelated arguments in that good relationships (with owners of prospective acreage) gives access to the best acreage, where best is synonymous with acreage with the lowest unit costs.[1] The arguments are, however, slightly different in that they imply access to proven petroleum resources as opposed to access to acreage with potential.

---

1  We are focusing on upstream arguments here. These arguments are also relevant to the downstream phases of the industry.

A basic tenet of modern competitive strategy literature (see Porter, 1980, 1990) is that we need to look at the larger *value system* of activities and actors in order to evaluate the potential of an industry and understand effective competitive strategies. Suppliers and buyers, and not only direct competitors, affect both how much value is created and who gets what share of the value created by the value system.

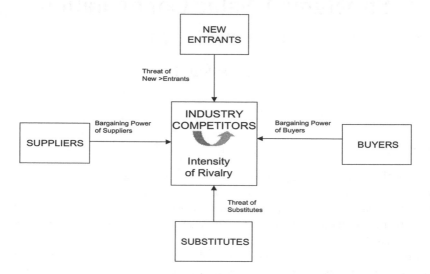

**Figure 6.1    5-forces framework for analysis of an industry (Porter, 1980)**

Figure 6.1 shows the elements of Porter's (1980) 5-forces framework for the analysis of industry structure. Threat of new entrants, threat of substitutes, bargaining power of buyers, bargaining power of suppliers and intensity of rivalry between competitors are the five forces. These forces are shaped by structural attributes of the industry such as economies of scale, concentration and mobility barriers.

Consider the PC industry. It is now very competitive, with small margins. Intel, however, has been able to obtain extremely good returns. The 5-forces framework explains this as due to Intel's near monopoly position as supplier of micro-processor chips.

Application of the 5-forces framework involves defining the focal industry, delineating the relevant value system and thus the main existing (and potential) actors in the industry. You then evaluate the structural forces that shape value created and who appropriates what share of this value. Understanding the industry in terms of competitive forces not only gives a picture of the attractiveness of the industry. It is also used to identify effective competitive strategies. Porter (1980) argues that there are only two basic, alternative competitive strategies: cost leadership and differentiation.[2]

---

2    Porter argues that trying to pursue both a cost leadership strategy and a differentiation strategy leads to getting 'stuck in the middle' with poor long term prospects. This raises the

We report here on research that started from the idea that much of modern competitive strategy literature was primarily relevant to industries that were dominated by a manufacturing logic (see Stabell and Fjeldstad, 1998; see also Afuah and Tucci, 2000). Our initial focus was on the firm-level analysis of competitive advantage. We suggested that Porter's value chain framework (1985) was relevant to manufacturing firms, but much less so to firms that sell problem solving services (think consulting and engineering services) and that sell mediation services (think financial, transportation and communication services). However, our work has also suggested that the different business logics of problem solving services and mediation services implies differences in terms of industry structure and in terms of what are effective competitive strategies. And the petroleum industry is increasingly an industry where all the three different business logics interact and define the competitive arena.

In what follows we first outline the new competitive strategy theory of alternative value creation logics, or what can be labeled value configuration theory. We then apply the distinction between the three business logics to the petroleum industry. Particularly when we focus on different segments of the industry, we see clearly the role of the different value configurations and how they both interact and co-exist. We then apply the models to two alternative perspectives on the upstream petroleum industry. In one, it is an industry of firms that explore and produce petroleum, getting their revenues from the sale of petroleum. In the other perspective, upstream petroleum is increasingly an industry of firms that sell a problem solving service directed at finding and producing petroleum for owners of prospective assets.

## Value configuration theory

Value configuration theory focuses firm-level competitive advantage. It starts from the premise that competitive advantage cannot be understood by looking at the firm as a whole. Competitive advantage stems from the many discrete activities a firm performs in generating and delivering value (Porter, 1985). Each of these activities can contribute to a firm's relative cost position and create a basis for differentiation. There is a fundamental distinction between primary and support activities. Primary activities deliver value to the customer. They define the firm's business model. Support activities (such as R&D, HRM, purchasing) support primary activities and impact customer value solely through their impact on current (and future) primary activities.

According to value configuration theory there are three basic, alternative ways that firms create value. In addition to Porter's initial formulation with the value chain (Figure 6.1), value configuration theory proposes that there is the value shop and the value network (see Figures 6.2 and 6.3). While the value chain is a template for the analysis of firms that deliver value by transforming inputs into goods, the value

---

issue of whether the mega-mergers will result in firms that are stuck in the middle, or is the petroleum industry an arena where Porter's ideas are refuted?

shop is a template for the firms that deliver value by solving a customer's problem. The value network is a template for firms that deliver value by mediating between customers.

Value configuration theory provides a systematic basis for analyzing and developing competitive advantage in all types of firms. A firm is broken down into value activities where costs and value generated are allocated and estimated, either using the value chain template for manufacturing firms, value network template for mediators, or value shop template for problem solving service firms. The results of this activity-directed review are used to identify the competitive strengths and weaknesses of the firm.

A second order and more fundamental analysis focuses the drivers of activity cost behavior and value delivered by activities. Drivers are structural properties of activities such as scale, location, learning and timing. Drivers are also structural properties of relationships between activities in the firm and activities in other firms in the value system. An example of a structural property of the relationship between activities is how input quality assurance impacts activity rejection costs in manufacturing. Another example is how documentation activities in prospect evaluation affects value delivered by post-drilling evaluation activities.

We distinguish between cost drivers and differentiation drivers (Porter, 1985). Differentiation drivers affect the unique value delivered by the activity and thus the premium price that the customer is willing to pay. The logic of the value chain implies a focus on cost drivers, while a value shop business is more concerned about differentiation.

Table 6.1 (from Stabell and Fjeldstad, 1998) summarizes key attributes of the three value configurations.

**Table 6.1    Differences across value configuration logics in petroleum industry**

|  | Chain | Shop | Network |
|---|---|---|---|
| Value creation logic | Transformation of inputs into goods | (Re) solving customer problems | Linking customers |
| Petroleum industry example | Petroleum production, oil refining | Drilling services, engineering services, consulting | Gas and oil transportation, oil and gas exchanges, brokering |
| Primary technology | Long-linked | Intensive | Mediating |
| Key cost drivers | • Scale<br>• Capacity utilization |  | • Scale<br>• Capacity utilization |
| Key value drivers* |  | Reputation | • Scale<br>• Capacity utilization |
| Primary value system relationships | Interlinked chains | Referred shops | Layered and interconnected networks |

\* We see that Porter is right that scale and capacity utilization is a dominant driver for the largest industries in the modern economy. But he misses that it can be both a value and a cost driver. Note also that reputation/success is similar to scale in that effective scale also implies success?

The repertoire of three alternative value configurations is important in order to both understand and analyze business logics across firms and industries. However, we argue that industry structure and forces are also different when we move from manufacturing to mediation and problem solving industries. Industry structure mirrors the logic of value creation. Differences in value creation logic are also reflected in differences in industry structure and dynamics.

Simply stated, industry structure reflects the structure of relationship between actors. The basic structure of relationships in a manufacturing industry is the dyadic buyer-seller relationship. The relationship replicates between the firm and its suppliers as well as between the firm and its buyers. In both mediation and problem solving industries, on the other hand, there is a many-to-many relationship between actors. Buyers are serviced concurrently (or virtually) by more than one supplier. Actors interchange buyer and supplier roles in the course of their interactions and exchanges.

Consider gas mediation. A gas pipeline company mediates gas between suppliers and users of gas. The pipeline company might, however, also connect with a potential competitor in order to mediate gas between the pipeline company's suppliers and the competitor's customer/user of gas. Similarly, the pipeline company might assist their competitor in mediating gas to one of its own customers. In terms of the structure of the mediation industry, rivals not only compete but also need to bargain in terms of their interconnected buyer-supplier relationships. And the structure of mediations across customer sets relative to mediations within customer sets is an important determinant of relative bargaining power.

This dual competitive and cooperative interaction among rivals is even more prevalent in problem-solving industries. Rivals compete for problems, but also refer, subcontract and jointly solve problems. Reputation and rankings structure competition in a setting (that is, industry) where winners often appear to take all (or at least the best problems and opportunities).

Before we develop this last point in more detail, let us take a closer look at the different kinds of value creation logics in the petroleum industry.

*Value creation in the petroleum industry*

In order to apply value configuration theory to the analysis of the petroleum industry we need to define the key activities and actors. Figure 6.2 shows the value system for the industry that serves end-users of petroleum products. The value system model only considers the actors directly involved in the discovery, development, production and distribution of petroleum products. This is what we label the primary petroleum value system.

**Figure 6.2    The primary petroleum value system**

Historically firms (the majors) that were vertically integrated over the whole petroleum value system dominated the petroleum industry. The integrated petroleum firm has a manufacturing (chain) logic.

With the creation of spot markets and the deregulation of the different intermediate activities, most importantly the market for crude oil, the integrated petroleum industry has been de-coupled along the different stages in the value system. With this de-coupling we see the emergence of actors with quite different business logics. At the level of the combined upstream and downstream petroleum industry, we see primarily two main classes of actors: manufacturers and mediators (see Figure 6.3).[3]

| | Acquire Assets | Explore | Develop & Produce | Transport | Refine | Distribute | Retail | |
|---|---|---|---|---|---|---|---|---|
| Independent (Apache) | ■ | ■ | ■ | | | | | CHAIN |
| Shipper (OMM) | | | | ■ | | | | NET |
| Refiner (Lyondell) | | | | | ■ | ■ | | CHAIN |
| Pipeline (Union Pacific) | | | | | | ■ | | NET |
| Retailer (Quick Trip) | | | | | | | ■ | CHAIN/ NET |
| Integrated Major (Shell) | ■ | ■ | ■ | ■ | ■ | ■ | ■ | CHAIN |

**Figure 6.3    Prototypical actors in the primary petroleum value system**

De-coupling together with competitive pressures has led even the majors to outsource activities. For example, majors used to transport oil using their own tankers. This activity is now outsourced. However, a percentage of the crude is still transported on tankers owned by the majors. This tapered vertical integration maintains a credible bargaining position in addition to provide knowledge and information on the activity.

Gas pipeline transportation has been outsourced through regulatory initiatives. Requirements for third party access has led to the establishment of pure gas mediators. Our analysis (Fjeldstad, Stabell and Kolbjørnsrud, 1998) suggests that this liberalization will lead to not only cheaper gas to end-users, but also to an

---

3    It is interesting to note that historically, the industry giants succeeded by controlling the mediation activity: Standard Oil through its control of pipelines and Shell through its innovation in tankers for shipment of petroleum products. Their move upstream into exploration and production was designed to secure supplies and effective operation of refineries.

increase in supply from smaller fields. Competitive pressures and drivers of value and cost, however, seem to push vertical integration of pure gas mediators upstream into gas resources or downstream into retailing.

*Problem solvers in upstream petroleum*

We do not see any problem-solvers (value shops) in our map of the petroleum industry value system. They are, of course, present all over as suppliers of problem solving services such as consulting services and engineering services. But these firms do not figure in the core petroleum industry value system in the sense that they are directly involved with the transformation of petroleum in the ground to the final consumption of petroleum products.

To see the whole range of alternative value configurations, we focus a more limited segment of the petroleum value system. Figure 6.4 illustrates the upstream segment of the petroleum industry. The focal firm is the petroleum exploration and production (E&P) company. The buyer is a spot market for crude and the suppliers include the suppliers of both equipment and services.

| Suppliers | Industry Competitors | Buyers |
|---|---|---|
| • Owners of prospective assets<br>• Exploration goods and services<br>• Field development goods and services<br>• Field operation goods and services | *Petroleum E&P companies* | • Spot market for crude and gas<br>• Transporters<br>• Refiners |

**Figure 6.4    Upstream petroleum as a manufacturing industry**

Table 6.2 presents an overview of the different categories of suppliers in upstream petroleum. One category that is missing is the owners of prospective assets. They are here not viewed as creators of value, but rather as owners of value.

One might argue that many equipment vendors (chains) also sell problem solving services. Should they therefore also be categorized as shops?

Value configurations are defined for strategic business units (SBU). In other words, value configurations are linked to distinct businesses, although these businesses might all reside in the same corporation. The critical issue is to what extent the problem solving service sold by equipment manufacturers is a distinct business unit or is it primarily a means to sell their equipment? In the latter case, the primary value configuration remains the chain. In the former case, the corporation might cover two value configurations, although not necessarily defined as two distinct business units.

Brokers of asset and data swaps and sales are the only mediators defined in the segment of upstream petroleum that is focused here. It is instructive to see that our examples of mediators are relatively new Internet-based service providers. We could also have included providers of transportation and telecommunication services as relevant mediators.

**Table 6.2    Value creation logic of suppliers in upstream petroleum**

| Actor | Examples | Role | Value Creation logic |
|-------|----------|------|----------------------|
| Seismic services | PGS, GecoPrakla, TGS-NOPEC | Supplier of services that produce seismic data for both exploration and exploitation decisions | Shop |
| Drilling services | Transocean, Parker | Supplier of drilling of exploration and exploitation wells | Shop |
| Production equipment manufacturer | ABB, Coflexip Stena, FMC | Supplier of petroleum production equipment | Chain |
| Engineering service | Aker Maritime, Kværner | Supplier of field development solutions | Shop |
| Vendor of IT systems | ROXAR, Paradigm Geophysical | Supplier of interpretation and geoscience systems | Chain |
| Broker | IndigoPool, DiscoveryPlace | Broker of asset and data exchanges | Network |

An even more focused look at upstream E&P identifies value shops in the core petroleum assets and equity petroleum focused part of the petroleum value system. If we consider solely petroleum exploration, we see at least three alternative exploration shops (that is, where petroleum exploration is a strategic business unit distinct from petroleum exploitation):

- PROSPECT GENERATOR: identifies interesting prospects and presents them to potential investors that both acquire the prospective assets and finance exploration. Is paid through some form of carried interest or outright sale of ideas.
- ASSET PLAYER: identifies and invests in prospective acreage. Is paid through some form of carried interest.
- PROSPECT EVALUATION SERVICE: sells service to assist asset owner or prospect generator in evaluation of prospects. Is paid for service.

Figure 6.5 summarizes the differences between the three business models in terms of both scope of activities and revenue model. The asset player takes a greater risk than the prospect generator, but has also a higher percentage of the upside. Asset players differ to the extent that they are active and make further investments later in the exploration cycle. The prospect evaluation service shop takes no risk, but is also only paid for a service.

The distinctive aspect here is to what extent the petroleum exploration shop owns acreage. It is only by owning acreage that the shop can appropriate a significant share of the value of their efforts to find petroleum.

| | Scouting | Acquisition of acreage | Seismic | Exploration drilling | Appraisal drilling | Revenue model |
|---|---|---|---|---|---|---|
| Prospect generator | | | | | | Carried or bonus |
| Asset player | | | | | | Carried |
| Asset player | | | | | | Carried |
| Evaluation service | | | | | | Fee |

**Figure 6.5    Alternative exploration shops**

Actors involved in selling services and equipment in upstream petroleum can also become involved in the risks and returns of equity oil. For example, a field development solution provider might take some of its revenue in a share of equity oil. This can promote convergence between the interests of the asset owner and the field development solution provider.[4] It can also be a means for the oil equity owner to finance exploration and development activities. Taking such a position, however, requires that the solution provider also cover the necessary subsurface expertise. And the tight relationship between equity owner and supplier might limit the supplier's access to other petroleum E&P customers.

It is also possible to consider an extension of the exploration shop concept where the service provider also solves the problem of exploiting a discovery. We are then at the stage where the service provider overlaps the whole upstream activity set. Revenue might be in equity oil or it can be in a risk service contract. This is an alternative perspective on the role of the upstream petroleum exploration and production company, where it is contracted on behalf of the asset owners (typically national government or national oil company).

*Alternative perspectives on upstream petroleum*

This brings us to an illustrative application of the alternative value configurations at the industry level. Building on the work of Stenseth and Powell (1998), we contrast a view of the upstream oil and gas as a problem solving industry with a view of it as an industry that manufactures petroleum. In the former case, the industry is solving the problem of finding, developing and producing petroleum for clients (nations) that own prospective petroleum assets. In the latter (and traditional perspective), upstream petroleum is an industry where the focal firms are in the business of producing and selling petroleum. Acquisition of prospective assets, exploration for petroleum and development of discoveries are support activities.

---

4    Note as there comes a market for assets, then there are more reasons to separate service providers and those that own equity oil.

*Upstream petroleum as a manufacturing industry*

The key distinctive aspect of upstream petroleum as a petroleum manufacturing industry is that the revenue model is petroleum sales. Following our overview of the petroleum value system (Figure 6.2), this implies that the focal firm is the producer of petroleum. Acquisition, exploration and development of petroleum assets is required as petroleum reserves are depleted.

The market for petroleum defines the downstream limits of the industry (see Figure 6.4). In our analysis we will assume that the market is efficient. We will also assume an efficient market in petroleum assets. This would appear to be valid for many onshore assets in the US and Canada.

Assumptions of efficient markets for both petroleum assets (that is, potential or identified petroleum in the ground) and petroleum at the well head limit the basis for competitive advantage. We identify three bases: differential expectations, control of complementary facilities and activities that can prove to be bottlenecks with rapid shifts in the demand for their services, and new technologies (see Fjeldstad, Stabell, Sheehan and Powell, 1998).

Differential expectations can be concerning both asset prospectivity and future petroleum prices. Complementary activities involve first and foremost drilling, transportation and refining. New technologies can be both in petroleum exploration and in petroleum exploitation. In our study of the Canadian Heavy Oil Industry, we considered the competitive potential of proprietary extraction technology.

Control of transportation and distribution is obviously one effective competitive strategy for the upstream petroleum firm. It is in fact so effective that government regulation has had to intervene throughout the history of the industry, first with the breakup of Standard Oil and then with the regulation of gas pipeline companies.

Another effective strategy is to actively position oneself in potentially prospective areas before they have become recognized as such. Shell's early positioning in the deepwater Gulf of Mexico based on differential expectations concerning potential developments in both exploration and exploitation technology is an example of such a play.

In summary, asset owners and owners of constraining capacity will benefit most from increases in the demand for petroleum or by significant technological innovations in the upstream petroleum manufacturing industry. Competitive forces and marginal production costs will define average margins in periods of stable demand and gradual innovation.

*Upstream petroleum as a problem solving industry*

Now consider an alternative perspective where upstream petroleum is viewed as a problem solving industry. With this perspective, the industry consists of firms that assist clients in solving the problem of exploring and exploiting clients' hydrocarbon resources (see Figure 6.6). This is the view implied by the Production Sharing Agreements that regulate revenue of the petroleum companies: the petroleum companies do not own the petroleum resources that are found and exploited, but are rather paid for their services through a combination of cost recovery oil and profit share oil. The clients are most often national governments, but can also be national petroleum companies that act as their agents.

| Suppliers | Industry Competitors | Buyers |
|-----------|---------------------|--------|
| • Professionals<br>• E&P Service and goods | • Integrated petroleum E&P companies<br>• Exploration shops | • Owners of prospective assets |

**Figure 6.6    Upstream petroleum as a problem solving industry**

Before we apply a problem solving industry perspective to upstream petroleum, let us review briefly the main characteristics of the generic problem solving industry.

Problem solving services involve the application of more or less formalized and scientific knowledge. Problem solving industries vary to the extent that they are professionalized. Professionalization implies certification and accreditation. This regulation reflects the need to protect the client in an exchange where there is potentially strong information asymmetry. Regulation also represents a barrier to entry.

There is extensive cooperation among competitors, both in terms of developing the knowledge base of the industry (profession), to promote and support effective training, and in terms of referrals. The amount of cooperation and openness will depend on the novelty of the field. A new and expanding problem domain will be the place where there is most to benefit from sharing knowledge, but where also first mover advantages are the greatest. Differentiation is the primary competitive strategy. Size becomes a means to differentiate in terms of being able to solve large problems, internalize problem recruiting and signal success.

Differentiation in the generic firm that sells problem-solving services is linked to the quality and reputation of the professionals in the firm. Problem solving services are labor intensive. Individual professionals have relatively large bargaining power. This limits profit margins for external owners. We therefore also see that problem-solving services are often organized as partnerships where the principals are producing professionals (Stabell, Fjeldstad and Sheehan, 1999).

Now consider the upstream oil and gas industry as a problem solving industry. The client is the owner of the prospective assets and the petroleum companies sell a petroleum exploration and exploitation service. Problem solving is risky as location and quantity of petroleum is most often highly uncertain. Exploration contracts are no-cure-no-pay: the petroleum company does not recover its exploration investment if the result is a dry well. However, clients also lose if they have 'incompetent' service providers: they will not get the rewards of profit oil and other taxes nor will they get the derivative economic benefits of an active petroleum industry.

Clients are typically government agencies. They will have some technical expertise (and they will engage their own experts to evaluate the 'solutions' offered and/or negotiate the terms of the contract). When choosing among competitors, the client will often consider the petroleum company's track record, ability to solve the whole problem (both exploration and exploitation of petroleum resources) and the firm's commitment to give the problem their full attention (through exploration plans). Commitment is of such importance that it is formalized in a work program. Clients define the barriers to entry through beauty contests and bidding rounds.

Clients must however also compete for the attention of oil and gas companies. This competition is defined by the perceived prospectivity of assets, by the fiscal terms offered and by the costs of exploring and exploiting the assets.

Firms compete through differentiation, by alliances (for example with national oil companies), and through mergers and acquisitions. Petroleum companies try to get in before the prospectivity of assets has been proven (as discoveries can immediately change the terms offered) and try to get in position to develop a whole play should their 'solution' turn out to be successful.

In frontier areas or areas with apparent low prospectivity, clients need to consider firms' ability to promote their problem (as an opportunity) and firms' ability to mobilize resources (partners). Promoters are an effective way to bootstrap from a less interesting problem (low prospectivity expectations) into a problem that catches the interest of the best firms in the industry.

Firms boost their competitive position through alliances, through mergers and acquisitions. Partnering is also used to spread the risk in exploration. The non-operator is then an investor, although a non-operator may also contribute important expertise.

In summary, in the problem solving industry, the network of reputations are critical. There is also a network of clients, where some are more highly valued. Different reputation classes in terms of both petroleum firms (competitors and cooperators) and in terms of asset owners (clients) form sub-groups in the industry.

## Conclusion: contrasting perspectives: an alternative view of mega-mergers

Now we are ready to contrast the two perspectives. As noted, the perspectives potentially cover two different segments of upstream petroleum. Thus while the manufacturing perspective implies a sector where prospective assets are traded in a market, the problem solving service industry perspective implies a sector where ownership of prospective assets are not traded and remain in the hands of the original (national) owner.

The two industries focus different clients. They imply quite different competitive situations and competitive strategies. The manufacturing perspective focuses potential competitive advantage from differential expectations. The problem solving perspective focuses the role of reputations as a key strategic lever.

Picking up on the recent mega-mergers in the petroleum industry (that obviously involve more than upstream petroleum), how can these mergers be understood when framed in terms of the two alternative perspectives on the upstream petroleum industry?

The manufacturing perspective would seem to see both differential expectations and the ability to exploit the opportunities presented by these expectations as a driver for size. New frontiers require large investments for exploration and exploitation. They also require an ability to be able to play on expectations by acquiring a sufficient amount of prospective assets to profit from the realization of expectations.

The problem solving perspective would see size as a strong reputation signal in terms of not only ability to discover but also exploit resources.

To the extent that the different perspectives apply to different segments of upstream petroleum, one might see mega-mergers as a means to trade in assets that are not traded. Instead of being able to buy into prospective assets managed through problem solving (production sharing) contracts, firms merge with competitors so as to get possession of their contracts.

**References**

Afuah, Allan and Christopher L. Tucci (2000), *Internet Business Models and Strategies. Text and Cases*, McGrawHill.

Fjeldstad, Øystein, C. Stabell and V. Kolbjørnsrud (1998), 'Gas Mediators in Europe: A New Competitive Landscape?', Norwegian School of Management, unpublished discussion note.

Fjeldstad, Øystein, C. Stabell, N. Sheehan and L. Powell (1998), 'Canadian Heavy Oil Industry: Attractiveness and Competitive Implications', Norwegian School of Management, unpublished discussion note.

Porter, M. (1980), *Competitive Strategy. Techniques for Analyzing Industries and Competitors*, New York: Free Press.

Porter, M. (1985), *Competitive Advantage. Creating and Sustaining Superior Performance*, New York: Free Press.

Porter, M. (1990), *The Competitive Advantage of Nations*, New York: Free Press.

Porter, M. (1991), 'Towards a Dynamic Theory of Strategy', *Strategic Management Journal*, Winter Special Issue, 12, pp. 95-117.

Stabell, C.B. and Ø. Fjeldstad (1998), 'Configuring Value for Competitive Advantage: On chains, shops and networks', *Strategic Management Journal*, 19(5), pp. 413-437.

Stabell, C.B., Ø. Fjeldstad and N.T. Sheehan (1999), 'Reputation, Tangible Assets and Governance in Problem-Solving Firms: Differential strategic positioning options for search, diagnosis and design shops', Paper presented at SMS Conference, Berlin, Fall 1999.

# PART 2
# Present and Future Challenges

# Chapter 7

# Transnational Energy Companies' Investment Allocation Decisions[1]

Petter Osmundsen, Magne Emhjellen
and Morten Halleraker

## Introduction

Because fixed area costs will incur when entering into a country or new area, the size of the expected net present value (materiality) of E&P investments must be substantial enough to cover these costs. If the new project itself is not able to cover the area costs, the company must then expect a sufficient net present value potential from other projects in the country or area. The combination of fixed area cost and company resource constraints emphasises the importance of the materiality of the expected net present value for the company capital budgeting decision. The materiality issue therefore not only becomes an issue for the investing company, but also an issue for governments in countries possessing exhaustible natural resources, interested in attracting and maintaining corporate investments. Thus, our analyses are of interest both for portfolio managers and tax authorities.

Since materiality is the size of the net present value of the project after tax, and traditional valuation by companies is defined as the discounted cash flow method, materiality becomes a function of expected after tax cash flow and the discount rate. The expected after tax cash flow is related to the size of the project itself, the company's equity share in the project and the tax level. The discount rate is the appropriate required rate of return dependent on the systematic risk (non diversifiable risk) of the project. Consequently, company approval of an investment will depend on the perceived risk of the project (the non diversifiable portion), the project size, the company's equity share and the tax level. In addition to these materiality variables companies are aware that there might be option values related to projects. Option value(s) are therefore an additional materiality variable that might affect companies' investment incentives.

In the chapter we examine the materiality requirement with the standard net present value method in a setting with company constraints and fixed area costs. Using real project oil exploration data obtained from the oil industry it will be demonstrated

---

1 This chapter has been included in the Papers and Proceedings, The International Association of Energy Economics (IAEE) Houston Conference, April 25-27, 2001.

how materiality will be important for company capital allocation decisions when company constraints and fixed country costs are included in the analysis. Data and illustrations are from the Norwegian Continental Shelf, but the insights are of a general nature. The results might help explain the recent strategy trend by oil exploration companies to focus their activity in particular geographic areas where the materiality conditions are favourable. Consequently, materiality is an important factor in order for countries to be competitive and attract foreign investments. Due consideration of materiality must therefore be taken when governments are making policy decisions regarding the energy industry.

## Materiality

Materiality is a concept which is linked to selection of investment projects when the company has a given investment budget and limited resources in the form of management and employees with specialised competence. Materiality – also referred to as financial volume or critical mass – implies that projects need to be above a certain size (in terms of after-tax net present value) in order for them to be interesting to multinational oil companies. A small project can be unattractive even if it is able to show a high expected return (internal rate of return).

Materiality requirements – requirements for minimum level of after-tax net present value – can be justified on the basis of different academic disciplines. Corporate strategy, accounting, corporate finance, management and investment analysis can all provide arguments for there to be a certain critical mass in connection with investment decisions. The petroleum companies' increasing materiality requirement is closely connected with their focusing strategies. They concentrate scarce resources on fewer activities, focus on those areas where they have comparative advantages. In return, they demand larger contributions after tax, measured in absolute value, from each of these selected activities. Thus, a positive net present value is, in connection with such allocation strategies, only an entrance ticket to transnational companies' ranking of projects on a global basis. It is a necessary yet not sufficient condition for realisation. The materiality requirements may also be looked upon from a finance and management theory setting. There is an increasing recognition that corporations incur certain amount of costs that for different reasons are not included in the expected project cash flow. One way to make allowances for these extra costs generated by a project is to demand a certain minimum size for the present value of projects.[2] One may envisage far more sophisticated methods by which to rectify this problem, but simple, implementable management systems are often the preferred solution by companies.

Materiality requirements may also follow directly from traditional economic decision analysis, if one recognises the fact that the real decision problem is non-linear and non-divisible, with a number of scarce factors and fixed costs. In the

---

2   See for instance Zimmerman (1979).

investment cases presented below, materiality and its importance in practical decision making is illustrated. We employ data from actual petroleum projects on the Norwegian Continental Shelf. The insight into materiality is general, however, and may appear in a more conventional model. The materiality result does thus not depend on our specific assumptions regarding price development, discounting interest and so on. We do not claim the example to be of universal validity, though. There may be situations in which constraints on scarce factors do not bind and in which the fixed area-dependent costs are low. However, in view of the petroleum companies' focusing strategy, there is reason to believe materiality considerations play a central role in the companies' allocation and localisation decisions.[3]

Materiality is particularly important in the petroleum industry, an industry dominated by a few profitable players. Through their international mobility and access to private information[4] these companies succeed in capturing part of the resource rent generated from scarce petroleum resources. The taxation never reaches 100 per cent, the companies keep a mobility rent and an information rent; see Osmundsen, Hagen and Schjelderup (1998). This is also valid for industries' that exploit non-mobile natural resources, since the input factors and the companies are mobile.[5] Large discoveries in new basins, opening of established, producing countries for transnational petroleum companies, and a reduction in the number of players through mergers and acquisitions, have increased competition between different producing countries to attract the most competent companies. This will make the fiscal terms more important, particularly in countries where the remaining acreage must be expected to yield economically marginal fields, that is, where the resource rent is falling over time. For a description of international tax and fiscal competition, see Zodrow and Mieszkowski (1986), Gresik (2000), and Olsen and Osmundsen (2000).

## Non-linear optimisation

Materiality is not modelled in elementary investment analysis or in existing taxation theory. These models consider capital to be the primary scarce factor, in which case the internal rate of return becomes the relevant decision-making criteria. In conventional examples based on internal rate of return, however, a number of simplifying and unrealistic assumptions are made. One assumes that other scarce factors are fully reflected in prices, one assumes full divisibility of projects and that all relevant costs are included in the calculation. In reality, there is often a small number of larger projects, and many scarce factors and bottlenecks. One such relevant scarce factor is qualified experienced professionals. For example, only few individuals possess

---

3   Wood Mackenzie (1999) point this out.

4   See Osmundsen (1995, 1998).

5   The companies do not need to move all of the operations physically. The transnational oil companies' international activity is to a considerable extent managed from the head office.

the necessary qualifications and experience to manage complex development projects in the North Sea. Furthermore, competent geologists and geophysicists are scarce. Usually, managerial capacity is also a scarce factor. The companies will, in consequence, look at what values (present value after tax) the companies can retain, compared to the input of professional resources and managerial capacity which could, alternatively, have been invested in projects in countries where the companies are allowed to retain a larger portion of the value created. The various projects also have to bear all area-dependent fixed costs and make contributions to the payment of overhead costs at the corporate level. An analytical approach to this decision problem will be to use portfolio analysis to arrive at the portfolio of projects with greatest combined present value for the company, with consideration to fixed costs and resource and capital constraints. For practical reasons however, one often uses simpler decision-making tools. One important reason is that recommendations and often decisions are made, not at the corporate level, but at a divisional level where not all constraints and costs are known. A practical way of paying consideration to scarce factors and area-dependent costs is therefore for the head office to demand a minimum size for a project's net present value after tax. Even though portfolio models are not necessarily used explicitly to deduce the optimal investment portfolio, such considerations may – via materiality requirements – be underpinning the choice of what core geographical areas the companies wish to invest in and how large equity shares the companies wish to go for. Simple capital allocation models, like a fixed investment budget and requirements of a certain financial volume, may act as a proxy or as an implementation mechanism for more advanced portfolio models.

Why, then, are these inputs scarce? If managers or professionals create values beyond the costs generated by them, one would think the companies would hire more staff until the last employee just barely satisfies his or her marginal cost. One reason why this is not automatically possible is that scarcity often does not concern professionals or managers as a group, but those that are highly qualified. It is argued that companies typically have a limited number of professionals and managers that are crucial to success and others that are important in completing the task to be undertaken. Due to asymmetric information – the fact that the individual employee knows more about his or her own skills than potential employers – it may be difficult to provide new such staff as and when required. Most likely one has to overstaff in order to be reasonably sure to capture some of the best individuals. Given a relatively rigid labour market, this is an expensive strategy, which is why the companies prefer to keep their organisation slim. Due to fluctuating level of activity and costs of restructuring, one is reluctant to build up capacity that will subsequently have to be down-scaled.

Not only present value per scarce factor is important when companies decide where to invest. Beside the obvious elements such as prospectivity, level of cost, tax burden and acreage availability, the costs associated with being present in a region or country may be substantial and therefore the minimum profitable activity must be of a certain volume. Furthermore, most companies learn that a simple structure with management focus on a few matters is important. Areas which as such are commercial, but which do not generate much value after tax (make small contributions to payment of overhead costs) can thus be rejected so as to allow management and professional employees to focus on those areas where values are generated for the company. Reference is often made to materiality considerations, and there is reason to take these seriously. Norwegian branches or subsidiaries of transnational companies are arguing that projects of a small scale in a corporate context, often represented by expected present value after tax being low, have difficulties in attracting attention – and thus investment funds – from the head office. This line of reasoning has gained a foothold also in the Norwegian companies, in parallel with their growing international activity. Note that even though the total project may be large, materiality can nonetheless be limited viewed from the perspective of a large international corporation if the company holds a low equity share.

**Factors determining the materiality of a project**

Materiality can be analysed at two main levels: 1) project level, and 2) basin level. Both issues are argued to be relevant. For example, as far as the project level on the Norwegian Continental Shelf is concerned, there is a development towards smaller fields. In an international context, though, these fields will still be considered large. New Norwegian fields are, on average, several times the size of fields on the UK Continental Shelf. Recently, there has been a marked shift to positive exploration results, also including large discoveries.

The fact that there in a mature area gradually will be vacant capacity within processing and pipeline transportation as established fields are phased out, may make it highly profitable to develop satellite fields. This presupposes that one is able to keep down the costs of operation and maintenance on old production facilities. However, in some new potential discovery areas, one is facing problems with long distances from existing infrastructure. Tightened cost control in development projects will also be of importance for the profitability of new field developments.

Other factors influencing materiality, both at project and basin level, are the scope and prospect of exploration acreage, the tax system and the distribution of equity shares in the licences. A high marginal tax causes lower portions of the total cash flow to be retained by the companies. A similar reduction in cash flow is caused by the fact that companies most often hold a limited equity share in the licence. Other companies' equity shares and the Norwegian State share via the State's Direct Financial Interest (SDFI) reduce the share of the net cash flow (and the investments) to each individual company. This reduces the size of NPV to each company. The internal rate of return, however, remains unchanged provided the company is in a tax paying position. Taxation does thus not reduce the profitability of the investment, but is instrumental in scaling down the project for each individual company. This reduces net present value after tax and thus the materiality of the project. The scheduled commercialisation of the SDFI (sale of equity shares from the State to privately run companies) could, in consequence, help bring about a substantial improvement in materiality for the companies on the Norwegian Continental Shelf. A change in the licensing policies, involving larger equity shares for the privately run companies, has also improved the materiality conditions on the Norwegian shelf.

There is reason to distinguish between localisation decisions faced by the company *before* and *after* they have built up a substantial organisation, infrastructure and specific competence in a certain producing nation. A company that has been present in a country for a long time and acquired substantial local competence that may not have the same value in a different country. The company then has a number of irreversible investments that are immobile. The materiality consideration will therefore be different before and after a substantial activity has been established. This works in the favour of established producing nations. This argument however, should not be overvalued since mobility can still be high to the extent that there is a second-hand market for oil leases and infrastructure. Also, there might be substantial area-dependent annual (avoidable) fixed costs associated with being established in a country.

Interesting to note, for governments, is that companies differ in their materiality requirements, with large companies typically having a higher demand for financial volume in projects than smaller companies. Thus, governments may be able to keep a larger share of the resource rent if they attract smaller petroleum companies. This is a policy currently pursued by Norwegian authorities. However, large and small companies differ in their financial strength and technical competence, and the authorities would have to trade off price (demand for financial volume) against quality (for example, resource extraction rate). We may expect to see a division of labour between larger and smaller companies, with the former developing larger reservoirs at deep water, whereas the latter focus on smaller, stand-alone reservoirs and tail extraction.

### The behavioural hypotheses of tax theory

Economic tax theory typically presumes that a company will realise any project with a positive net present value (materiality is irrelevant).[6] If the capital is scarce, the company will allocate its investments where the profitability (internal rate of return) is highest. According to these behavioural assumptions,[7] the fact that the company's cash flow is scaled down, should have no negative impact on the investment decision. However, somewhat more sophisticated portfolio investment theory does not prescribe the use of internal rate of return as decision-making criterion, but rather the use of portfolio models to arrive at the portfolio of projects with the largest accumulated present value to the company (with consideration paid to resource and

---

6    See, for example, Atkinson and Stiglitz (1980).

7    This neutrality property is only valid if we can ignore the probability that the company, for instance due to low oil prices, falls out of tax position, or if the tax system has perfect loss offset. These conditions are not satisfied in practice.

capital constraints). This theory is also more in line with company practice.[8] Several scarce factors, fixed costs and divisibility problems may favour projects with good materiality. It will therefore be of interest to extend the existing tax models so as to capture materiality considerations. The general tax implications of materiality, if not the detailed tax design, however, are also clear without the use of formal models. In order to secure the participation of competent companies one must – in situations of reduced expected basin profitability – give the companies higher equity shares and gradually lower average tax for new fields. This is simply to state that the tax and licensing conditions must be curtailed to the present level of resource rents generated.

## Case analysis

Based on exemplifying project cases, the effect on project decisions of capital constraint, organisational constraints and project-external corporate costs will illustrated by project data from the Norwegian Continental Shelf. We use oil project data received from Statoil, and used previously in Emhjellen (1999) and Emhjellen and Alaouze (2000). Table 7.1 shows expected production, investments and operating costs for five different oil projects.

*Assumptions and calculations*

Revenues are based on a real oil price of USD 15 per barrel. The reason why a real oil price of USD 15 has been chosen as the basis for calculation of incomes is that, despite a very high oil price at the moment, this price assumption is more in line with the oil companies' long-term expectations. The company is assumed to be one hundred percent equity-financed and to require a 10 percent real return on capital after tax. The results prove to be robust with respect to assumptions on oil price and required return on capital.

It is assumed for illustrative purposes that the project portfolio of these five petroleum projects is available in two different countries. The purpose of assuming identical projects in pairs in the two countries is to separate out the effects of geological prospectivity and cost level, to be able to isolate the effects of tax and licensing policy. Calculations are therefore shown for a total of ten projects, of which projects 1 to 5 are in country 1, whereas projects 6 to 10 are in country 2. Project 1 in country 1 corresponds to project 6 in country 2, project 2 in country 1 is identical to project 7 in country 2, and so on. In country 1, we assume the existence of strict fiscal conditions with an equity share of 20per cent and an effective marginal tax rate of 75per cent, whereas for country 2, we assume more favourable framework conditions with an equity share of 50per cent and a marginal tax rate of 40per cent. The calculation of tax is simplified – in order to be able to focus on aspects of materiality

---

8    Simplified approaches – like NPV per unit of scarce factor – is used in some companies to rank investment opportunities.

– by assuming the tax is paid on the pre-tax cash flow and that the company, in the case of a negative pre-tax cash flow – is able to consolidate this negative cash flow against other income in the company. The project thus has a positive tax effect in the case of a negative cash flow before tax. Shown in Table 7.2 are cash flow before tax, cash flow after tax and present value for each project in country 1. As shown by the results in Table 7.2, the net present value parameter in country 1 varies from USD 6.2 million (project 3) to USD 17.7 million for project 2. Similarly, Table 7.3 shows the results in country 2. The net present values in country 2 are varying from USD 37.3 million (project 8) to USD 106.2 million (project 7). Due to a higher equity share and lower tax rate, the present values are generally higher in country 1. However, the internal rate of return is equal in the two countries. With a fully linear tax system (negative tax possible), the State carries an equal portion of expenses as it captures of incomes. Return on investments is thus not influenced by taxes. Based on standard assumptions in tax theory, such a tax system will not influence the investment allocation. We will, however, show that this standard assumption does not hold if the company is facing constraints and fixed area costs.

*Results*

Table 7.4 sums up net present value and the sum of investments for the projects based on the project data and assumptions. Column 1 shows project number, column 2 shows tax rate, column 3 shows internal rate of return (equal for all), column 4 shows net present value in USD, column 5 shows equity share in project and column 6 shows the sum of investments.

   As illustrated by the table, internal rate of return is equal between the pair-wise projects in country 1 and country 2. However, the net present value of the projects is substantially lower (yet positive) in country 1 as a result of a higher tax rate and a lower equity share (weaker materiality). Without any sort of capital constraint or materiality evaluations, that is, a linear decision-making situation, all projects would be approved by the oil company.

## Table 7.1  Project data

| | Project 1 | | | Project 2 | | | Project 3 | | |
|---|---|---|---|---|---|---|---|---|---|
| Yr | Oil production Mill.bbl. | Real inv. cost $mill. | Real oper. cost $mill. | Oil production Mill. bbl. | Real inv. cost $mill. | Real oper. cost $mill. | Oil production Mill. bbl. | Real inv. cost $mill. | Real oper. cost $mill. |
| Sum | 80.1 | 350.4 | 348.7 | 156.3 | 772 | 604.2 | 162.9 | 881.9 | 817.7 |
| 1 | | 7.3 | 0.3 | | | | | 4.3 | |
| 2 | | 93.1 | 6.1 | | 8.9 | 0.6 | | 97.1 | 1.4 |
| 3 | 3.7 | 161.6 | 21.7 | | 58.4 | 2.9 | | 471.4 | 4.3 |
| 4 | 14.8 | 86.1 | 53.8 | | 291.7 | 10.3 | 1.9 | 221.4 | 29.7 |
| 5 | 14.8 | 2.3 | 48.5 | 13.7 | 312 | 35 | 17.5 | 50 | 81.2 |
| 6 | 14.8 | | 48.8 | 31.4 | 97.7 | 77.6 | 23.3 | 37.7 | 80.2 |
| 7 | 14.3 | | 48.7 | 31.9 | 3.3 | 83.2 | 24.2 | | 82.3 |
| 8 | 9.1 | | 44.9 | 26.2 | | 83.2 | 24 | | 84.5 |
| 9 | 5.1 | | 39.8 | 19.9 | | 80.5 | 21.5 | | 82.8 |
| 10 | 3.5 | | 36.1 | 14.7 | | 78.6 | 14.8 | | 77.7 |
| 11 | | | | 10.3 | | 76.7 | 11.5 | | 75.4 |
| 12 | | | | 8.2 | | 75.6 | 9.2 | | 73.8 |
| 13 | | | | | | | 7.9 | | 72.9 |
| 14 | | | | | | | 7.1 | | 71.5 |

| | Project 4 | | | Project 5 | | |
|---|---|---|---|---|---|---|
| Yr | Oil production Mill. bbl. | Real inv. cost $mill. | Real oper. cost $mill. | Oil production Mill. bbl. | Real inv. cost $mill. | Real oper. cost $mill. |
| Sum | 314.5 | 982.4 | 1742.7 | 119 | 508.6 | 596.6 |
| 1 | | | | | | |
| 2 | | 184.8 | | | 120.6 | 6.1 |
| 3 | | 182.6 | 10.6 | | 163.4 | 5.4 |
| 4 | | 236.1 | 17.1 | | 181 | 22.5 |
| 5 | 9.4 | 94.5 | 71.9 | 18.2 | 43.6 | 77.5 |
| 6 | 15.1 | 115.8 | 94.3 | 18.2 | | 78.4 |
| 7 | 20.8 | 78.1 | 113.8 | 18.2 | | 76.2 |
| 8 | 23.3 | | 121.1 | 18.2 | | 77.1 |
| 9 | 23.3 | 51.7 | 122.5 | 18.1 | | 76.5 |
| 10 | 23.3 | 38.8 | 122.5 | 12.3 | | 59.7 |
| 11 | 23.3 | | 122.5 | 7.3 | | 45.2 |
| 12 | 23.3 | | 122.5 | 4.9 | | 37.9 |
| 13 | 23.3 | | 122.5 | 3.6 | | 34.1 |
| 14 | 23.3 | | 122.5 | | | |
| 15 | 23.3 | | 122.5 | | | |
| 16 | 23.3 | | 122.5 | | | |
| 17 | 23.3 | | 122.5 | | | |
| 18 | 23.3 | | 122.5 | | | |
| 19 | 12.9 | | 88.9 | | | |

As illustrated by the table, oil production in million barrels per year is shown for each project under column 1, investment costs in million USD (fixed) under column 2 and operating costs in million USD (fixed) under column 3.

## Table 7.2  Cash flows and present values in country 1

| Yr | Project 1 Real b/tax CF (project) $mill. | Real a/tax CF (company) $mill. | Project 2 Real b/tax CF (project) $mill. | Real a/tax CF(company) $mill. | Project 3 Real b/tax CF (project) $mill. | Real a/tax CF (company) $mill. |
|---|---|---|---|---|---|---|
| Sum | | **11,2** | | **17,7** | | **6,2** |
| 1 | -7,6 | -0,4 | | | -4,3 | -0,2 |
| 2 | -99,2 | -5,0 | -9,5 | -0,5 | -98,5 | -4,9 |
| 3 | -127,8 | -6,4 | -61,3 | -3,1 | -475,7 | -23,8 |
| 4 | 82,1 | 4,1 | -302,0 | -15,1 | -222,6 | -11,1 |
| 5 | 171,2 | 8,6 | -141,5 | -7,1 | 131,3 | 6,6 |
| 6 | 173,2 | 8,7 | 295,7 | 14,8 | 231,6 | 11,6 |
| 7 | 165,8 | 8,3 | 392,0 | 19,6 | 280,7 | 14,0 |
| 8 | 91,6 | 4,6 | 309,8 | 15,5 | 275,5 | 13,8 |
| 9 | 36,7 | 1,8 | 218,0 | 10,9 | 239,7 | 12,0 |
| 10 | 16,4 | 0,8 | 141,9 | 7,1 | 144,3 | 7,2 |
| 11 | | | 77,8 | 3,9 | 97,1 | 4,9 |
| 12 | | | 47,4 | 2,4 | 64,2 | 3,2 |
| 13 | | | | | 45,6 | 2,3 |
| 14 | | | | | 35,0 | 1,8 |

| Yr | Project 4 Real b/tax CF (project) $mill. | Real a/tax CF (company) $mill. | Project 5 Real b/tax CF (project) $mill. | Real a/tax CF (company) $mill. |
|---|---|---|---|---|
| Sum | | **16,1** | | **9,8** |
| 1 | | | | |
| 2 | -184,8 | -9,2 | -126,7 | -6,3 |
| 3 | -193,2 | -9,7 | -168,8 | -8,4 |
| 4 | -253,2 | -12,7 | -203,5 | -10,2 |
| 5 | -25,4 | -1,3 | 151,9 | 7,6 |
| 6 | 16,4 | 0,8 | 194,6 | 9,7 |
| 7 | 120,1 | 6,0 | 196,8 | 9,8 |
| 8 | 228,4 | 11,4 | 195,9 | 9,8 |
| 9 | 175,3 | 8,8 | 195,0 | 9,8 |
| 10 | 188,2 | 9,4 | 124,8 | 6,2 |
| 11 | 227,0 | 11,4 | 64,3 | 3,2 |
| 12 | 227,0 | 11,4 | 35,6 | 1,8 |
| 13 | 227,0 | 11,4 | 19,9 | 1,0 |
| 14 | 227,0 | 11,4 | | |
| 15 | 227,0 | 11,4 | | |
| 16 | 227,0 | 11,4 | | |
| 17 | 227,0 | 11,4 | | |
| 18 | 227,0 | 11,4 | | |
| 19 | 104,6 | 5,2 | | |

## Table 7.3  Cash flow and present values in country 2

| Yr | Project 6 Real a/tax CF (comp.) $mill | Project 7 Real a/tax CF (comp.) $mill | Project 8 Real a/tax CF (comp.) $mill | Project 9 Real a/tax CF (comp.) $mill | Project 10 Real a/tax CF (comp.) $mill |
|---|---|---|---|---|---|
| Pr.value | **67,5** | **106,2** | **37,3** | **96,5** | **58,9** |
| Sum | | | | | |
| 1 | -2,3 | | -1,3 | | |
| 2 | -29,8 | -2,9 | -29,6 | -55,4 | -38,0 |
| 3 | -38,3 | -18,4 | -142,7 | -58,0 | -50,6 |
| 4 | 24,6 | -90,6 | -66,8 | -76,0 | -61,1 |
| 5 | 51,4 | -42,5 | 39,4 | -7,6 | 45,6 |
| 6 | 52,0 | 88,7 | 69,5 | 4,9 | 58,4 |
| 7 | 49,7 | 117,6 | 84,2 | 36,0 | 59,0 |
| 8 | 27,5 | 92,9 | 82,7 | 68,5 | 58,8 |
| 9 | 11,0 | 65,4 | 71,9 | 52,6 | 58,5 |
| 10 | 4,9 | 42,6 | 43,3 | 56,5 | 37,4 |
| 11 | | 23,3 | 29,1 | 68,1 | 19,3 |
| 12 | | 14,2 | 19,3 | 68,1 | 10,7 |
| 13 | | | 13,7 | 68,1 | 6,0 |
| 14 | | | 10,5 | 68,1 | |
| 15 | | | | 68,1 | |
| 16 | | | | 68,1 | |
| 17 | | | | 68,1 | |
| 18 | | | | 68,1 | |
| 19 | | | | 31.4 | |

## Table 7.4  Results given project data and assumptions

| Project | Tax rate | IRR | NPV | % share | Investment | Project (0,1) |
|---|---|---|---|---|---|---|
| 1 | 75 % | 39 % | 11,2 | 20 % | 70,1 | 1 |
| 2 | 75 % | 35 % | 17,7 | 20 % | 154,4 | 1 |
| 3 | 75 % | 15 % | 6,2 | 20 % | 176,4 | 1 |
| 4 | 75 % | 17 % | 16,1 | 20 % | 196,5 | 1 |
| 5 | 75 % | 22 % | 9,8 | 20 % | 101,7 | 1 |
| 6 | 40 % | 39 % | 67,5 | 50 % | 175,2 | 1 |
| 7 | 40 % | 35 % | 106,2 | 50 % | 386,0 | 1 |
| 8 | 40 % | 15 % | 37,3 | 50 % | 441,0 | 1 |
| 9 | 40 % | 17 % | 96,5 | 50 % | 491,2 | 1 |
| 10 | 40 % | 22 % | 58,9 | 50 % | 254,3 | 1 |

*Capital constraint* As an essential part of their finance management, transnational petroleum companies are often operating with investment budgets. These work as efficient constraints on investment decisions. Two different designs of capital budgets are being employed, in which maximum investment amount can be calculated either in the form of pre-tax or after-tax values.

*After-tax capital constraint* A constraint in after-tax investment amount is a rational option if capital constitutes the only scarce factor. By making calculations after tax, one will capture the circumstance that the State is, in fact, carrying a substantial part of the investment cost if the company is in tax-paying position (or if one has a fully linear tax system). When setting out to rank projects, one will look at returns after tax, viewed in relation to after-tax investment amount, i.e., maximising the value per scarce factor. One fraction often computed is referred to as The Present Value Index (PVI). Internal rate of return will not work as a ranking criterion because one does not capture the time dimension (a project with high profitability for twenty years may be better than a project having a higher return but which is of shorter duration). Since we typically have large-scale non-divisible projects (non-linear optimisation), it is not certain that one will be able to use the entire capital available. Also, with binding capital constraint(s), some projects with positive present values will typically not be realised. High-tax countries will not perform worse than low-tax countries, in this setting, if both countries have neutral tax systems.

*Pre-tax capital constraint:* Some transnational petroleum companies are operating with binding investment budgets on a pre-tax basis. These do not capture the circumstance that the company will cover a lower share of the investments in high-tax countries. The capital constraint will, in other words, bind more strongly in such countries since one includes tax in the calculation of cash flow excluding investments (in the present value index, one makes allowance for tax in the numerator but not in the denominator). Such a system for allocation of investment funds must be taken to mean that capital is not really what constitutes the scarce factor of the company, but rather that investments before tax are a proxy for other company scarce factors, for example, professionals or managerial capacity. As shown below, this allocation mechanism also gives similar project rankings as if one had been operating with more explicit constraints on other scarce factors. The latter approach would be more difficult to implement, though, explaining why fixed capital budgets are often used. The rationale of having an investment budget on a pre-tax basis is that this serves to best reflect the magnitude and occupation of scarce resources of the projects. A project in a country with a high marginal tax calls for just as many professionals and just as much administrative follow-up as a project in a country with a low marginal tax.

Below we illustrate the effects of introducing capital constraint in the form of an investment constraint, where the sum of investments before tax shall not exceed USD 1.4 billion. In Table 7.5, we can see how an oil company will maximise portfolio present value given the constraint on investment level. The oil company will now select the portfolio composition giving the highest accumulated present value. In Table 7.5, we can read under column 7 that this causes projects 2 to 5 (country 1) not to be approved for implementation and project 8 (country 2) not to be approved, because of too weak materiality. The total investment constitutes USD 1376.8 million and the total present value constitutes USD 340.4 million.

**Table 7.5    Capital constraints**

| Project | Tax rate | IRR | NPV | % share | Investment | Project (0,1) |
|---|---|---|---|---|---|---|
| 1 | 75 % | 39 % | 11,2 | 20 % | 70,1 | 1 |
| 2 | 75 % | 35 % | 17,7 | 20 % | 154,4 | 0 |
| 3 | 75 % | 15 % | 6,2 | 20 % | 176,4 | 0 |
| 4 | 75 % | 17 % | 16,1 | 20 % | 196,5 | 0 |
| 5 | 75 % | 22 % | 9,8 | 20 % | 101,7 | 0 |
| 6 | 40 % | 39 % | 67,5 | 50 % | 175,2 | 1 |
| 7 | 40 % | 35 % | 106,2 | 50 % | 386,0 | 1 |
| 8 | 40 % | 15 % | 37,3 | 50 % | 441,0 | 0 |
| 9 | 40 % | 17 % | 96,5 | 50 % | 491,2 | 1 |
| 10 | 40 % | 22 % | 58,9 | 50 % | 254,3 | 1 |

As a consequence of the capital constraint of USD 1.4 billion for investments, country 1 with the highest marginal tax and the lowest equity share will not be competitive compared to country 2. In country 1 only one project is included, whereas all projects except for project 8 are approved in country 2. Sensitivity calculations performed with an oil price of USD 13 and 17 per barrel show that the above results do not change within this oil price interval. Also, a change in the required real rate of return within the interval 8–12per cent does not change the results.

*Organisational constraints* Organisational constraint is here defined as an internal constraint in the company which causes the management to initiate only a limited number of projects. Table 7.6 shows an example in which an organisational constraint is illustrated by allowing the company to only have seven qualified project managers available. There may, in real-life situations, be a scarcity of many types of professionals. Table 7.6 therefore only shows a simplified example. Many simultaneous development projects with management and controller resources scattered over a large number of projects, is one of the factors explaining the recent years cost overruns on the Norwegian Continental Shelf. It is, for the sake of simplicity, assumed that each development requires a separate project manager. As can be seen from the table, projects 1, 3 and 5 in country 1 with the lowest after-tax present value will not be approved as a consequence of this constraint. This illustrates the importance of materiality in connection with organisational constraints.

*The Changing World of Oil*

Sensitivity calculations performed with an oil price of USD 17 per barrel or a change in the required real rate of return within the interval 8–12per cent does not change the above results. However, with an oil price of USD 13 per barrel the net present value of project 8 turns negative (USD -7,6 million) while the net present value of project 1 is reduced to USD 6,7 million. Project 8 is consequently not included because it is more oil price sensitive than project 1. The country with the highest materiality, however, still receives the majority of the investments.

**Table 7.6  Organizational constraints**

| Project | Tax rate | IRR | NPV | % share | Investment | Project (0,1) |
|---|---|---|---|---|---|---|
| 1 | 75 % | 39 % | 11,2 | 20 % | 70,1 | 0 |
| 2 | 75 % | 35 % | 17,7 | 20 % | 154,4 | 1 |
| 3 | 75 % | 15 % | 6,2 | 20 % | 176,4 | 0 |
| 4 | 75 % | 17 % | 16,1 | 20 % | 196,5 | 1 |
| 5 | 75 % | 22 % | 9,8 | 20 % | 101,7 | 0 |
| 6 | 40 % | 39 % | 67,5 | 50 % | 175,2 | 1 |
| 7 | 40 % | 35 % | 106,2 | 50 % | 386,0 | 1 |
| 8 | 40 % | 15 % | 37,3 | 50 % | 441,0 | 1 |
| 9 | 40 % | 17 % | 96,5 | 50 % | 491,2 | 1 |
| 10 | 40 % | 22 % | 58,9 | 50 % | 254,3 | 1 |

*Company costs* As mentioned above, company costs can be of decisive importance in connection with materiality evaluations. The reason for this is that there often are company costs involved in initiating new projects, when establishing new offices in new areas or countries or when continuing activity in a country. These are costs which are usually not included in the anticipated cash flow for a project but which are important when an investment decision is to be made. Examples of company costs may be use of resources in the form of man-hour costs by corporate staff, travels made by corporate staff and management, and the establishment and operation of a head office. When expected materiality is relatively low, even limited company costs may cause the company not to elect to venture into a new country or area. It may also result in rejection of a new project in an existing area, or possibly a total shutdown of the activity in an area.

Below we calculate two cases. One where company costs fully reduces taxable income in the two countries (Table 7.8) and one where the costs are not deductible (Table 7.7). In reality the most likely case would be somewhere in between these assumptions, and varying from country to country. Some company costs may reduce taxable income locally while other company costs, like 'overheads' in the mother company, may be harder to get approved for local tax deduction. Calculated costs for use of scarce management resources will typically be difficult to deduct. The company costs are assumed to be equally distributed between the five projects (USD 2 million on each). The example illustrated in Table 7.7 assumes a company cost of USD 10 million per year as a consequence of venturing into or staying on in country 1 and a similar cost for country 2. The company costs are assumed not to reduce taxable income in the two countries.

Table 7.7 shows that in country 1 only project 2 still has a positive net present value. However, an overall evaluation of the present value potential in country 1 causes the company not to be able to initiate or uphold activity in country 1. The overall activity is unable to cover the area-dependent costs. The conclusion that can be taken on the basis of Table 7.7 is that the company must have relatively high materiality in the form of anticipated present value after tax in its project calculations (that is, excluding company costs) before it is willing to venture into a new country or area, or a new project in an existing area. When consideration is paid to fixed company costs, materiality becomes important for the decision. Sensitivity calculations performed with an oil price of USD 13 show that project 8 will not be profitable. At high oil price (USD 17) country 1 is close to becoming interesting due to higher net present values in the projects. A sensitivity with a low required return (8per cent) also make country 1 interesting. With a required return of 12per cent the main results in Table 7.7 are not changed. As shown, the materiality conditions in the form of ownership share is important. The ownership share must be large enough to cover the company costs.

In the case that company costs can fully reduce taxable income, the results in Table 7.8 show that the projects in country 1 will not have negative net present value before company costs exceed USD 35 million per year, compared to only 10 million in Table 7.7. The reason for this is the assumption of a linear tax system where the State covers the tax part of all costs.[9]

**Table 7.7    Company costs (not recoverable)**

| Project | Tax rate | IRR | NPV | % share | Investment | Project (0,1) |
|---|---|---|---|---|---|---|
| 1 | 75 % | 4 % | -3,0 | 20 % | 70,1 | 0 |
| 2 | 75 % | 12 % | 2,1 | 20 % | 154,4 | * |
| 3 | 75 % | 3 % | -10,5 | 20 % | 176,4 | 0 |
| 4 | 75 % | 9 % | -2,6 | 20 % | 196,5 | 0 |
| 5 | 75 % | 4 % | -6,4 | 20 % | 101,7 | 0 |
| 6 | 40 % | 31 % | 53,2 | 50 % | 175,2 | 1 |
| 7 | 40 % | 29 % | 90,6 | 50 % | 386,0 | 1 |
| 8 | 40 % | 12 % | 20,5 | 50 % | 441,0 | 1 |
| 9 | 40 % | 15 % | 77,8 | 50 % | 491,2 | 1 |
| 10 | 40 % | 18 % | 42,7 | 50 % | 254,3 | 1 |

---

9   Again, it should be noted that the company must be in tax paying position.

**Table 7.8     Company costs (tax recovery)**

| Project | Tax rate | IRR | NPV | % share | Investment | Project (0,1) |
|---|---|---|---|---|---|---|
| 1 | 75 % | 8 % | -1,3 | 20 % | 70,1 | 0 |
| 2 | 75 % | 14 % | 4,0 | 20 % | 154,4 | * |
| 3 | 75 % | 4 % | -8,4 | 20 % | 176,4 | 0 |
| 4 | 75 % | 10 % | -0,3 | 20 % | 196,5 | 0 |
| 5 | 75 % | 6 % | -4,4 | 20 % | 101,7 | 0 |
| 6 | 40 % | 24 % | 37,5 | 50 % | 175,2 | 1 |
| 7 | 40 % | 24 % | 73,4 | 50 % | 386,0 | 1 |
| 8 | 40 % | 10 % | 0,5 | 50 % | 441,0 | 1 |
| 9 | 40 % | 14 % | 57,2 | 50 % | 491,2 | 1 |
| 10 | 40 % | 14 % | 24,9 | 50 % | 254,3 | 1 |

**Conclusion**

The examples demonstrate that each of the three possible causes of materiality – capital constraint, organisational constraint and company costs – may be sufficient for a project's or area's materiality to be important for decision-making purposes. In real-life situations several of these constraints may bind simultaneously thereby reinforcing the importance of materiality for the companies investment and localisation behaviour. Sensitivity analyses indicate that the materiality results are robust. They illustrate the general result that investments go where materiality conditions are favourable. Thus, materiality considerations are therefore essential for governments in order for their countries to stay competitive and attract investments.

In our analysis we have assumed that the company's scarce inputs are homogenous. If there are quality differences between different inputs, for instance professionals or management, an additional quality distortion in favour of the country with high materiality is introduced. The best resources will be allocated where the potential gain is largest.

In our case illustration of corporate costs, we obtained the result that the activity level was fluctuating with the oil price level in the country offering low license shares and high taxes. This country was only able to attract investments when the oil price was high. A strongly fluctuating activity level may make it difficult to develop or maintain a national oil industry.

**References**

Atkinson, A.B. and J.E. Stiglitz (1980), *Lectures on Public Economics*, McGraw-Hill.

Emhjellen, M. (1999), *Valuation of Oil-Projects Using the Discounted Cash Flow Model*, Thesis for Doctor of Philosophy, University of New South Wales.

Emhjellen, M. and M.C. Alaouze (2000), 'Project Valuation When There Are Two

Cash Flow Streams', *Discussion paper* 00/02, School of Economics, University of New South Wales.

Gresik, T. A. (2000), 'The Taxing Task of Taxing Transnationals', forthcoming in *Journal of Economic Literature*.

Olsen, T. and P. Osmundsen (2000), 'Strategic Tax Competition; Implications of National Ownership', forthcoming in *Journal of Public Economics*.

Osmundsen, P. (1995), 'Taxation of Petroleum Companies Possessing Private Information', *Resource & Energy Economics*, **17**, 357-377.

Osmundsen, P. (1998), 'Dynamic Taxation of Nonrenewable Natural Resources under Asymmetric Information about Reserves', *Canadian Journal of Economics*, **31**(4), 933-951.

Osmundsen, P., K.P. Hagen and G. Schjelderup (1998), 'Internationally Mobile Firms and Tax Policy', *Journal of International Economics,* **45**, 97-113.

Wood Mackenzie (1999), *Comparative Fiscal Regimes Study*, report prepared for the Norwegian Ministry of Oil and Energy.

Zimmerman, J. (1979), 'The Cost and Benefits of Cost Allocations', *The Accounting Review*, July, 504-521.

Zodrow, G.R. and Mieszkowski, P. (1986), 'Pigou, Tiebout, Property Taxation, and the Underprovision of Local Public Goods', *Journal of Urban Economics,* **19**, 356-370.

Chapter 8

# Liberalisation, Integration and Specialisation: The Restructuring of the European Oil Industry

Øystein Noreng

## Purpose of the chapter

The overall aim of the chapter is to analyse the forces that contribute to changing the European oil industry in the direction of privatisation and competitive markets, distinguishing between upstream and downstream operations. The first part of the chapter discusses the general European trend toward deregulation and privatisation of the oil industry, within the context of general conditions that provoke changes in the worldwide oil industry, emphasising the role of the European Commission in imposing such changes on often recalcitrant EU member states. The second part of the paper will focus on conditions in the North Sea oil industry, emphasising differences between Norway and the United Kingdom in coping with oil industry change, and the potential impact of electricity and gas market liberalisation. The objective is not to present a firm picture of the future structure of the European oil industry, but rather to present the dynamics that lead to continuous change.

At the global level, problems of access to equity crude oil and natural gas, price instability and demanding financial markets put pressure on the oil industry to restructure, aiming at economies of scale and the consolidation of positions in oil products markets. The effect is a more centralised industry structure. The gradually advancing maturity of the resource base, forcing the industry toward deeper waters, less accessible areas, more complex and often smaller prospects represents a contrary pressure, opening opportunities for smaller oil companies, specialised in upstream operations. The effect is a less centralised industry structure. Both trends have been prevalent in the North Sea. Mergers and acquisitions among major oil companies, such as Total-Fina-Elf, Exxon-Mobil, Conoco-Phillips and Shell-Enterprise, have created larger units operating across the Norway-UK borderline. On the other hand, the shifting resource base is providing new chances for smaller oil companies, old hands as well as newcomers.

From the perspective of industry structure, in UK waters the emergence of smaller companies seems to have a stronger impact than the consolidation of the large companies, the overall result being a more decentralised oil industry structure. By contrast, in Norwegian waters, the overall effect seems to be a more centralised oil industry structure. The 1999 acquisition of Saga Petroleum, Norway's third oil company, by Norsk Hydro and Statoil, Norway's second and first oil companies, has been decisive. At the time of writing, summer of 2005, smaller oil companies also seem to be strengthening their position in Norway, but not sufficiently to offset the consolidation of the larger oil companies, so far at least.

## Oil liberalisation and privatisation

In the energy business, liberalisation of markets and privatisation of companies go together.[1] Insofar as a segment of the energy market is sheltered from competition, to secure supplies or shelter consumers in markets with allegedly imperfect competition, it makes sense to serve the market by a public monopoly, owned by the state, or by regional or local authorities. The supposed aim is to have the economic rent accruing from a monopoly or oligopoly position benefit public sector treasuries rather than private investors. Insofar as the reasons for sheltering the particular segment of the energy market disappears and competition is introduced, it makes little sense to keep a publicly owned company whose position will be undermined by private competitors.

Publicly owned companies usually suffer from a competitive disadvantage through inherent inefficiency due to the absence of capital market monitoring, lack of simple and precise targets, and soft budget constraints because the public owner usually demands a low return on capital employed.[2] In practice, publicly owned companies are less accountable to their government owners than are corresponding private companies in relation to the capital market. Although this may represent a short-term advantage in terms of managerial discretion, in the longer run it usually turns out to be a drawback because of weaker efficiency incentives. In a dominant or monopoly position these companies may give priority to expansion and organisational growth, rather than efficiency, driving up costs.

Hence, in an open and competitive energy market, keeping a wholly or partly publicly owned company in principle makes little sense. The public owner will suffer in terms of a low return on capital, while the public risks suffering in terms of higher prices. Instead, the rational solution would be to enhance the public interest by promoting competition and privatising the public energy companies. This presupposes, however, that markets are transparent and competitive, that security of supply is not an issue, and that governments are able to enforce competition. In some circumstances, as to protect infant industries, there may be good arguments for a state participation in an energy company, but it usually has a cost in terms of

---

1   Horsnell, Paul (1999) 'Issues in Deregulation, Privatization and Reregulation of Energy Industries', *Privatization and Deregulation in the Gulf Energy Sector*, Abu Dhabi: The Emirates Center for Strategic Studies and Research (69-83).

2   Jean-Jacques Laffont and Jean Tirole (1993) *A Theory of Incentives in Procurement and Regulation*, Cambridge, Mass.: The M.I.T. Press.

loss of efficiency and market valuation. In mature markets and industries, there is a strong case for the government to assume an active role as a regulator, supervising competition, and to discontinue any company ownership. This reasoning applies to oil as to electricity and gas.

In this perspective, liberalising energy markets logically should be followed up by privatisation, with a profound effect on the company structure. A public monopoly will be replaced by a multitude of private companies with shifting market shares. Electricity and gas in the United Kingdom UK are telling examples, and so is oil in many European countries.

The European Union (EU) is presently a driving force in opening member countries' electricity and gas markets for competition, thus paving the way for privatisation, but historically it has been instrumental in opening the oil markets of many European countries. The most striking success has been in the oil and oil products markets of France, which had to abandon its import and refining quota system in 1978. The French system had been put in place in 1928 due to concerns over oil supply security and imperfect competition in the world oil market.[3]

These concerns may have been legitimate in the 1920s and 1930s, but were less so in the 1960s and 1970s. Although the national companies were successful in providing oil and France avoided the oil supply problems that affected other European countries during the 1973 oil crisis, the cost was high. By attributing import and refining licenses, the French government gave the lion's share to the two national companies, CFP-Total and Elf, with smaller shares to a select number of international companies. By regulating market shares, the government stifled competition, while close cooperation with oil companies gave strong incentives to collusion and high consumer prices.[4] Indeed, a parliamentary inquiry commission described French consumers as victims of an effective cartel headed by the two national oil companies, both of which were partly owned by the government.[5] To a large extent, the public companies seem to have made public policy, for their own benefit.[6] Following the deregulation, supermarket chains entered the French motor fuels market, taking a high market share through price competition. Subsequently, both CFP-Total and Elf were progressively privatised. Nevertheless, the French government kept a 'golden' share that permitted it to enforce a merger with Total when Elf was looking for a partner in 1999.

When joining the EU in 1981, Greece had to abandon its oil import monopoly. The same was the case for Portugal and Spain in 1986 and for Finland in 1995. Between 1989 and 1997 the Spanish government sold its shares in the erstwhile national

---

3   Nowell, Gregoryn P. (1994), *Mercantile States and the World Oil Cartel 1900-1939*, London: Cornell University Press.

4   Sheahan, John (1963) *Promotion and Control of Industry in Postwar France*, Cambridge, Mass.: Harvard University Press.

5   Rapport de la commission d'enquête parlementaire (1974), *Sur les sociétés pétrolières opérant en France* Paris : Union Générale d'Éditions.

6   Feigenbaum, Harvey B. (1985), *The Politics of Public Enterprise*, Princeton, N.J.; Princeton University Press.

oil company Repsol. The Finnish deregulation was overdue, as the oil import and refining monopoly had been instituted after the Second World War to handle imports of Soviet crude under the auspices of the Finnish-Soviet Treaty of Friendship and Trade. The Treaty was suspended after the collapse of the Soviet Union in 1991, making the oil import monopoly redundant. Subsequently, the Finnish national oil company Neste was merged with the state power company IVO to make Fortum, which subsequently has been privatised.

The EU today essentially has open and competitive crude oil and products markets, with large-scale cross-border trading, although taxes, duties and hence, consumer prices vary markedly. Trading patterns also differ, as, so far, the French supermarket sales of motor fuels have hardly spread to other countries. Nevertheless, the open market has facilitated oil industry restructuring, of which the TotalFina merger is the most spectacular cross-border case. More is likely to follow.

Currently, electricity and gas market liberalisation is advancing at an accelerating pace in Europe. Driving forces are the EU Commission and its Electricity and Gas Directives, as well as the maturity of the markets. With infrastructure in place and essentially depreciated, there is little justification for high margins in intermediary merchant and transmission companies as well as in local distribution companies. These margins amount to monopoly rents that might have had some justification at a historical stage when these industries were infant and investment needed protection, but in the present situation with a considerable excess capacity at many stages, they distort energy markets at consumer expense.

Hence, the explicit motive behind the EU efforts to open electricity and gas markets is enhance European competitiveness through lower energy costs resulting from liberalisation and enhanced competition.[7] In principle, opening electricity and gas markets should transfer economic rents from companies controlling the infrastructure to producers and consumers, with a potential gain for traders. The immediate ambition is to establish an EU-wide electricity market, where in principle any consumer would be able to choose any supplier. In practice, this would require transparency and unbundling of integrated power companies as well as low transmission tariffs and equal access, preferably regulated by an independent public autority. This is no simple task and experience shows that vested interests able to resist and distort reform, at times helped by governments reluctant to enforce radical change, although mandated by the EU. France has provoked EU prosecution by delaying and diluting implementation of the Electricity Directive. The German government has, so far, chosen not to regulate transmission tariffs, with the result that power market competition occurs at producer expense, while the transmission tariffs have remained practically unchanged. To sum up, EU electricity market reform still has a long way to go. The UK was early in reforming the electricity system, but with privatisation preceding liberalisation, to the detriment of consumers. Indeed, the financial motive of the Thatcher government in practice amounted to selling an

---

7    European Commission (1999), *European Union Energy Outlook to 2020*, Brussels: EU Directorate General for Energy.

integrated national public monopoly to regional private monopolies, with consumers paying higher prices.[8]

Nevertheless, the resistance to electricity market liberalisation seems to be a losing battle. The current wave of power industry mergers and acquisitions, especially in Germany, can be seen largely as defensive moves facing a more competitive and more risky future. Large companies try to consolidate positions, as with the mergers of VEBA and VIAG, and RWE and VEW in Germany, and with the Électricité de France, EdF, purchase of a stake in German EnBW. It is telling that local and regional governments, especially in Germany, are selling their stakes in erstwhile energy monopolies. In the Netherlands and the UK, the power industry was at first fragmented, then largely taken over by foreign investors. The overall trend is toward consolidation and oligopolistic competition, but with openings for niche players. The structure of the European power industry is under increasing pressure. There are new business opportunities pertinent to the oil industry, especially as gas is concerned. Open electricity markets favour gas-based power generation over coal or nuclear because of low capital costs, short-lead times and limited economies of scale. The UK precedent is important in this respect, as competition in the electricity market has strongly favoured gas in power generation.

The historical system of gas trading in Europe can be described as *de facto* mutual monopolies either under government ownership or government guarantee. The reality of monopoly trading has been ever present, in spite of formal differences and apparent diversity in organisation. Indeed, the difference between the French vertical integration and the German vertical control has been more formal than real. The model was in many ways the electricity industry. In order to foster gas trade, the gas merchant companies, which were also transporters, were either by law or in practice given exclusive rights. At the same time, local gas distribution has also been exempt from competition.

The historical European system of gas trading is under attack from several corners. The key element of change is demand for energy in general. As the European economies grow and become technologically more advanced, with employment increasingly in services, the bulk of energy demand moves from industry to the residential and commercial sector. More than a volume growth, this represents a qualitative change in the sense that energy demand becomes decentralised on a large number of consumers with individual requirements and load patterns, taking out a rising part of their energy consumption in the form of electricity. Such a heterogeneous market is more difficult to service by a monopoly than a more homogeneous market with the bulk of demand in industry with more even load patterns. In continental Europe, as has been the case in the UK, chances are that a liberalisation of the electricity market will set an irresistible precedent for the gas market.

Implementing gas market liberalisation is, however, likely to prove even more difficult because of the high import dependency and concerns for security of supply

---

8    Thomas, Steve (1997), 'The Privatization of the Electricity Supply Industry', *The British Electricity Experiment*, ed. John Surrey, London: Earthscan Publication (40-66).

through long-term take-or-pay, TOP; contracts. So far, excepting the UK, European gas trading has been reminiscent of monopsonies, single buyers, confronting an oligopoly, a few sellers. Barring major changes in the gas sales organisation of Algeria, Norway and Russia, Europe's gas supplies are likely to be increasingly dependent upon the oligopoly, as demand rises and domestic output subsides. Hence, for the EU to pursue gas market liberalisation with the same consistency as for power risks compromising the purchasers' bargaining position. As a major importer, Europe would perhaps simply be best served by a few strong gas merchants, such as those that until now have dominated the various national markets. This would, however, be contrary to the spirit of competition and undermine the power market reform, which aims at improved conditions for gas-based power generation, meaning access to gas at lower prices and at more flexible terms also for smaller power generators.

Against this backdrop, supply security becomes the lynchpin. Security of supply can be seen as a private commercial or as a public regulatory issue. As a private commercial issue, the task is to diversify risk and eventually pay a premium for priority deliveries in case of a crunch. Monopoly trading makes this difficult, as users have no choice of supplier and monopolies have few incentives to offer premium contracts. As a public regulatory issue, the question is what customers are to have priority in case of a crunch, at what cost. In this perspective, competition may imply an enhanced risk through uncertainty and reduced investment. Instead of competing suppliers, the solution may be regulations and emergency plans, including storage requirements. The priority among users then becomes a question of substitutability and alternatives.

In principle, there is little difference between demand rising in relation to constant supplies or supplies falling in relation to constant demand, abstracting differences in timing and abruptness. In both cases a shortfall should lead to price rises. The question is whether the cost should be distributed by regulators or by the market. The market solution may be more brutal, but also more efficient and less costly in the longer run. Provided the system is sufficiently integrated through infrastructure and general access to storage facilities, a shortfall at one point should be distributed fairly evenly and the cost be limited for any single user. The problem in today's European gas market is, however, that insufficient infrastructure between the various gas importers and the reliance on bilateral take or pay contracts enhance the supply risk for each importer through a low degree of actual diversification and a low degree of potential diversification in case of a crisis. Hence infrastructure development and more flexible trading could considerably reduce the supply risk for all gas users, enhancing the attractiveness of gas as a fuel. Such measures could also be in the interest of the established suppliers.

Indeed, the gas market is not a zero-sum game. The interest of the suppliers is to reach a large market at low transportation cost. The interest of the buyers is to diversify supply risk and hedge bargaining positions. In the present, segmented European gas market, where different areas are served by different TOP contracts, often with limited diversification the supply risk today in each case is unnecessarily high, due to insufficient infrastructure and rigid trading patterns. In a market more integrated by infrastructure, freer access and more open trading, the risk connected with each supplier would be spread out on a much larger area, with much smaller potential effects of a shortfall. It would also strengthen the buyers' bargaining position.

The restructuring of the European gas industry and the battle for positions has barely commenced, but the mature UK gas industry has seen major upheavals. The continental gas industry is unlikely to stay untouched for long. The salient questions are which new actors will emerge in the hitherto state-dominated gas markets of France and Italy and which elements will disappear from the complex German gas industry. As in the oil and electricity industries, mergers and acquisitions are likely to be the order of the day also in the European gas industry. More pertinently, rising gas demand in power generation is likely to induce cross-industry mergers and acquisitions not only between electricity and gas companies, but with oil companies as well. Indeed, oil companies with equity gas are likely to be in a preferential position, securing supplies and diversifying risk. In this perspective, Europe's electricity and gas market liberalisation seems to offer a new arena for the oil industry.

### Oil industry restructuring and the European downstream

In the late 1990s, the international oil industry has undergone profound changes, which have strongly affected the oil companies operating in Europe.

The first major merger, BP and Amoco, has affected the European upstream oil industry, leading to a larger and more consolidated North Sea producer. Prior to the merger, BP was the leading oil producer in UK waters, with considerable production also in Norway, whereas Amoco was relatively more important in Norway. The addition, Arco, had sold its Norwegian assets, but retained UK production. The outcome, BP Amoco, is on some accounts the leading North Sea oil producer. The effect on the downstream part of the business is smaller, as Amoco only had outlets in the UK and was absent from the rest of Europe.

The second major merger, Exxon and Mobil, also affected the concentration of assets in the North Sea. Whereas Exxon had a large share of UK oil production, Mobil had a relatively stronger position in Norway. The combination is a fairly strong North Sea producer. In this case, the result is also a stronger concentration of market power, as both companies had refineries and outlets in a number of European countries, including the UK.

The third major merger, Total and Petrofina, subsequently with the addition of Elf, has a strong impact upstream as well as downstream. Upstream, the combination of the Norwegian and UK acreage of the three companies makes a large North Sea oil producer. Indeed, the merger of the three companies' North Sea assets represents a quantum leap. Moreover, this merger has a strong effect on oil products markets by consolidating downstream operations, with a strongly enhanced market power especially in Belgium and France. Indeed, in parts of France the new company appears have a quasi-monopoly position, only challenged by the supermarkets.

Finally, the acquisition of Saga by Norsk Hydro and Statoil has reduced the number of large Norwegian oil companies from three to two, enhancing upstream concentration. As Saga was an exclusively upstream company, the acquisition had no downstream effect.

Multiple forces have driven the recent oil industry transformation and the precise rationale differs from case to case, as circumstances vary. The general feature is, however, the need for return on capital employed. Focus is increasingly on value added for investors, but the 1990s have been disappointing for most oil companies because of low volume growth, declining reserves, rising costs and a lower pace of technological change. Investor value added can happen through volume growth, efficiency gains, synergy through complementarity, competence, and by mergers and acquisitions.

The stagnant oil market of the 1990s combined with efficiency gains caused a crowding-out effect in the industry. For some companies to grow and show a performance acceptable to investors, others had to shrink or disappear. Hence, facing the low oil prices of 1997-99, some companies were eagerly looking for partners with which to merge to provide growth. Failing to do so, investors could realise value added by selling the company to another one willing to buy.[9] Hence, the more successful oil companies take over the less successful, whether it is called a merger or an acquisition. The process also portrays a certain unwillingness to take upstream risk by fresh exploration in view of oil price uncertainty or to break into new markets. Even efficient oil companies highly valued by the market, such as Mobil and Petrofina have preferred merging with a stronger partner rather than risk a continued independent life with a limited growth potential.

Against a backdrop of slow market growth and uncertain oil prices, the mergers and acquisitions are likely to continue. As in the recent past, the precise circumstances and motives are likely to diverge. The pursuit of volume growth will propel reserve acquisitions as well as the take-over of competitors.[10] The pursuit of shareholder value through efficiency and return on capital employed will lead to the slimming and discarding operations seen as less valuable. The large oil companies have grown because they are efficient, they are not profitable just because of size.

Around 2000, there is a fairly clear relationship between size and market value in the oil industry, but that was not the case around 1990 and will not necessarily be the case ten years hence. The change is largely due to a small number of large mergers. BP and Amoco were each around 1990 two large not very profitable oil companies. At first BP cut costs vigorously and then absorbed Amoco, whose staff largely was discarded. The outcome is a large and profitable oil company. The merger of Exxon and Mobil was followed up by a massive cost reduction, so that the new company is

---

9   Wood-Collins, John (2000), 'Mergers, Size and Value', *Oxford Energy Forum*, 1, May 2000 (11-12).

10  Sieminski, Adam and J.J. Traynor, (2000), 'Mergers, Size and Value', *Oxford Energy Forum*, 1, May 2000 (12-15).

both larger and more profitable than the previous ones. The merger of Total and Fina likewise led to a streamlining of operations and massive cost cutting.

This is, however, hardly the end of history. The shedding of assets by the largest oil companies by necessity provides opportunities for the others. To sustain their efficiency, the large oil companies are likely to become increasingly selective in upstream engagements, but more generally seek market power downstream. Hence, there seems to be a growing playing ground for smaller and medium-sized upstream oil companies. Differences in resources, strategies and costs make for an increasing potential for trading upstream assets. Through the purchase of assets, mergers and acquisitions there is thus a growing potential for new, medium-sized international oil companies, mostly in the United States, but also in Europe. Moreover, the development of the Russian oil industry will have an international impact. Finally, insofar as smaller oil companies have cost advantages over larger ones, they may be attractive investment objects.

Stricter environmental regulations are likely to put a further squeeze on downstream operations in Europe. Further restrictions on emissions from refineries and fuels will cause heavy investment that the large oil companies may easily finance, but whose burden will increase inversely with size. Hence, the stage seems set for a continued consolidation of the downstream oligopoly, but the upstream may look quite different. Moreover, gas may give a new lease of life to smaller and medium-sized oil companies, especially if they benefit from market opening.

**The European upstream: the North Sea**

The discussion will be limited to the North Sea, essentially Norway and the UK, which today represent the bulk of European oil production.

Europe also has a record of state participation in the upstream oil industry. The concessionary regimes of Norway and the UK are based on discretionary licensing, giving the government virtually free hands in selecting companies and attributing petroleum licenses. For a long time, British and Norwegian governments favoured national oil companies, whether private or public. British Petroleum, BP, was until privatisation in the late 1980s up to 68 per cent state owned. The state participation dated back to 1914, aiming at securing oil supplies, at which the company has been successful. Royal Dutch Shell, although private with a British minority ownership, is also generally considered a UK oil company. The two companies have been the most successful in UK oil licensing since the mid 1960s, being awarded about thirty per cent of all operator task, but accounting for more than forty per cent of capital expenditure, indicating that they have got access to larger than average fields, and hence, economic rent. Since the early 1970s, British Gas, a wholly nationalised company, had the sole right to land, transport and sell natural gas in the UK. From 1975, the UK also practised a form of direct state participation, through the British

National Oil Company, BNOC. The aim was to capture economic rent through a majority ownership of all fields.[11]

Norway has a more remarkable record of resource nationalism. Three Norwegian companies, two of which are wholly or partly state-owned, together were awarded 65 per cent of operator tasks since the mid 1960s, accounting for 70 per cent of capital expenditure. Statoil, which is wholly state owned, established in 1972, got 35 per cent of all operator tasks awarded since 1965, accounting for 46 per cent of total capital expenditure. Norway's second oil company, Norsk Hydro, had a 51 per cent government ownership from 1968 to 1999.

For a number of reasons, the UK government involvement in the offshore oil and gas industry was reduced during the 1980s. The most apparent motive was the Thatcher government's need for money, which seems to have been stronger than the ideological urge to privatise oil and gas.[12] In any case. During the 1980s, the UK government embarked on selling the shares in BP, BNOC and the oil assets British Gas. By 1988 the process was completed and the UK upstream oil and gas industry was in private hands. By this time, output had peaked for the first time and it was evident that the UK was a mature oil province, so that remaining prospects would essentially be either small or in deep waters, costly to develop. This realisation set the stage for a change in oil industry regulations and taxation that contributed to a remarkable structural change in the UK oil industry, with the advent of newcomers.

Norway, at least in the North Sea, is reaching a relative stage of resource maturity, with the remaining prospects being of modest size or in deep waters. In the Norwegian Sea, recent large discoveries indicate a less advanced maturity. In any case, the Norwegian government has recently announced changes in licensing terms with the intent to boost exploration, development and production.[13]

The development of North Sea oil and gas fields, essentially the willingness to invest, can be measured by several indicators, the most important of which are the number of prospects committed for development, the number of barrels committed for development and the investment capital committed. These three indicators give different results as to the willingness to invest.

The number of prospects committed for development shows a persistent rise from the mid 1960s to the end of the century. This measurement abstracts any differences between types of prospects, so that satellite fields are counted equally with independent, major prospects. The methodological defence is simplistically that the law of large numbers applies, so that differences will tend to even out. The rise in activity has apparently been strong in Norway, where only one field was developed between 1965 and 1973, against ten fields in UK waters. During the whole period 1965-98, close to two hundred prospects were committed for development in

---

11  Hoopes, Stephanie M. (1988), *Oil Privatization, Public Choice and International Forces*, London: Macmillan.

12  Hoopes, (1988).

13  St.meld,nr. 39 (1999-2000), *Olje- og gassvirksomheten*, Oslo: Ministry of Oil and Energy.

UK waters and almost fifty in Norwegian waters. In terms of prospects committed annually, Norway in the 1990s had yet to catch up with the UK level of activity of the late 1970s.

**Table 8.1     Number of prospects committed for development**

| Period | UK Total | Norway Total | UK Per year | Norway Per year |
|---|---|---|---|---|
| 1965-73 | 10 | 1 | 1,1 | 0,1 |
| 1974-79 | 19 | 3 | 3,2 | 0,5 |
| 1980-86 | 21 | 9 | 3,0 | 1,3 |
| 1987-98 | 136 | 35 | 10,5 | 2,7 |
| 1965-98 | 186 | 48 | 5,5 | 1,4 |

*Source*: Norwegian School of Management

The petroleum resources, oil and gas, committed for development, show a smaller difference, but trends are more diverging. Over the whole period the UK has committed about 37 billion barrels of oil and gas for development, against slightly over 34 billion barrels for Norway. The UK committed more than half during the early periods, from 1965 to 1979, apparently followed by a paucity of investment decisions between 1980 and 1986, but with activity catching up again since 1987. Norway presents a more gradual evolution. The striking contrast is that Norway since 1980, has committed markedly more petroleum resources for development than the UK.

**Table 8.2     Resources committed for development. Billion barrels of oil and gas (converted to oil equivalents)**

| Period | UK Total | Norway Total | UK Per year | Norway Per year |
|---|---|---|---|---|
| 1965-73 | 9570 | 3565 | 1063 | 396 |
| 1974-79 | 10893 | 5323 | 1816 | 887 |
| 1980-86 | 3569 | 6278 | 510 | 897 |
| 1987-98 | 13028 | 19083 | 1002 | 1468 |
| 1965-98 | 37060 | 34249 | 1090 | 1007 |

*Source*: Norwegian School of Management

Hence, with a much smaller number of fields, but almost as much petroleum committed for development, it is not surprising that Norway has on the average been developing much larger oil fields than has been the case in the UK. For the whole period, the average Norwegian field developed has been about three and a half times the size of the average UK one. Indeed, in terms of maturity measured by average field resources, Norway in the 1990s seems to be at the stage of the UK in the late 1970s.

**Table 8.3    Average petroleum resources in fields committed for development. Billion barrels of oil and gas (converted to oil equivalents)**

| Period | UK bbls/field | Norway bbls/field |
|--------|---------------|-------------------|
| 1965-73 | 957 | 3565 |
| 1974-79 | 573 | 1774 |
| 1980-86 | 170 | 698 |
| 1987-98 | 96 | 545 |
| 1965-98 | 199 | 714 |

*Source*: Norwegian School of Management

The larger field size has permitted Norway to commit much less capital, less than two thirds, to develop almost the same amount of petroleum resources as the UK. Another contrast is between the fairly gradual rise in average annual investment commitment in Norway and the uneven development in the UK. Indeed, in the UK, average annual investment commitment peaked in the late 1970s, slumped in the 1980s and rose again in the 1990s. In Norway, there was a significant rise in investment commitment in the late 1970s; it rose again in the 1980s and the 1990s. Still, it is below the UK level.

**Table 8.4    Capital investment committed 1965-98. Million 1999 $**

| Period | UK Total | Norway Total | UK Per year | Norway Per year |
|--------|----------|--------------|-------------|-----------------|
| 1965-73 | 19033 | 7286 | 2114 | 809 |
| 1974-79 | 53025 | 10788 | 8838 | 1798 |
| 1980-86 | 19043 | 22228 | 2721 | 3175 |
| 1987-98 | 66909 | 56026 | 5147 | 4310 |
| 1965-98 | 158011 | 96329 | 4648 | 2833 |

*Source*: Norwegian School of Management

Against this backdrop it is not surprising that the average investment committed per barrel has been consistently higher in the UK than in Norway. In hindsight, it is surprising that the average capital commitment per barrel did not rise after the 1973-74 oil price increase, but only after the second one, in 1979-80. A remarkable contrast is that in the 1990s, average investment commitment per barrel has risen significantly in the UK, whereas it has actually fallen in Norway. In these terms, measured by constant money investment commitment per barrel, Norway in the 1990s seems to be about the stage of the UK in the late 1970s. This corresponds to differences in field sizes indicated above.

**Table 8.5    Capital investment committed per barrel. 1999 $/bl.**

| Period | UK | Norway |
|---|---|---|
| 1965-73 | 3,87 | 2,05 |
| 1974-79 | 3,21 | 2,03 |
| 1980-86 | 4,26 | 3,54 |
| 1987-98 | 5,92 | 2,93 |
| Average | 4,26 | 2,81 |

*Source*: Norwegian School of Management

A final contrast is in the move towards the deep offshore. Until 1973, both the UK and the Norwegian oil industry operated in waters now considered shallow, until 100 metres of depth. The 1973-74 oil price rise apparently stimulated the industry to move into deeper waters, but in the early 1980s, the bulk of activity in the UK was again in shallow waters. In the 1990s, measured by average water depths of new prospects, the UK oil industry has moved slightly toward deeper waters, whereas in Norway there has apparently been a quantity leap into the deep. The reason is a number of huge prospects in deep waters, such as for example the Troll gas field.

**Table 8.6    Average ocean depth. Metres**

| Period | UK | Norway |
|---|---|---|
| 1965-73 | 82 | 73 |
| 1974-79 | 135 | 129 |
| 1980-86 | 82 | 126 |
| 1987-98 | 108 | 253 |
| Average | 106 | 206 |

*Source*: Norwegian School of Management

Analysing capital costs of North Sea oil field development, a few salient factors should be taken into account:

- Field size, as a parameter of the potential economic rent, as economies of scale indicate that unit capital costs diminish with size
- Ocean depth, as an indicator of field development adversity
- Year of development start-up, as an indicator of technological progress that makes unit capital costs diminish over time

Only by correcting for these factors can costs be compared between companies. Historical costs have been converted to 1999 US dollars.

In the following analysis, categories are as follows:

- Field size:
  1. Small: < 100 million tonnes of oil equivalent, mtoe

    2. Medium: 100-500 mtoe
    3. Large: 500 mtoe<
  • Ocean depth:
    1. Shallow: < 100 metres
    2. Medium 100-200 metres
    3. Deep: > 200 metres

  • Construction start-up:
    1. Early: until 1979
    2. Intermediary: 1980-1989
    3. Late: since 1990

A preliminary conclusion is that in UK waters smaller oil companies seem to have an advantage in smaller fields in shallow waters and that large oil companies have their advantage in large fields in deep waters. This has only been apparent in the 1990s, however. The general tendency is for the large oil companies to consolidate their dominance with deeper waters, and that the importance of the smaller ones diminishes. So far, smaller and medium-sized oil companies are absent in deep waters. Another trend is for capital costs per barrel to decline with company size, when the whole period 1964-97 is considered.

Field sizes matter, as capital costs per barrel are higher for smaller and medium-sized fields than for the large ones. The medium-sized fields may, however, have relatively high capital costs because of water depth and construction start-up. Smaller and medium-sized companies generally have a large share of small fields in their portfolio.

**Table 8.7    Capital costs per barrel of oil equivalent developed by operator company category and field sizes, UKCS, 1964-97**

| Company category | Capital cost/bl. (1999 USD) Field sizes | | | | | |
|---|---|---|---|---|---|---|
| | Small (0-100) | N | Medium (100-500) | N | Large (500+) | N |
| Small | 4,77 | 27 | 5,56 | 14 | 4,01 | 4 |
| Medium | 4,63 | 40 | 5,95 | 14 | 3,24 | 5 |
| Large | 5,10 | 38 | 5,24 | 31 | 3,36 | 11 |
| | | 105 | | 59 | | 20 |

*Source*: Norwegian School of Management, BI, data from WoodMackenzie

The analysis also shows that it has been between 15 and 40 per cent more costly, measured on the average, per barrel, to develop fields in water depths between 100 and 200 metres than in fields in water depths of less than 100 metres. Smaller companies have about two thirds of their prospects in shallow waters, against about one half for the large oil companies. When the whole period is considered, the large oil companies have the lowest capital costs per barrel in shallow and medium-deep waters. This observation does not take into account, however, that the large oil companies generally have had larger fields than smaller and medium-sized oil companies.

**Table 8.8    Capital costs per barrel of oil equivalent developed by operator company category and water depths, UKCS, 1964-97**

| Company category | Capital cost/bl. (1999 USD) Water depth | | | | | |
|---|---|---|---|---|---|---|
| | Shallow waters (0-100) | N | Medium (100-200) | N | Deep waters (200+) | N |
| Small | 4,23 | 28 | 5,78 | 17 | 0,00 | 0 |
| Medium | 4,09 | 34 | 4,69 | 25 | 0,00 | 0 |
| Large | 3,31 | 41 | 4,34 | 36 | 4,90 | 3 |
| | | 103 | | 78 | | 3 |

*Source*: Norwegian School of Management, BI, data from WoodMackenzie

To some extent, the impact of technological development seems to have been greater on smaller and medium-sized oil companies than on the larger ones. The general trend for technology development in the offshore oil industry is to reduce costs, so that fields developed in the late 1990s would have lower costs than similar fields developed around 1970. The analysis shows a marked increase in the number of prospects developed and that the predominance of the large oil company as operators of the early period has gradually ceded to a more even balance between the three types of companies, measured by the number of operator responsibilities.

On prospects developed until 1979, the large and medium-sized oil companies have an evident cost advantage over small oil companies. On prospects with a development start-up between 1980 and 1989, the large oil companies appear as the least cost effective, while the medium-sized companies appear as the most cost effective. In the late period, on prospects with a development start-up since 1990, the small oil companies appear as the most cost effective, while the medium-sized ones now are the least cost effective.

**Table 8.9    Capital costs per barrel of oil equivalent developed by operator company category and development start-up, UKCS, 1964-97**

| Company category | Capital cost/bl. (1999 USD) Development start-up | | | | | |
|---|---|---|---|---|---|---|
| | Early (-1979) | N | Intermediary (1980-89) | N | Late (1990-) | N |
| Small | 4,53 | 5 | 5,27 | 12 | 4,64 | 28 |
| Medium | 3,52 | 8 | 4,45 | 8 | 5,82 | 43 |
| Large | 3,38 | 16 | 6,00 | 17 | 4,96 | 47 |
| | | 29 | | 37 | | 118 |

*Source*: Norwegian School of Management, BI, data from WoodMackenzie

Comparing capital costs on small prospects developed during the 1990s, by water depths, gives a clearer picture. The analysis shows that on small prospects in shallow waters, small oil companies do appear to have a cost advantage. In shallow and medium-deep waters, until 200 metres, the tendency is for capital costs to increase with company size. By contrast, for the large oil companies, capital costs seem to decline as waters get deeper. Other field characteristics may be decisive in this respect.

**Table 8.10   Capital costs per barrel of oil equivalent on small prospects by operator company category and water depths, UKCS, 1990-97**

| Company category | Capital cost/bl. (1999 USD) | | | | | |
|---|---|---|---|---|---|---|
| | Ocean depth | | | | | |
| | Shallow waters (0-100) | N | Medium (100-200) | N | Deep waters (200+) | N |
| Small | 4,85 | 11 | 3,73 | 8 | N/A | |
| Medium | 4,90 | 25 | 3,76 | 12 | N/A | |
| Large | 5,32 | 26 | 4,80 | 11 | 4,70 | 1 |
| | | 62 | | 31 | | 1 |

*Source*: Norwegian School of Management, BI, data from WoodMackenzie

A preliminary conclusion is that during the 1990s on the UK continental shelf, small oil companies have proved to be particularly cost effective, especially with small and medium-sized prospects in shallow waters.

The licensing history is a necessary reference for analysing present relative cost patterns in the North Sea oil industry. The large oil companies were favoured in the early licensing rounds and hence, got the largest and most prospective acreage. By comparison, the small and medium-sized oil companies as latecomers for the most part got the leftovers, the acreage that had been discarded by the large ones. Hence, their share of the total acreage is comparatively small. Moreover, their acreage is generally less productive, as measured by oil and gas output per square kilometre of area licensed.

Against this backdrop, it should not surprise that the large oil companies on the average have the lowest capital costs, because field sizes matter for unit costs. Correspondingly, the less productive acreage represents an additional incentive for the smaller and medium-sized oil companies to be more cost-effective, which is a matter of survival. Hence, they also have to invest more selectively than do the large oil companies. Data indicate that the smaller and medium-sized oil companies on the whole have succeeded in cost-effective specialisation. The small oil companies each operate only one or a few small fields, but with a high equity share. By contrast, the large multinational oil companies usually operate a number of large fields, but with a comparatively low equity share in each. The medium-sized oil companies are in an intermediary position. Hence, equity also seems to be an important incentive to cost effectiveness.

Hence, the key issue is the company structure and the criteria for allocating licenses as the resource base matures, technology develops, and markets and the oil industry change. The rational exploitation of the resources of a mature oil province requires more open competition, more active partners and more flexibility, as well as better incentives. With maturity, the interest of the government landowner is to use the infrastructure in a rational way and to develop smaller prospects. By experience, the large, established oil companies have a limited interest to engage in marginal prospects.

The recent wave of mergers strengthens the concentration in the North Sea oil industry, with a paradoxical result. On one hand, the new, large companies have a large part of their resource base and their production in the North Sea. On the other hand, their size and resources indicate that their future upstream interest may be less in the North Sea than in more challenging less mature oil provinces, such as offshore Africa and Brazil, the Middle East and parts of the former Soviet Union. The outcome could be that the large companies keep an interest in North Sea gas, especially if beachhead value in North-West Europe should increase, but less so in smaller oil fields. This may enlarge the playing ground for smaller oil companies, but if successful they could also become targets of take-over by larger companies.

Norway seems to be in a contradictory situation, with the mature North Sea contrasting with the Norwegian Sea. Insofar as rules and eventually taxation are adjusted to provide incentives for North Sea activity and smaller companies, the Norwegian Sea could become a highly attractive area for the large ones. Indeed, compared to the UK, judging by maturity, the Norwegian oil industry may have decades ahead, especially if gas becomes more valuable in relation to oil. The figures on concentration of production should be seen with reference to the 'Rest' category, which in Norway contains the large State Direct Financial Investment, SDFI, and in the UK a host of smaller companies.

**Table 8.11    Before the mergers: production 1998**

| Norway | Thousand bbls of oil equivalent/day | | | Share of total | | |
|---|---|---|---|---|---|---|
| | Oil | Gas | Total | Oil | Gas | Total |
| BP | 81,504 | 5,38 | 86,884 | 2,5 % | 0,6 % | 2,1 % |
| Amoco | 19,496 | 5,11 | 24,606 | 0,6 % | 0,6 % | 0,6 % |
| Exxon | 138 | 49,25 | 187,25 | 4,3 % | 5,3 % | 4,5 % |
| Mobil | 73 | 7,83 | 80,83 | 2,3 % | 0,8 % | 2,0 % |
| Elf Aquitaine | 122 | 41,79 | 163,79 | 3,8 % | 4,5 % | 4,0 % |
| Petrofina | 48,4 | 15,24 | 63,64 | 1,5 % | 1,7 % | 1,5 % |
| Total | 38,6 | 12,59 | 51,19 | 1,2 % | 1,4 % | 1,2 % |
| Saga | 125,96 | 20,16 | 146,12 | 3,9 % | 2,2 % | 3,5 % |
| Hydro | 206,36 | 59,24 | 265,6 | 6,4 % | 6,4 % | 6,4 % |
| Statoil | 423,44 | 125,66 | 549,1 | 13,2 % | 13,6 % | 13,3 % |
| Rest | 1933,24 | 580,09 | 2513,33 | 60,2 % | 62,9 % | 60,8 % |
| Grand total Norway | 3210 | 922,34 | 4132,34 | 100,0 % | 100,0 % | 100,0 % |

| UK | Thousand bbls of oil equivalent/day | | | Share of total | | |
|---|---|---|---|---|---|---|
| | Oil | Gas | Total | Oil | Gas | Total |
| BP | 385 | 170 | 555 | 13,6 % | 9,8 % | 12,1 % |
| Amoco | 85 | 52,62 | 137,62 | 3,0 % | 3,0 % | 3,0 % |
| Exxon | 328 | 123,79 | 451,79 | 11,6 % | 7,1 % | 9,9 % |
| Mobil | 62 | 105,96 | 167,96 | 2,2 % | 6,1 % | 3,7 % |
| Elf Aquitaine | 104 | 73,62 | 177,62 | 3,7 % | 4,2 % | 3,9 % |
| Petrofina | 58,96 | 35,56 | 94,52 | 2,1 % | 2,0 % | 2,1 % |
| Total | 34,3 | 43,48 | 77,78 | 1,2 % | 2,5 % | 1,7 % |
| Saga | 31,36 | 5,68 | 37,04 | 1,1 % | 0,3 % | 0,8 % |
| Hydro | 0 | 0 | 0 | 0,0 % | 0,0 % | 0,0 % |
| Statoil | 14,47 | 10,77 | 25,24 | 0,5 % | 0,6 % | 0,6 % |
| Rest | 1734,55 | 1118,34 | 2852,89 | 61,1 % | 64,3 % | 62,3 % |
| Grand total UK | 2837,64 | 1739,82 | 4577,46 | 100,0 % | 100,0 % | 100,0 % |

**Table 8.12    After the mergers: production 1998**

| Norway | Thousand bbls of oil equivalent/day | | | Share of total | | |
|---|---|---|---|---|---|---|
| | Oil | Gas | Total | Oil | Gas | Total |
| BP Amoco | 101 | 10,49 | 111,49 | 3,1 % | 1,1 % | 2,7 % |
| Exxon Mobil | 211 | 57,08 | 268,08 | 6,6 % | 6,2 % | 6,5 % |
| TotalFinaElf | 209 | 69,62 | 278,62 | 6,5 % | 7,5 % | 6,7 % |
| Hydro Saga | 332,32 | 79,4 | 411,72 | 10,4 % | 8,6 % | 10,0 % |
| Statoil | 423,44 | 125,66 | 549,1 | 13,2 % | 13,6 % | 13,3 % |
| Rest | 1933,24 | 580,09 | 2513,33 | 60,2 % | 62,9 % | 60,8 % |
| Grand total Norway | 3210 | 922,34 | 4132,34 | 100,0 % | 100,0 % | 100,0 % |

| UK | Thousand bbls of oil equivalent/day | | | Share of total | | |
|---|---|---|---|---|---|---|
| | Oil | Gas | Total | Oil | Gas | Total |
| BP Amoco | 470 | 222,62 | 692,62 | 16,6 % | 12,8 % | 15,1 % |
| Exxon Mobil | 390 | 229,74 | 619,74 | 13,7 % | 13,2 % | 13,5 % |
| TotalFinaElf | 197,26 | 152,66 | 349,92 | 7,0 % | 8,8 % | 7,6 % |
| Hydro Saga | 31,36 | 5,68 | 37,04 | 1,1 % | 0,3 % | 0,8 % |
| Statoil | 14,47 | 10,77 | 25,24 | 0,5 % | 0,6 % | 0,6 % |
| Rest | 1734,55 | 1118,35 | 2852,9 | 61,1 % | 64,3 % | 62,3 % |
| Grand total UK | 2837,64 | 1739,82 | 4577,46 | 100,0 % | 100,0 % | 100,0 % |

**The balance: impact on competition and economic rent distribution**

On the balance, the European oil industry seems to head for greater diversity, driven by liberalisation, integration and specialisation. Strong forces drive the industry toward a more oligopolistic structure downstream. The major oil companies moving heavily into the European gas and power industry, as is happening in the United States would enhance this trend. Few electricity companies or gas transporters or distributors would have the resources to out-compete the major oil companies in gas and eventually electricity trading. Moreover, most electricity companies have little competence in gas trading. Hence, for the major oil companies moving into general energy markets, there is a prospect of at least an oligopoly rent. By such a move they will also show growth and investor value added.

The flip side of the coin is that the more the major oil companies engage in downstream operations, whether in oil, gas or electricity, the more their crude or gas deficit is likely to grow. Hence, they are likely to remain large net buyers of oil and gas, but remaining selective in their upstream engagements. This could be blessing for the smaller and medium-sized companies that are squeezed out of downstream operations. Consumers will foot the bill unless Europe develops more aggressive and more independent regulatory and anti-trust agencies like the United States.

**References**

European Commission (1999), *European Union Energy Outlook to 2020*, Brussels: EU Directorate General for Energy.

Harvey B. Feigenbaum (1985), *The Politics of Public Enterprise*, Princeton, N.J.; Princeton University Press.

Stephanie M. Hoopes (1988),. *Oil Privatization, Public Choice and International Forces*, London: Macmillan.

Paul Horsnell 1999), 'Issues in Deregulation, Privatization and Reregulation of Energy Industries', *Privatization and Deregulation in the Gulf Energy Sector*, Abu Dhabi: The Emirates Center for Strategic Studies and Research (69-83).

Jean-Jacques Laffont and Jean Tirole (1993), *A Theory of Incentives in Procurement and Regulation*, Cambridge, Mass.: The M.I.T. Press.

Gregoryn P. Nowell. (1994), *Mercantile States and the World Oil Cartel 1900-1939*, London: Cornell University Press.

Rapport de la commission d'enquête parlementaire (1974), *Sur les sociétés pétrolières opérant en France*, Paris : Union Générale d'Éditions.

St.meld. nr. 39 (1999-2000), *Olje- og gassvirksomheten*, Oslo: Ministry of Oil and Energy.

John Sheahan (1963), *Promotion and Control of Industry in Postwar France*, Cambridge, Mass.: Harvard University Press.

Adam Sieminski and J.J. Traynor (2000), 'Mergers, Size and Value', *Oxford Energy Forum*, 1, May 2000 (12-15).

Steve Thomas (1997), 'The Privatization of the Electricity Supply Industry', *The*

*British Electricity Experiment,* ed. John Surrey, London: Earthscan Publication (40-66).

John Wood-Collins (2000), 'Mergers, Size and Value', *Oxford Energy Forum,* 1, May 2000 (11-12).

Chapter 9

# Future Oil Resources and Oil Company Strategies: The Clash between Geologists and Economists and What it Means for the Industry

Jerome Davis

## Introduction: how much oil – a recurrent problem?

The 2004 issue of the authoritative *BP Statistical Review of World Energy* gives a thumbnail indication of the issues involved in this chapter. Firstly, it notes a division between economists and geologist as to the extent of oil resources. Referring to the concept of ultimate recoverable resources (URR), the estimate of 'the total amount of oil that will ever be recovered and produced' (Ibid), it notes:

> Whilst some consider URR to be fixed by geology and the laws of physics, in practice estimates of URR continue to be increased as knowledge grows, technology advances, and economics change. Economists often deny the validity of the concept of ultimately recoverable reserves as they consider that the recoverability of resources depends on changing and unpredictable economics and evolving technologies (*Ibid*).

Clearly any discussion of much oil (and natural gas) takes place in a 'house divided'.

Furthermore, the *Statistical Review*, perhaps the most cited recorder of global oil reserves states that 'nobody knows or can know how much oil exists under the earth's surface or how much it will be possible to produce in the future'. Yet if this is the case why is it that perhaps the most vitriolic debate in the oil world today is focussed on the question of 'how much'? BP approaches this question indirectly in its discussion of reserves replacement, the replacing of utilized resources by the finding and development of new reserves:

> [Global] proved oil reserves at the end of 2003 are estimated to have been 1147.7 billion barrels. That represented an increase of around 12% over the end-1993 figure of 1023.6 billionn barrels, despite a cumulative production of almost 264 billion barrels during the intervening years, ie. reserves replacement amounted to almost 400 billion barrels between end-1993 and end-2003 (*Ibid*).

What exactly are 'proved reserves'? The *Statistical Review* defines these as follows:

> Although there is no single, commonly accepted technical definition of proved reserves, a commonly used description is as follows: 'the estimated quantities of oil which geological and engineering data demonstrate with reasonable certainty to be recoverable in future years from known reservoirs under current economic and operating conditions' (Ibid).

This defines the so-called deterministic method in the calculation of reserves as it is differentiated from a definition based on a probability calculations (where proved reserves are defined by a probability 'cutoff' where it is 90 percent or more certain that they exist). Yet there are several severe caveats.

Firstly, the *Statistical Review* makes it clear that even with these definitions, discrepancies appear: 'Although every effort is made to come up with a consistent series for reserves based on a common definition, in reality different countries use different methodologies and the data have varying levels of reliability' (Ibid).

Secondly, the editors of the *Review* are very much aware of the legal implications of what they are doing:

> The reserves series does not necessarily meet the United States Securities and Exchange Commission definition and guidelines for determining proved reserves, nor necessarily represent BP's view of proved reserves by country. Caution needs to be exercised in attempting precise comparisons between nations or analyses of time series (*Ibid*).

These statements reflect a common set of problems in dealing with the issues of 'how much oil and gas'. It is a contentious, highly sensitive question.

What follows in this chapter is an attempt at an objective view of the issues involved in determining estimates of ultimate recoverable reserves (if, indeed, such a concept is valid). Essentially, the battlelines are drawn between a relatively small number of retired oil executives, geologists, and petroleum engineers organized in various groupings, the most prominent of which is the Association for the Study of Peak Oil (ASPO) on the one hand, and the economists and what might be termed the 'oil and gas establishment', on the other, with many individuals taking a middle ground between the two sides. (There are many issues here where one can be sceptical of the status quo without agreeing with ASPO.) The structure of the chapter largely follows the themes of the *BP Statistical Review* as discussed to this point.

The first section looks at the question of estimating ultimately recoverable reserves and the various methods by which reserve calculations are made. This is a highly complex field and many details are, of necessity, left out. (One of the more significant details, the debate over reserve 'growth' is covered in more detail in appendix 9A.) Key in this discussion is how the current debate might be leading to newer and better means of reserve calculations.

Yet, it is not methodologies alone that are the subject of debate. As indicated above, there are problems with calculating the resource base. One can without overly exaggerating state that reserve calculations are also subject to politics, a main reason for the fact that there are over 150 different national reserve classification systems (Sever, 2004). This 'political element' is also a subject for debate, in that it is claimed differing national practices, particularly those of the United States, distort calculations of ultimately recoverable reserves.

Finally, where are the oil companies in all this? In the final, concluding section we review the arguments of those who claim that oil companies may have been 'fudging' their reserve booking practices, and that, over-all, the companies are having increasing problems with replacing the reserves consumed with new reserves on which they can draw on in the future. The evidence here, while inconclusive, is presented for the sake of thoroughness.

## How much is enough? An introduction

How much IS enough? A clue to this answer is given in Table 9.1 (next page). This table contrasts the estimates of the US Geological Survey, arguably the best official source of ultimate resource estimation with those of two retired senior petroleum geologists, perhaps the most prominent members of ASPO. Some explanation is needed to understand the significance of the table.

Firstly, the size of the ultimate recoverable reserves are calculated differently. The calculations presented by Wood et al (2004) are divided into probabilities, generally conforming to those adopted by the Society of Petroleum Engineers (SPE), the World Petroleum Congress (WPC), and the American Association of Petroleum Geologists (AAPG) (although with the notable exception of the 5 percent probable classification).

These professional organizations classify reserves as follows: 'proved reserves' are those deemed 90 percent probable of recovery, 'probable reserves' are those judged to be more than 50 percent probable of recovery, and 'possible reserves' are those thought to be recoverable with more than a 10 percent probability. (It is this classification system which, unless otherwise noted, we will utilize in the balance of this chapter). Wood et al's figures are those of the United States Geological Survey (USGS) year 2000 study and are arrived at through separate Monte Carlo runs for US and 'rest of world' (ROW) reserve estimates, the two of which are then added together.[1] Calculations by Campbell are based on statistical means; those of Laherrère on a minimum-mean-maximum basis, and those of the 1994 on statistical modes.

---

1    This addition procedure is a somewhat dubious means of calculation. As the US Geological Survey itself states: 'Fractiles are additive under the assumption of perfect positive correlation.' (United States Survey, 2003) The U.S. Geological Survey therefore utilizes only mean figures for their world undiscovered totals. This practice does not seem to have been followed by Wood, Long, and Morehouse.

**Table 9.1** Contrasting estimates: ultimately recoverable reserves and timing of world production 'peaks' (conventional oil and NGLs)

| Estimator | Ultimately Recoverable Reserves | Timing of Peak[a] | | |
|---|---|---|---|---|
| | | 2 pct.growth/decline[b] | Graphed curve[c] | R/P=10[d] |
| | $10^9$ bbls/oil | year of peak | | |
| Wood, Long & Morehouse[e] | | | | |
| EIA/USGS (2004)[f] | | | | |
| 95 pct probable | 2,248[f] | | | 2026[a] |
| 50 pct. mean(?) | 3,003[f] | 2016[a] | | 2037[a] |
| 5 pct. probable | 3,896[f] | | | 2047[a] |
| Masters et al (1994) | | | | |
| U.S. Geological Survey | | | | |
| Mode | 2,272 | -- | ---- | -- |
| Campbell (2003) | | | | |
| Mean | 1,850 | | 2008 | |
| Laherrère(2001b) | | | | |
| Minimum | 1,900 | | | |
| Mean | 2,250 | | ca. 2010-2020 | |
| Maximum | 4,000 | | | |

*Key*:

[a]assuming a constant 2 percent growth in demand.

[b]assuming 2 percent growth to peak/2 percent decline thereafter.

[c]see text.

[d] R/P= reserves/production ratio. Here the global production path is determined by corporate maintenance of a target reserve/production ratio of 10.

[e]Wood, Long and Morehouse (2004) based upon the US Geological Survey, *World Petroleum Assessment 2000* (2003).

[f]Potential reserves within a 30 year time frame.

Secondly, what is measured is different. Table 9.1 covers conventional oil (i.e. excludes Albertan tar sands), but even here there are differences. Campbell's estimates exclude conventional polar and deep water reserves in addition to 'heavy oils'. Laherrère's figures exclude 'extra heavy oils' (personal correspondence, October 17, 2004).

What is the significance of these figures? Taking the most probable outcome (50 percent probability for Wood et al, may actually be a median figure rather than a mean), the mode calculations (1994) or statistical means (Campbell, Laherrère), we find that figures range from a high ultimately recoverable of 3003 billion bbls to a low of 1850 billion barrels. Note that the differences between Laherrère and the 1994 US Geological Survey results may not be that far off from each other, depending on the differences in calculation, 2250 billion barrels being only slightly less than 2272 billions.

Is the world going to run out of oil tomorrow? Global consumption currently stands at around 83 million bbls/day for all liquids (including NGLs, and refinery 'growth'). This is somewhat above the daily figure for crude oil alone. Even assuming 5 percent per annum compounded growth in world demand, it would take 30 years for global consumption to reach 1888 billion bbls, in excess of only the most pessimistic estimates of ultimately recoverable reserves.

More significant is what is illustrated to the right in Table 9.1, the various estimates as to the year when world oil production, based on the totals cited in the right hand column, is anticipated to peak. These 'peaks' vary on how they are calculated. All assume a 2 percent annual growth in global demand for conventional oil, but then they differ. Campbell and Laherrère use the curve derived by Hubbert to establish their 'peak year' estimates. The study by Wood, Long and Morehouse derives its two peaks in two different manners. One peak is based on fitting a curve assuming 2 percent annual growth to the peak and a 2 percent decline thereafter within the overall 3,003 billion barrel figure. The other curve assumes that all oil producers retain a production/reserves ration of 1 to 10, and will do so into the future, their production decreasing as their reserves become fewer and fewer. Looking at these estimates, one can begin to see what the controversy is about. Depending on the assumptions, a 'peak' may be reached as early as 2008 or as late as 2047.[2]

### How much is enough? The problems of method

Simplifying considerably, there are two differing, overlapping methods for calculating oil and gas reserves. Geologists are agreed in that the only way to be certain about resource size is through the actual drilling up of oil and gas reserves and producing from these over time. Ten wells drilled on a structure can, for example, convince explorationists that their original estimates that structure holds 50 million barrels of oil are valid; an eleventh 'delineation well' on the same structure may prove a 'duster'. Estimated reserves would then be revised downwards from 50 millions. Reserve estimates are, therefore, estimates, made on the basis of probabilities that the following observed data are valid (Morehouse, 1997, ix):

- Reservoir rock porosity (amount of hydrocarbons contained in rock pores)
- Reservoir rock permeability (flow rate of hydrocarbons through the sourcerock)
- Data on the production of fluids from one or more wells

---

2   What is particularly interesting is the shape of the resulting curves. Here the curve depending on an annual production/reserves ratio of 1:10 is particularly disquieting as it has a steeply declining 'post peak' slope.

- Geologic mapping of the extent and breadth of the structure which is (again) inferred from well, geophysical, and geological data
- Data on reservoir temperature and pressure.

Generally speaking the longer the operating history on a given oil or gas field, the higher the probability that the data cited above are correct, the better the estimates of reserves. Conversely, the less that is known about the structure in terms of its data, the higher the probability that the reserve estimate will be inaccurate.

With regard to known but undrilled structures, for example, there are two estimating methods used: a nominal method which bases the reserves estimate on a 'rule of thumb' or an analogy to other reservoirs (or oil provinces) believed to be similar to the structures under investigation, or a more accurate volumetric method applying a 'rule of thumb or analogy based recovery factor to an in-place volume of oil or gas estimated from geologic and engineering data (Morehouse, 1997, p. ix)' With drilled structures, various estimating methodologies using well and reservoir production data can be used.

In all these methods a high degree of reliance is placed on the estimator's judgement. How does one judge rock and fluid properties? The determination of the reservoir volume? The nature and type of a reservoir drive mechanism? What trend line most adequately describes a reservoir decline? And these judgemental factors pale beside those needed of a geologist/geophysicist in assessing undiscovered resources in a province.

To this point, all experts are more or less in agreement. What causes debate in petroleum geologist circles are two factors:

- Whether, when (if ever) the production of oil will 'peak' and then go into decline, and
- The reliability of the data which are used in making ultimate recoverable reserve calculations.

## How much is enough? Hubbert's peak and resource estimations

Wrestling with the problems of US reserve estimates in 1956, a petroleum geologist, W. King Hubbert, discovered a relationship between past reserve discoveries current production figures and oil province decline. By aggregating historic discovery data, and the resulting production figures, he claimed he could define a point in the future where additions to US reserves would decline in the face of rising consumption. Hubbert made a famous prediction about oil and NGL reserves in the 'lower 48 states' (excluding Hawaii and Alaska). Taking then existing estimates of ultimately recoverable reserves at 150 billion bbls. (low estimate) and 200 billion bbls.(high estimate) he plotted production versions of a logistic curve for these quantities. On this basis, he predicted that production would peak either in 1966 (low estimate) or in 1971 (high estimate). Lower 48 production in fact peaked in 1971.

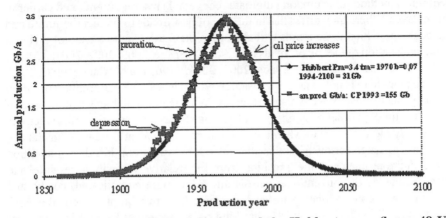

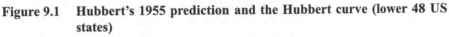

**Figure 9.1    Hubbert's 1955 prediction and the Hubbert curve (lower 48 US states)**

*Source*: Laherrère, 1997, p. 3.

Laherrère's version of the Hubbert peak illustrates the Hubbertian argument well. As can be seen from Figure 9.1, oil production from the lower 48 states is fitted to a symmetrical curve, a variation of a logistical curve. Variations from the curve are explained in terms of OPEC (oil price increases), and US policies (prorationing) and the 1930s depression.

The success of Hubbert's projections gave him close to legendary status among petroleum geologists. Even today's sceptics give him credit for his work:

Hubbert deserves much credit for his predictions which were based on more realistic criteria than those used by many of his contemporaries, but the conclusion of some that Hubbert's methodology and assumptions must have been correct because his predictions were 'accurate' is not logical (McCabe, 1998, p.2121).

Much has been made of the nature and the shape of Hubbert's curve. Hubbert himself did not produce a mathematical explanation for the shape of his curve until 1981. In the meantime, he speculated that the curve might be bell-shaped, a speculation which his sceptics have turned against him (see, for example, McCabe, 1998). At other times it is claimed that the curve was a logistical curve (Bentley, 2002). Other interpretations exist (see for example, Deffeyes, 2001; Laherrère, 2001a, 2001b, and, of course, Wood, Long and Morehouse, 2004).

What is significant in this context is that a series of geologists have carried on and developed variations of his method utilizing world wide field production data, supplementing these with other forms of trend analysis. This has led at least one USGS geologist to dismiss them as 'trendologists' (Charpentier, R.R., 2003), warning about the dangers of relying extrapolations of past trends as a means of prediction. In fact both ASPO adherents and the their opponents largely agree on the geological methods of estimating ultimate recoverable reserves mentioned earlier in this chapter. Where they differ lies in the use of past trends to predict the future and the degree to which these trends will change in the future due to technology. (For a good explanation of the use of trends here, see Laherrère, 2003, 2002, 2001a, 2001b, 1996. For critical reviews, see Lynch, 2003, 2001, 1996, and McCabe, 1998.)

The point here is not to agree or disagree with this ASPO/King Hubbert tradition of analyzing ultimately recoverable reserves. What is indisputable is that a group of (largely retired) petroleum engineers and geologists has introduced a new vivacity to a relatively old debate as to when the 'oil will run out'. What is new to this debate, and must be taken seriously, is that this relatively little group has drawn attention to the future problems of the transition from the (relatively) easily accessible, and cheap resources of conventional petroleum to the more complicated, costly, and uncertain non-conventional petroleum sources. One may argue whether a peak exists, if at all, and, if does exist, what kind of peak it might be, and in what year it might occur. One can argue over the what the 'driving forces' behind the peak might be. One can distinguish between a longer run depletion of oil and a shorter run capacity constraint. What has happened is that there exists a new awareness about the problems of oil supply.

Yet another credit to the 'neo Hubbertians' is that their focus on shortages may have contributed to the US Geological Survey's careful retooling of its means of estimating future oil and gas resources, a topic to which we shall now turn.

*How much is enough? The US Geological Survey: newer and better methodology?*

The US Geological reserve estimates mentioned in Table 9.1 (Wood, Long and Morehouse from the *Survey World Petroleum Assessment 2000*) are based on a method which encompasses up-to-date developments in petroleum and geological knowledge. Whereas previously, the US Geological Survey had based its evaluations on the contents of world petroleum basins, and (for the US only) on geological 'plays', the *Assessment 2000* introduced a new and revolutionary concept, that of 'Total Petroleum Systems'(TPS), 'the essential elements (source rock, reservoir rock, seal rock and overburden rock) and processes (generation-migration-accumulation and trap formation) as well as all genetically related petroleum that occurs in seeps, shows and accumulations, both discovered and undiscovered, whose provenance is a pod of closely related pods of active source rock' (US Geological Survey, 2004, p. PS-4). This definition was the result of a decade of work 'identifying, mapping, and naming' its elements (ibid). Characteristic of the system was its orientation towards the fluid element, distinguishable by the different characteristics of known crude types, and working away from the specific crude type and its source (pod) rock to identify known and potential resources from the latest petroleum geological and engineering knowledge, This allowed the mapping of the individual TPS in 'three dimensional space thorough time to locate, define, and evaluate' its potential for undiscovered hydrocarbons. 159 TPSs were identified and analyzed on a worldwide basis, exclusive of the USA. These were analyzed on an Assessment Unit (AU) basis, allowing for discovered fields within the AU to be 'the basis for the discovered history segments which along with additional trap characteristics, were used to help estimate the number of grown, undiscovered oil and gas fields in that AU' (ibid, PS-6). The results were digitalized. The methods used were reviewed by the American Association of Petroleum Geologists, the National Academy of Science and members of the World Energy Congress. And when *World Petroleum Assessment 2000* was published, there were no fewer than 30 000 pages of texts, diagrams, maps, and tables made available for public perusal either through the provision of free CD diskettes or as web documents. The US Geological Survey was unequivocal in its results: 'The grand total of the known volumes [oil and natural gas] from each TPS is 2.4 trillion BOE [barrels of oil equivalent]' (ibid.)

There were three other characteristics of *World Petroleum Assessment 2000* of interest here: firstly, geological characteristics were the sole set of criteria for resource assessment, socio-economic factors being deliberately eschewed (US Geological Survey, 2000, p. IN-5). Secondly, the USGS deliberately did not attempt to assess ultimate recoverable resources: rather what was done was to 'forecast the potential for additional reserves to be added in a 30 year time frame, 1995-2025' (ibid, pp. IN-5-IN-6). Finally, the USGS may have 'thrown caution to the winds' in estimating 'reserve growth' based on USreserve accounting practices and tacking it onto their TPS estimates for the rest of the world (see Appendix 9A on this debate).

The US Geological Survey, in adopting a 30-year time frame, neatly sidestepped the question of whether their calculations were really a form of ultimate reserve estimates. Neither did the USGS give any clue as to any possible relationship between the two variables. Most importantly, the USGS has neither given any information as to the costs necessary to exploit the resources remaining in these TPSs, nor has the USGS any form of scenario for a global peak production. (The peak estimates in Table 9.1 are derived from *World Petroleum Assessment 2000* by the US Energy Information Administration.)

But, perhaps the most serious criticisms of this study have been made as to its inclusion of 'reserve growth' figures. 'Reserve growth' is the phenomenon in which estimates as to the amount of oil or gas recoverable from a field tend to grow over time. Lacking information as to possible world wide reserve growth rates, it has been charged, the USGS simply took the US history of reserve growth and applied it to their world figures inflating them by perhaps as much as 44 percent. If one deflates USGS figures in Table 9.1 by 44 percent, it would place them at or below Campbell's and Laherrère's ultimate reserve estimates of 1900 to 2250 billion barrels.

**How much is enough? Data reliability issues**

Whether or not one believes in the reliability of the Hubbert curve in predicting the timing of a production peak, the issues of data reliability deserve consideration. Of the many reliability issues here, two stand out in importance: the calculation of national oil reserves (and their implications for calculating world-wide reserves), and the issues behind corporate 'booking' and 'rebooking' of the reserves in their inventories.

*How much is enough? The problem of reserves and politics*

The very process of calculating global reserves is fraught with difficulties. Firstly, one must ask oneself, what is the nature of what is being counted. Is it crude oil, or crude oil and natural gas liquids (NGLs) many of which are critical refinery inputs? What conversion factors are being used for different qualities of oil? In calculating reserves, should one take into account the additions to reserves made through the refining process. Is the authority including only 'conventional' oil, or 'nonconventional oil' (i.e. crude refined from Athabascan tar sands or the Orinoco deposits in Venezuela)? Some examples might suffice here. In 2002 the *Oil and Gas Journal* (December 23) added Canada tar sands reserves to its reserve figures, but omitted the Orinoco heavy oil reserves. The *BP Statistical Review*, another key resource in this regard, did not follow the *Oil and Gas Journal*'s lead and did not include tar sands in its reserve figures, but it did include this unconventional oil in its production figures. The following year the *BP Statistical Review* included both figures.

Secondly, most of the world's future reserves are owned by governments. There is considerable evidence that nationally reported oil and NGL reserve statistics may be politically biased.

Perhaps the best case in point here is the so-called 'OPEC paper barrel puzzle' illustrated in Table 9.2. In introducing their quota systems, the OPEC producers took nationally reported reserves as an allocation device: the more the reserves, the higher the allocation As can be seen, in the period 1985 through 1989, the major OPEC producers upgraded their 'proved reserves' from 363.7 billion bbls. to 725.4 billion barrels. While there may be other explanations to this upward revision, reserve analysts have been quick to note that the timing of the revisions was convenient.

**Table 9.2    Calculating reserves – The OPEC 'proven reserve paper barrels puzzle'**

|  | Saudi Arabia | Abu Dhabi | Iran | Iraq | Kuwait | Venezuela |
|---|---|---|---|---|---|---|
|  | | | billion bbls. crude | | | |
| 1982 | 163.4 | 28 | 58 | 31 | 65.4 | 17.9 |
| Year of change | (1989) | (1987) | (1987) | (1988) | (1985) | (1986) |
| 1990 | 257.5 | 92.2 | 92.9 | 100.0 | 90.0 | 56.3 |
| 2000 | 259.2 | 92.2 | 89.7 | 112.5 | 94.0 | 77.8 |

*Source*: Simmons (2003)

This criticism is not limited to a few members of ASPO. For instance, the US Geological Survey, in making their global estimates of 1994, comment succinctly on the revised Saudi Arabian figures, 'We could not account for 66 billion barrels included in Saudi Arabia's published reserve numbers' (Masters et al, 1994, p.4). (An indication of the size of this discrepancy is that 66 billion bbls alone is roughly one-and-half times the size of the total probable reserves of the North American Continent.)

Also significant here could be the fact that while Saudi Arabia and Kuwait increased their reserves by a total of 118 billion barrels, their jointly owned reserves located in the Neutral Zone were not upgraded. One might note as well that while reserves were upgraded by over 90 percent, actual OPEC discoveries during this period were on the order of 10 billion bbls of oil (Laherrère, 2004, p. 5). It is therefore unlikely that these upgrades are the result of drilled evidence alone.

It is unlikely that OPEC countries alone are 'playing politics' with reserve figures. Such figures can be far too important for other national objectives to prevent national governments from tinkering. For example, in Russia, Special Law #153, November 11, 2003, has classified all information dealing with in-place reserves, production or consumption of oil and gas as state secrets, the revelation of which can lead to criminal prosecution. In 2004 this law was used against BP for publishing such figures in the widely circulated *BP Statistical Review*, reportedly for underestimating Russian proved reserves at some 60 billion barrels.

Evidence of such political tampering has led some to argue that world oil resources are vastly overstated. Campbell (2003), relying on field data provided by Petroconsultants (now IHL), for instance, has argued that politics has led to an overvaluation of world proved reserves by a factor of 35 percent.

Another related, but receding, problem is that of recording reserves. More and more nations are reporting oil reserves in terms of a mean or mode probability value, enabling some consistency in figures across countries. The US (since Canada's defection in 2003) is the only nation to rely solely on proved reserves as the basis for its national reserve calculation.

While designed to please the US Securities Exchange Commission (SEC) and the oil companies (Wall Street wants certainties, not probabilities), the US system creates problems on a global scale. As the major independent government source for calculation of global oil and gas remains the US Department of the Interior's Geological Survey (USGS), the source for half of the estimates in Table 9.1, the USGS data sources are heavily dependent on US data. This is particularly the case with the controversial problem of 'reserve growth', a concept which is being used in the rest of the world (ROW) and accounts for much of the differences in the figures in Table 9.1.

Nor is the United States the only 'miscreant'. The countries of the Former Soviet Union are still using the Soviet reserve classification system. Here reserves are classified into two categories, 'explored' (with subcategories A, B, and C1) and 'preliminarily estimated' (category C2). What is important in this context is that the private Russian oil companies are increasingly conforming to Society of Petroleum

Engineering/World Petroleum Congress specifications enabling their figures to be more easily aggregated in an international context.

## How much is enough? The problem of bookings

Ultimately, most governmental oil reserve calculations are based on the reserve 'booking' practices of the oil companies. Also dependent on the annual recording of corporate oil reserve depletion and gains are the equity markets on which shares of privately owned oil companies are traded. In this latter case, the annual booking of corporate oil reserves is vital for estimating the market value of its traded shares. This 'booking' and 'rebooking' of proved reserves is a highly specialized field. Virtually all the professional petroleum engineering associations have strict codes of conduct which are to be followed by estimators and auditors alike.

Perhaps nowhere are 'booking' practices so closely followed as they are in the United States. Here the US Securities Exchange Commission has particularly precise rules as to what categorizes various types of proved reserves. (It should be noted here that this precision is also open to interpretation, a major complaint of the submitting firms.)[3] The annual 20F forms required by the SEC require information on worldwide holdings of the registering companies often run into the hundreds of pages. It is not unheard of for the SEC to require changes in corporate annual bookings.

Thus, although with certain reservations, one could expect that the degree of success of corporate exploration programs might be found in their equity market reports as this information is critical for. US equity market corporate valuations. Here there are two sorts of evidence available as to how registering firms increase their resource base, over-all systemic evidence based on analyses of SEC 20F forms, and the recent difficulties which the super majors individually have had with the booking system.

With regard to systemic trends, there are two studies which are of some interest. The first of these, a recent US Energy Information Administration (2004a) study of the 20 major oil firms in the US has found that one can divide oil firms into two categories: 'makers' and 'buyers'. 'Makers' are those firms 'making' additional reserves through development of properties which they have either leased or owned. 'Buyers' are those firms which tend to 'buy' reserves through corporate acquisitions. It was hypothesized that the difference between 'buyers' and 'makers' lay in their

---

3    For example, in deciding whether an increase in proved reserves through improved recovery qualifies or not, the SEC has the following principles: 'Reserves which can be predicted economically through application of improved recovery techniques (such as fluid injection) are included in the proved classification when successful testing by a pilot project, or the operation of an installed recovery programme in the reservoir provides support for the engineering analysis on which the project or programme was based. In a few limited circumstances, such as in the case of certain fields in the North Sea, the Office of Engineers of the SEC will review estimates of Proved Reserves attributable to fluid injection, in light of the strength of the evidence presented by the registrant in support of a contention that enhanced recovery will be achieved (Heiberg et al, 2002).

finding costs, 'buyers' tending to have higher finding costs than 'makers'. The results of their analysis are summarized in Table 9.3. It was hypothesized that the buyers would substitute merger acquisition of 'makers' for investing in exploration and development themselves. those firms for which finding costs for their own reserves are relatively high, while 'makers' tend to be tempting targets for 'buyers'. While the statistical significance of this 'substitution' (buying for making) hypothesis is just below the threshold of significance, it is likely that the 'finders' have higher over-all rates of return, an additional attraction for the 'buyers'.

**Table 9.3    Average finding cost and return on investment for the twenty largest US oil firms, 1997–2002**

| Company Type | U.S. Finding Costs ( $/bbl oil equivalent) | Return on Investment (pct) |
|---|---|---|
| Makers | 6.83 | 12.71 |
| Buyers | 7.88 | 10.25 |

*Source*: U.S. Energy Information Agency (2004a), p. 82

A second study, performed by Laherrère, has found on the basis of booking data, that proved reserves in the true 90 percent probability classification have in fact been falling rapidly. Laherrère took the annually booked increases in proved reserves in the period since 1970 and divided these by the total of the newly booked and downwardly revised reserves on an annual basis. This calculation should yield a percentage of 90 percent, with, of course, annual variations. Yet, on this basis (see Graph 9.2 on next page) Laherrère has found that 'proved reserves' were only 75 percent probable in the early 1970s and are 'trending towards 55 percent in 2005' (Laherrère, 2004, p. 9).

Nor have the super majors fared exceptionally well in recent years. That equity markets have a major role to play was made obvious in Royal Dutch Shell's re-evaluation of their 'proved reserves' first announced on January 9, 2004. At issue was their reduction of proved reserves from 20 billion bbls of oil equivalent (boe) by some 3.9 billion bbls oil equivalent (2.7 billion bbls of crude, 7.2 trillion ft$^3$ natural gas). Royal Dutch Shell's problems were not made any easier when a few months later, they again revised their proved reserves figures downwards – reportedly due to reserve revisions of the Macaroni and Brutus fields in the Gulf of Mexico, and natural gas (Maui field in New Zealand, the Norwegian Ormen Lange field , Sable Island in Canada). Total downward revisions in 2004 were some 4474 million boe. The consequences of these moves have been dramatic, including a fall in share prices, the dismissal of leading executives, and the commencement of lawsuits against the 'offending parties'.[4] Royal Dutch Shell was also fined a total of 151 million dollars

---

4    Several factors have been seen as critical to this reserve reclassification: a lack of sufficient investment commitment (fields in Nigeria, Norway, New Zealand, and Australia); lack of market demand (gas fields in Australia), insufficient regulatory approval (the Kazakh Kashgan field, and fields in Italy and the Netherlands), overestimation of field performance

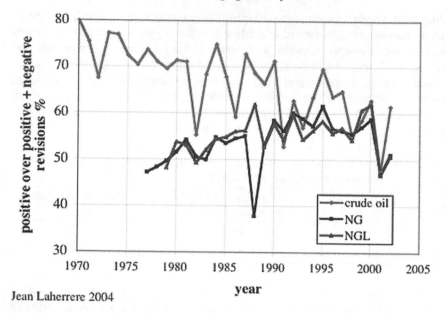

Jean Laherrere 2004

**Figure 9.2    US proved reserves: a downward trend?**

by the two investigative bodies, the US Security Exchange Commission and the British Financial Services Authority (Sever, 2004).

Nor is Royal Dutch Shell alone here. ChevronTexaco has increased its holdings of proved oil and gas reserves by 14 percent in the period 1998–2002. Yet at the same time, its production of oil and gas has fallen by 15 percent in the same period, despite repeated promises to increase its production (Berenson, 2004, p.F-2). This has the effect of improving the reserve replacement ratio, a measure by which Wall Street sets great store, but is an improvement due more to a decline in production than a de facto increase in exploration and development successes.

BP too may be having its problems. Its 2003 form 20F submission to the SEC reported a net loss in its reserves of 546 million barrels for the year. (This was decreased to a loss of only 523 million barrels at the insistence of the SEC.) BP did not reduce its estimates of proved reserves at the Norwegian Ormen Lange field as did its partners, but sold its field interests to the state-owned Danish Oil and Natural Gas Company in late 2004.[5]

---

(fields in the Middle East and Nigeria); and various failures to technically satisfy SEC requirements in reporting proved reserves.

5    While all agree that the natural gas reserves at Ormen Lange are in the order of 400 billion m³, the percentage of these regarded as proved has been downgraded. Royal Dutch Shell downgraded this portion from 60 percent to 20 percent, Norsk Hydro reduced its estimates

Of the four super majors, only ExxonMobil appears to have increased its proved reserves recently (from 10 953 million bbls in 1998 to 12 075 million bbls in 2003), while holding its annual production rate steady at around 890 million bbls per annum.

Yet, while cautionary, the Royal Dutch Shell story may be only a portion of the picture. Equity markets pay close attention to proven reserve figures and to the ratio between total proved reserves and corporate annual production, the reserve replacement ratio Royal Dutch Shell and BP were not the only firms encountering problems. Several smaller firms have written down their proved reserves, and more are expected to follow.[6]

The financial community has its share of sceptics about industry's current problems. Proved reserves, they point out, enable capitalization of huge projects which are becoming more and more typical of the industry. This in turn leads to optimism as to their definition, which is then  challenged by the US Securities Exchange Commission.

*How much is enough? Reserves and bookings – a cautionary note*

Do the problems of differing national reserve practices, and a recent wave of debookings support the more pessimistic evaluations of the world ultimate recoverable crude oil reserves? Here a word of caution is in order. Firstly, not all national booking practices are influenced by a political need to exaggerate ultimate reserves. For example, the omission of the Neutral Zone from the 'paper barrel' OPEC upgrades, mentioned earlier, can have alternative explanations (for example, it may have been difficult to renegotiate the terms under which the two countries share 'paper barrel' or other reserve gains from this petroliferous area).

Similarly, SEC bookings and debookings are common in the oil industry, normally occurring with the rise and fall of crude oil prices. They can also be due other factors than an inability to find oil. Thus, a transfer of proved hydrocarbon resources as part of a state participation agreement, agreements quite common in the international industry, would require SEC rebooking of that portion of proved resources transferred. What is interesting here, however, is that debookings normally occur in a period with falling oil prices. What has happened recently is that they are occurring in a period of rising oil prices. This has led to claims from the financial community that oil firms have been overly optimistic, and that a rash of debookings might be expected to continue (Sever, 2004).

---

by 30 percent. ExxonMobil and Statoil did not change their bookings which remained at 30 percent. BP alone has resisted this trend, insisting that its original booking of 80 percent is the correct estimate of proved reserves (Sever, 1984)

6   El Paso Corporation recategorized 35 percent of its reserves in February 2004 and underwent investigation by the SEC. Another US independent, Forest Oil, downgraded its proved reserves by 25 percent (Sever, 2004).

Finally, it is difficult to find out what exactly is happening due to the existence of multiple practices of reserve recording. The industry is irritated about the 'arcane' SEC definitions of proved reserves. Countries retain their own reserve classifications. Firms have their own reserve classifications which may or may not fit those of the different countries within which they operate.

*How much is enough? Towards a consensus?*

What is interesting about the oil resource debate is that despite its acrimony it might be said to be approaching a consensus, both with regard to the existence of a 'crisis in supplies' and to the problems of reserve classifications and bookings.

In looking at the 'supplies crisis' one can observe the following phenomena: Firstly, the US Geological Survey TPS has been praised by many Hubbert analysts as being an improvement on previous resource estimations, particularly with regard to their inventory methodology.[7] It is notable that much criticism of the US Geological Survey's 2000 figures rest on the problems of US and foreign reserve calculations, and on assumptions based on these which may or may not be questionable.

Secondly, the question of a 'peak' in oil consumption is now taken seriously by many on both sides in the debate. Many members of ASPO now regard themselves, not so much as neo Hubbertians, but as analysts of petroleum cycles and trends. They tend to be more multiple peakologists or plateau-ologists than strict adherents of Hubbert's original methodological approach. What separates ASPO and bodies such as the USGS today lies more in their disparate methods of arriving at ultimate recoverable reserve figures, than in whether future production may be constrained. The point is that there could well be a peak (or perhaps a series of peaks) and a consensus appears to be forming here.

Thirdly, the existence of a peak, a series of peaks, or a plateau does not mean that ample supplies of crude oil will not be available to those who can pay for them. The question is one of whether, given the volatility of world crude prices, markets can smooth the transition to other hydrocarbon (or non-hydrocarbon) fuels.

And, fourthly, that geology was the only criterion used in the *Survey 2000* is understandable, but, given that 77 percent of the TPSs with estimated volumes of more than 5 billion BOE (cumulative production plus remaining reserves) are located either in North Africa/Middle East or in the Former Soviet Union, the geopolitical facets of future sources of oil and gas are certainly challenging in and of themselves.

These factors (and others) have been characterised by the US Geological Survey's Magoon (2003) as the 'Big Rollover', a period of transition which will inevitably present the oil industry with some severe challenges.

---

7    On the other hand, the USGS departed from the Delphic method of making estimates, a better method than that used by the USGS to estimate ultimate reserves in this last study where estimates are based alone on six values estimated by a single geologist per TPS.

In addition to these developments on the crisis front, the degree of classification and statistical 'static' presently confusing the debate is likely to diminish, rather than increase in the future. This is most probable in the field of national reserve classification. The uniform measures that have been pushed by the efforts of the Society of Petroleum Engineers, the World Petroleum Congress, and the American Association of Petroleum Geologists has yielded fruit internationally. Here a committee of the United Nations has been working for eight years to address the problems of creating a uniform reserve and resource terminology. Similarly, the US Securities and Exchange Commission has voiced an interest in this process, and may eventually change its classifications system so that it is more in accord with agreed upon international norms. What is particularly encouraging here is that the financial and geological communities are attempting to establish a uniform reserve classification system which is better suited to the demands of the former.

**References**

Bentley, R.W. (2002), 'Viewpoint: Global Oil and Gas Depletion: An Overview', *Energy Policy*, **30**, pp. 189-205.

Berenson, A. (2004).'An Oil Enigma: Production Falls Even as Reserves Rise', *The New York Times*, June 6, p. F-2.

British Petroleum (2004), *Statistical Review of World Energy*, (London: British Petroleum).

Campbell, C.J. (2003), The Essence of Oil and Gas Depletion, (London: Multi-Science Publishing).

Charpentier, R.R. (2003), *The Future of Petroleum: Optimism, Pessimism or Something Else?* USGS Open-File Report 03-137.

Deffeyes, K.S. (2001), *Hubbert's Peak: The Impending World Oil Shortage*, New Jersey: Princeton University Press.

Heiberg, S., P. Blystad and E. Soendenaa (2002), 'Resource Accounts, National and International Standardization', ppt. presented at the *4th National Data Repository Meeting*, Stavanger, Norway, 5-7 March. Accessed October 5, 2004. http:/www.posc.org/technical/ndr/ndr4/Sigurd_Heiberg.ppt.

Hubbert, M.K. (1950), 'Energy from Fossil Fuels', The American Association for the *Advancement of Science Centennial*, Washington: American Association for the Advancement of Science, pp. 171-177.

Laherrère, J. (1997), 'Multi-Hubbert Modeling', July, available at http://www. hubbertpeak.com/Laherrère/multihub.htm. Accessed July 17, 2004.

_____(2001a), 'Comments', www.oilcrisis.com/Laherrère/Kuuskraa/. Accessed July 26, 2004.

_____(2001b), 'Estimates of Oil Reserves'presented at the EMF/IEA/IIASA meeting, Laxemburg, Austria, June 19, available at www.oil.crisis.com/Laherrère. Accessed July 17, 2004.

_____ (2004), 'Shell's Reserves Decline and SEC Obsolete Rules', article in preparation for Energy Politics, 27 February, available at www.oilcrisis.com/ Laherrère/ . Accessed July 26, 2004.

Lynch, M.C. (1996), 'The Analysis and Forecasting of Petroleum Supply', in D. H. El Mallakh, ed. *Energy Watchers VII*, International Research Center for Energy and Economic Development.

_____ (2001), 'Forecasting Oil Supply: Theory and Practice', *Quarterly Review of Economics and Finance*, 422, 2, pp. 373-389.

_____ (2003), 'The New Pessimism about Petroleum Resources: Debunking the Hubbert Model (and Hubbert Modelers)', *Minerals and Energy*, **18**(1), pp. 21-32.

McCabe, P.J. (1998), 'Energy Resources – Cornucopia or Empty Barrel?' *AAPG Journal*, **82** (11), November, pp. 2119-2134.

Magoon, L.B. (2002?), 'Are We Running Out of Oil?', USGS poster display, available at http://www.oilcrisis.com/magoon/ . Accessed November 4, 2004.

Masters, C., E. Attanasi and D. Root (1994), 'World Petroleum Assessment and Analysis' (US Geological Survey, National Center, Reston, Va) *Proceedings of the 14th World Petroleum Congress,* Stavanger, Norway, New York: John Wiley and Sons.

Morehouse, D.F. (1997), 'The Intricate Puzzle of Oil and Gas "Reserves Growth"' *Natural Gas Monthly*, US Energy Information Administration, July 1997, pp. vii-xx.

*Oil and Gas Journal* (2002), 'World Wide Reserves Increase as Production Holds Steady', December 23, pp. 113-144.

Sever, M. (2004), 'Booking and Rebooking Oil Reserves', *Geotimes* (September) 4pp. available at http://www.geotimes.org/sept04/resources.html. Accessed November 5, 2004.

Simmons, M.R. (2003), 'The Saudi Arabian Oil Miracle', ppt presentation at the 'Conference: Future of Global Oil Supply-Saudi Arabia', Washington D.C: Simmons & Company International for the Center for Strategic and International Studies, February 24, http://www.csis.org/energy/ . Accessed December 29, 2003.

United States Geological Survey (2003), *USGS World Petroleum Assessment 2000: New Estimates of Undiscovered Oil and Natural Gas, Natural Gas Liquids, including Reserve Growth outside the United States*, Reston, Virginia: USGS Fact Sheet FS-062-03, June.

_____ (2003–2004), *World Petroleum Assessment 2000— Description and Results*, US Geological Digital Data Series – DDS-60, energy.cr.usgs.gov/oilgas/wep/products/dds60/tables.html. Accessed July 26, 2004.

Wood, J., G. Long and D. Morehouse (2004), *Long Term World Oil Supply Scenarios: The Future is Neither as Bleak nor asRosy as Some Assert*, Washington D.C: US Department of Energy, Energy Information Administration www.eia.doe.gov/pub/ oil_gas/petroleum/feature_articles/2004/worldoilsupply/pdf/itwos04.pdf. Accessed November 10, 2004.

**Appendix 9A: The Puzzle of 'Reserve Growth'**

*What are the issues?*

Perhaps no other issue divides geologist reserve estimators more bitterly than does the issue of reserve growth. The term (also called 'ultimate recovery appreciation') refers to the phenomenon in which estimates as to the amount of oil or gas recoverable from a field tend to grow over time. In part, this is due to an initial tendency to conservatively estimate the amount of recoverable hydrocarbons. Such conservatism leads to upward revisions of what can be ultimately recovered as the field operators become better acquainted with the structures involved. Morehouse (1997) lists several causes for this upward revision:

- The proved area of a reservoir may be increased either by successful extension drilling or through development drilling experience;
- A new, hitherto unknown, economically productive reservoir may be discovered in a field;
- There may be a performance-based positive upward revision of a field's natural reserves;
- There may be completions within existing wells to utilize resources which were bypassed in the initial drilling plans; and
- The economics of recovery may improve to such a degree that it becomes profitable to 'drill up' the field more thoroughly (p.xiii).

Other factors affect such upward revisions: the physical complexity of the field concerned will affect the amount of time to 'prove it up'; technological advances may increase recovery factors; operating firm risk preferences may change reserve booking practices; environmental factors may delay field development or field physical isolation may prevent development until transportation or other infrastructure becomes available (ibid). The acute reader will note the use of the term 'proved reserves' in this context. In fact, the most thorough studies of reserve growth have been made in the United States, where the most extensive data (from around 25 000 fields) has been collected over the greatest length of time.

It is this statistical basis, in particular the necessity to calculate reserve growth on the ultra conservative 'proved reserves' definition, a definition which is the source of contention between the US Geological Survey and its critics, Campbell and Laherrère being the most outspoken. The question can be put simply. Assume two different national reserve 'booking' requirements: in one country, country A, 'proved reserves' are those reserves 90 percent probable of economic development; in the other, country B, 'proved reserves' are estimated as being those proved and probable reserves above a 50 percent probability level. For simplicity let us assume two identical fields, one in each country. In both countries, the owner running Monte Carlo simulations finds that with a 90 percent probability the field concerned contains at least 10 million bbls. And there are at least a total of 50 million bbls reserves at a

50 percent probability level. In country A, the owner looks at the reserves and books 10 million bbls recoverable at a 90 percent probability. In country B, the owner books 50 million bbls. (Note that the latter is the practice recommended by the SPE, the WPC and the AAPG.) Now, as the chances are 50 percent in both country A and country B that the fields hold more than 50 million bbls, and 50 percent that they hold less, the odds are that the fields each contain 50 million barrels. What will happen over time?

Assuming that technology is not an issue and that prices remain constant over time, in country A, the field reserve estimates are likely to increase over time, perhaps even by factor of four, from 10 million bbls to 50 million bbls even without improved recovery technologies, while in country B, they are liable not to increase at all. While there is nothing wrong with this, should one assume that because of country A's reserve growth of 40 million bbls, that reserves booked by the owner in country B will also grow by 400 percent, one could make a fundamental error.[8]

That this issue is vital to the different projections of ultimate recoverable reserves should be clear from the comparative estimates made by the U.S. Geological Survey in its 2000 and 1994 Assessments and those of Campbell and Laherrère in Table 9.1. Recall that the US Geological Survey upped its estimate from 2272 billion barrels in 1994 to 3003 billions in 2000. Recall as well that, for example, Laherrère's (2001) mean estimate was 2250 billion barrels, roughly the same as the 1994 USGS study.

As can be seen from Table 9A.1, reserve growth is the basis of a revised reserve classification system whereby the classification 'Identified Reserves' is replaced by two categories, 'Reserve Growth' and 'Remaining Reserves'. Reserve growth takes center stage in the new assessment. While generalizations are hazardous here in that the methods and means of calculation between the 1994 and the 2000 Survey Assessments have notable differences, it would appear that the mean estimate of worldwide undiscovered oil is increased from 582.6 billion barrels of oil to 732 billions. This is generally acknowledged to be an improvement due to the better methods employed in the petroleum system inventory classification utilized in the latter study. However reclassifying Identified Reserves in the manner indicated increases this reserve category (redefined) from 1103.2 billion bbls to 1579 billion bbls, an increase of 476 billion bbls, some 43.1 percent of the original total. Without this revision the total reserves for the 2000 Survey would be 2545 billion bbls. Such an estimate is not far off the 2272.5 billions estimate of the 1994 Survey or from the 2250 billion bbls estimated by the Laherrère (2001). In other words some 76 percent of the increase in conventional oil reserve estimates in the *Assessment 2000* is alone due to the results of this revised method of accounting.

---

8   Note, however, that this would not apply for company bookings if these were made in accordance with the US SEC. Here international companies must define their proved reserves uniformly throughout the world according to SEC standards. However, this has little to do with individual country estimates of proved reserves over-all, country by country. These would follow international practices more or less as described above.

**Table 9A.1 U.S. Geological Survey World Petroleum Assessments 1994 and 2000 compared**

|  | 1994 Assessment | 2000 Assessment | |
|---|---|---|---|
|  | World Total | ROW[a] | USA |
|  | billion bbls | | |
| Reserve Categories | | | |
| Cumulative Production | 698.6 | 539[c] | 171[c] |
| Identified Reserves[b] | 1,103.2 | -- | -- |
| Undiscovered[d,e] | 582.6[c] | 649[c] | 83[c] |
| Reserve Growth[d,f] | -- | 612[c] | 76[c] |
| Remaining Reserves | -- | 859[c] | 32[c] |
| Totals | | 2,659[c] | 362[c] |
| World Totals | 2272.5[g] | 3,021[c] | |

Notes: [a]ROW = Rest of World.
[b]Identified reserves = national variations of proved+probable+possible reserves.
[c]Mean values.
[d]Conventional oil reserves.
[e]1994 rock source method, 2000 petroleum system inventory classification.
[f]Remaining reserves =Known volumes – Cumulative production.
[g]Mode.

*Sources*: Masters, Attanasi, and Root (1994): U.S. Geological Survey (2003).

Two questions arise in this context: firstly, are there problems with the calculation of reserve growth? And, secondly, are there problems with the US Geological Survey's use of ROW reserves growth in its *Assessment 2000*, as these are based on US ratios in terms of past US reserve growth, what might be termed a 'US analogue'?[9]

*Are there problems modelling 'reserve growth'*

To begin with, there is evidence that there have been problems in the American modelling of 'reserve growth'. To understand these, mention will be first made of reserve growth models before proceeding to a discussion of the problems associated with these models.

Simplifying somewhat, all models of reserve growth are a variation of Arrington's pioneering 1962 study (Arrington, 1962). Using proprietary reservoir data and looking at each of his company's reservoirs year-by-year, Arrington mapped the percentage changes in each year's net change in his company's estimates of that reservoir's proved reserves. In graphical form, the 'Y' axis representing the growth in estimated proved reserves as a factor of the original estimates and the 'X' axis the number of post discovery years, reserve growth appeared as an asymptotic curve

---

9   A prominent ASPO geologist has compared this use of two different standards in proved reserve calculation with directly comparing measurements in inches and feet with those in the metric system without taking into account that the measures are not directly comparable.

with yearly percentage increases declining steadily. Since Arrington's study, many geologists and petroleum engineers have elaborated on his approach using differing mathematical models to arrange a 'fit' between their specific data and a reservoir 'growth' curve. However, few of these studies really attempted to come to grips with the nature of the data being 'pushed' through their models. (For a review of these studies, see Morehouse, 1997; Schmoker and Klett, 2003; Root, Attanasi, Mast and Gautier, 1996.)

As might be expected with any data series combining a enormous set of longitudinal corporate proprietary data series each influenced by individual corporate booking practices and calculation of 'proved reserves', there are not a few problems involved in calculating reserve growth. Morehouse (1997, p. xiv) lists the following:

- There appear to be problems with the early data series collected. This has led to highly erratic results in the intial periods for many of the early fields in the sampling.
- Appreciation rates for those fields where production commenced before 1947 are on average six times larger. This is important because oil production from those US lower 48 fields discovered in 1920–1930 account for 20 percent of *today's* total estimated recoverable reserves for the area.
- Difficulties seem to have been experienced in assigning discoveries to the proper year. (Note that this problem is one which reserve growth modelers share with the ASPO revisionists mentioned in Chapter 9.) This means that it becomes hard to place initial reserve calculations to a particular year in the development of those fields.
- Various series do not seem to correspond to each other. Thus, the American Gas Association data on the discovery and production of associated/dissolved gas found with oil yields nonsensical results when compared to the American Petroleum Institute's data for crude oil. Since the two should be associated with one another, this incongruence suggests that there may be something wrong with either or both data sets.
- There is a problem with 'outliers' in the data sets, in particular those fields which have had exceptional rates of reserve growth. While these fields are not the majority of the fields in models, they account for far more than their numbers to reserve growth trends for the fields in the data sets. This in turn leads to problems in the statistical 'smoothing' required for model projections of over-all reserve growth.
- Reserve growth tends to be different for different regions in the United States. Thus reserve growth rates for Texas are higher than those for the rest of the lower 48. (See, for example, the varying regional graphing results for the US in Klett, 2003; and Root, Attanasi, Mast and Gautier, 1996.)

*The 2000 assessment: are there problems with the US analogue?*

Given that there are statistical and methodological problems with the US practice, is the use of reserve growth calculations in the US Geological Survey's *World Petroleum Assessment 2000* justified? Here there also appear to be problems.

Firstly, what is the basis of the calculations being made? The 2000 Assessment is coy about this. In the US studies, the basis is 'proved reserves' plus the cumulative volumes exploited to that point. The first of these, 'proved reserves' is a rather shaky category as is evidenced in Chapter 9's discussion varying corporate interpretations of what constitutes 'proved'. The 2000 Assessment does not mention proved reserves. Rather the basis is 'known petroleum volume' which is defined as 'the sum of the cumulative production and remaining reserves' (USGS, 2003, p.AR-5). The definition of cumulative production is fairly clear, but nowhere is 'remaining petroleum reserves' precisely defined: 'For this assessment, remaining reserves were calculated by subtracting cumulative production from known volumes.' What one is left with is a circular definition of remaining reserves. One still does not know what remaining reserves are. Laherrère and others with access to the proprietary Petroconsult (now IHS) databases also used by the USGS have stated that 'remaining reserves' are in fact 'proved reserves'. Here, the question becomes one of defining proved reserves. This can be difficult to do if in other countries firms unlisted in the US stock exchanges do not book their reserves in a US Security Exchange Commission approved manner. If this is the case, are the 'remaining reserves' used by the USGS in its calculations at all compatible to US proved reserve figures? And if these two categories are incompatible, then the basis of the reserve growth rate for the Rest Of the World (in Table 9A.1) defined in terms of 'known volumes' is also incompatible.

On the other hand, if 'remaining reserves' are not proved reserves, then they could be the result of any of a multiple of forms of national or corporate reserve reporting, and, given that known petroleum volumes are the sum of remaining reserves and cumulative production, this international multiplicand will be even further off the US multiplicand used in conjunction with the US analogue 30-year reserve growth multiplier.

Secondly, there are the additional problems which the USGS and others have encountered in examining US reserve growth rate. Here, despite the advantages of being data from the one and same country, any calculation of US reserve growth rate has been beset with problems, as discussed in the previous section. Curiously, those responsible for the 2000 Assessment have used the same sources to justify their including reserve growth rates and to state that the statistical bases are insufficient. Thus, for example, Attanasi and Root (1993) are used as a justification for including reserve growth (USGS, 2003, p. RG-3) and simultaneously for the contention that 'successive field-size estimates were not sufficiently reliable to develop world-level reserve growth functions' (USGS, 2003, RG-10).

The end result is that the USGS comes down on the side of including a reserve growth dimension. '[A] greater error would be to not consider world-level reserve growth at all' (USGS, 2003, RG-11). Simplifying somewhat, the result was to multiply the known mean reserve volume, by 1.44, a single factor or 'Lower-48-Mean reserve growth function', for the entire world, to reflect world 'growth volume' over 30 years, the difference between growth volume and known petroleum reserve volume, or 612 billion bbls of oil being defined as 'reserve growth'. (See Table RGApp-1, in USGS (2003), p. RG-26.) Having made these assumptions, the *Assessment 2000* authors argue:

> The forecast of world potential reserve growth described here is considered to be preliminary. Much work remains to be done on the subject of world potential reserve growth. The present study is an attempt to provide a numerical hypothesis for world potential reserve growth that is valuable in itself, and will perhaps act as a stimulus for discussion and research aimed at reducing the uncertainty of world reserve-growth estimates (US Geological Survey, 2003, RG-4).

# References

Arrington, J.R. (1962), 'Predicting the Size of Crude Reserves is Key to Evaluating Exploration Programs', *Oil and Gas Journal*, **58**(9), pp.130-134.

Attanasi, E. D. (1998), 'Economics and the 1995 National Assessment of United States Oil and Gas Resources', *US Geological Survey Circular 1145*, Washington D.C: U.S. Government Printing Office.

_____ and D.H. Root (1993), 'Statistics of Petroleum Exploration in the Caribbean, Latin America, Western Europe, the Middle East, Africa, non-Communist Asia and the Southwest Pacific', *US Geological Survey Circular 1096*, (Washington D.C: U.S. Government Printing Office.

Klett, T.R. (2003), 'Graphical Comparison of Reserve-Growth Models for Conventional Oil and Gas Accumulations', *US Geological Survey Bulletin*, Denver, Colorado, January 2.

Laherrère, J. (1997), 'Multi-Hubbert Modeling', July, available at http://www. hubbertpeak.com/Laherrère/multihub.htm. Accessed July 17, 2004.

_____(2001), 'Estimates of Oil Reserves', presented at the EMF/IEA/IIASA meeting, Laxemburg, Austria, June 19, available at www.oil.crisis.com/Laherrère. Accessed July 17, 2004.

_____(2002), 'Modelling Future Liquids Production from Extrapolation for the Past and from Ultimates', presented at International Workshop on Oil Depletion, Uppsala, Sweden, May 23, http://www.hubbertpeak.com/laherrere/UppsalaJHL.pdf. Accessed July 19, 2004.

_____(2003), 'Future of Oil Supplies', presented at a seminar, Center of Energy Conservation, Zurich, May 7, http://www.hubbertpeak.com/laherrere/ZurichJHL.pdf. Accessed July 19, 2004.

_____ (2004), 'Shell's Reserves Decline and SEC Obsolete Rules', article in preparation for Energy Politics, 27 February, available at www.oilcrisis.com/

Laherrère/ . Accessed July 26, 2004.

Masters, C., E. Attanasi and D. Root (1994), 'World Petroleum Assessment and Analysis', US Geological Survey, National Center, Reston, Va), *Proceedings of the 14th World Petroleum Congress,* Stavanger, Norway, New York: John Wiley and Sons.

Morehouse, D.F. (1997), 'The Intricate Puzzle of Oil and Gas "Reserves Growth"', *Natural Gas Monthly*, US Energy Information Administration, July 1997, pp. vii-xx.

Root, D.H., E.D. Attanasi, R.F. Mast and D.L. Gautier (1996), 'Estimates of Inferred Reserves for the 1995 USGS National Oil and Gas Resource Assessment', *US Geological Survey Open File Report 95-75L*, (Reston, Virginia, January 7).

Schmoker, J.W. and T.R. Klett (1999), 'U.S. Geological Survey Assessment Model for Undiscovered Conventional Oil, Gas, and NGL Resources – The Seventh Approximation', *US Geological Survey Bulletin 2165*, US Department of the Interior, US Geological Survey.

_____(2003), 'Estimating Potential Reserve Growth of Known (Discovered) Fields: A Component of the USGS Petroleum Assessment 2000', *US Geological Survey Digital Data Series 60*, USGS: Reston Virginia.

United States Geological Survey (USGS) (2003), *USGS World Petroleum Assessment 2000: New Estimates of Undiscovered Oil and Natural Gas, Natural Gas Liquids, including Reserve Growth outside the United States*, Reston, Virginia: USGS Fact Sheet FS-062-03, June.

_____(2003-2004), *World Petroleum Assessment 2000 – Description and Results*, (US Geological Digital Data Series – DDS-60, energy.cr.usgs.gov/oilgas/wep/products/dds60/tables.html. Accessed July 26, 2004.

# Chapter 10

# 'Why Don't Oil Companies Commit to "Renewables"?' A Corporate Constraints Perspective[1]

Jerome Davis

'As sole trustee of the nation's second largest public pension fund, it is my fiduciary responsibility to consider all long-term investment risks including those associated with the proliferation of greenhouse gases' Alan Hevesi, Comptroller, State of New York and Sole Trustee of New York Common Retirement Fund (Millam, 2004).

## Introduction: corporate CEOs confront their shareholders

With few exceptions, the oil industry has not been enthusiastic about compliance with the strictures of the Kyoto Protocol on Greenhouse Gases (GHG). Yet, in spite of this lack of enthusiasm, there are signs of change, in part imposed by major shareholder activisim in conjunction with corporate Annual General Meetings (AGMs). Major institutional investors, for example, are becoming increasingly concerned about the super majors' future stance on the issues of greenhouse gasses and commitment to renewables technologies, those technologies which emit no carbon dioxide in their generation of energy (windmills, fuel cells, geothermal energy, solar, and solar electrical (photovoltaics)).[2] This has been reflected in the increasing number of GHG-related proxy resolutions, essentially amendments to the corporate management Annual Report proposals, proposed by shareholders (and in the US) cleared by the Security and Exchange Commission. While none of the proxy resolutions has been adopted (proxy resolutions are seldom adopted at AGMs as a general rule), a sizable minority is an embarrassment to management, and proxies are often the subject

---

1 Special thanks are due to Tora Skodvin (Oslo University) for her advice in dealing with this topic. The author would also like to thank colleagues from a Roskilde University 2004 technology policy seminar for their useful comments on earlier versions of this chapter.

2 This excludes, of course, the $CO_2$ emitted in their manufacture. 'Renewables' are seen here as different from 'greenhouse technologies' which are new or improved technologies which decrease $CO_2$ emissions. These may range from improved diesel engines, the manufacture of methanol to the use of compressed natural gas (CNG) for transport purposes.

of unpublicised negotiations between their initiators and the managements of the companies concerned, negotiations which can lead to corporate policy change.[3]

Reacting to a 2003 GHG-related proxy resolution receiving more than 25 percent of the votes cast, ChevronTexaco acted in 2004 to become a 'quiet industry leader on climate change' (CERES, April 24, 2004). [4] Four years earlier, BP, confronted with a shareholder revolt over its pledge to invest $50 million annually in solar energy over five years in its 2000 annual general meeting (Macalister, 2000), increased that amount significantly. The currently reported investment in solar photovoltaics is $500 million over three years (2000-2003). Nor have other super majors escaped criticism.[5]

Similarly, various reports sponsored by environmental interest groups have pointed out potential losses companies risk in not pursuing the opportunities offered by renewables technology. (See, for example, Duncan and Sauer, 2002; Mansley, 2002.) Most large oil companies today perceive of themselves as energy companies. As such, are they capable of doing their share in confronting and solving the problems engendered by the continuous increase in greenhouse gasses? Are the super majors, for example, capable of facing the immense tasks of developing new technologies, in particular those of renewable sources of energy, and of successfully introducing them to a market economy?

Whether interested in investing in renewables or not, oil firms face two severe organisational constraints which must be overcome to meet this goal.[6] The first set of constraints are those posed by the nature of existing corporate R&D in a vertically integrated mature industry. The second set of constraints is the need to coordinate renewable technologies so that these have the properties of being complements, 'a

---

3    For example, a major study of the correspondence behind 62 proxy resolutions initiated by the US Teachers Insurance Annuity Association-College Retirement Equities Fund against 43 firms has found that a negotiated agreement was reached with 42 firms, a success rate of 97.7 percent, despite the fact that only one of the proxy resolutions achieved a majority vote in an AGM (Carleton, Nelson and Weisbach, 1998).

4    Measures adopted by ChevronTexaco were: (1) being the first and only oil company to disclose its entire GHG footprint (this definition includes emissions by end users of ChevronTexaco products); (2) becoming the first oil company to incorporate the practice of assuming a $5 to $20/ton charge for $CO_2$ in its future investment decisions. ChevronTexaco also promised to make a major investment in renewables technology (CERES, April 28, 2004).

5    The website, Corporate Library (2004), keeps statistics on shareholder proxy proposals. For example for ExxonMobil, it lists eight proposals advanced in the 2004 'proxy season', of which one was related to the greenhouse gas (GHG) problem. Figures for the years 2003, 2002, 2001 and 2000 are 2 (out of a total of 12), 2 (out of a total of 8), 2 (out of a total of 8) and 2 (out of 7) respectively. That GHG concerns are real are reflected in that the two proposals voted upon in 2003 received respectively 22 and 21 percent of the votes cast.

6    Readers will recognise this as a diversification problem. For other theoretical approaches to this topic see Markides and Williamson, 1996; Prahalad and Bettis, 1986; and Simpert and Duhaime, 1997.

set of activities with the property that doing more of one set of activities raises the marginal returns on others sets of activities' (Milgrom and Roberts, 1992, p. 597).

In the following we will first review the policy stances of the super majors with regard to the Kyoto Convention and their consequent commitments to renewables technologies. Here, there is demonstrably a difference in super major stance on GHGs, a difference reflected in their renewables investments policies. Thereafter, we argue that critics of insufficient oil company investments in renewables underestimate the actual degree of oil company commitment, for three of the four super majors(critics tend to exclude the impact of external sources of innovation). This is followed by a section demonstrating the difficulties of achieving complements in the renewable technologies field, seen essentially as a coordination game. In the fifth section we briefly examine the rise of oil company hybrid organisational arrangements in the renewables field. We conclude with an evaluation of the viability of super major strategies in renewables.

## Renewables and the super major policy stances with regard to Kyoto

The policy stance of the super majors has been subjected to intensive scrutiny by political scientists (e.g. Levy and Rothenberg, 1999; Skjaerseth and Skodvin, 2001, 2002, 2003; Rowlands, 2000) and business economists (Levy and Kolk, 2002). Little (if any) correlation has been found between corporate dependency on carbon fuels and corporate policy positions. Rather, other variables, the nature of national regulatory systems, the environmental orientations of corporate 'home' countries, the 'iron cage' of corporate institutions and the role of CEOs (for example Lord John Brown of BP) have been seen as instrumental in diverging corporate GHG policy stances. Often the emphasis has been on the differences between North American based (ExxonMobil, ChevronTexaco) and European based (Royal Dutch Shell, BP) firms. While these studies yield valuable insights as to oil company positioning on the Kyoto Protocol and the GHG problem, the emphasis in our context is more directed at corporate strategic investment policies and the role which GHG R&D investments play in these policies.

Table 10.1 correlates super major policy stances on Kyoto Protocol to GHG-related investments. Not surprisingly, the table shows that those super majors most supportive of the Kyoto Protocol are also those which have been most active in pursuit of renewables R&D. This is seen by memberships in pro-active industrial environmental groupings such as the Pew Center, the World Business Council for Sustainable Development (WBCSD), and the Emissions Trading Association initiatives. This correlation also holds for the setting of quantitative GHG targets for their own exploration, production, refining, and marketing operations. Here as elsewhere, BP and, especially, Royal Dutch Shell can be distinguished from the two American based oil companies, ChevronTexaco and ExxonMobil. Only

**Table 10.1  Super major commitment to green technologies: positions and initiatives**

| Position/initiatives | BP | Exxon | Royal Dutch Shell | ChevronTexaco |
|---|---|---|---|---|
| Proactive partnerships | Pew Center, EPA Climate Wise Program, California Fuel Cell Partnership, trading system with EDF, EPA voluntary greenhouse gas reporting, WBSCD, International Emissions Trading Association | California Fuel Cell Partnership (2001–) | Pew Center, California Fuel Partnership, WBCSD, International Emissions Trading Association | California Fuel Cell WBSCD |
| Trading/monitoring of GHGs | Measurement and trading from 1997. External auditing from 6/1999 | Internal measurement of emissions data | Reporting $CO_2$ emissions from 1998 in externally verified HSE report. Launched internal trading in January 2000 | Internal measurement of emission data 2002 first emissions inventory. 2003 external audits |
| Quantitative GHG Targets | Reduce emissions by 10 pct. in 2010, relative to 1990 | NA | Reduce GHG emissions by >10 pct. by 2002 | |
| Investments in renewables | Owns Solarx. Invest $100 m. In online green retail electricity company | NA | Solar factories (Germany, Japan, Netherlands. 1997–2002 $500m. investment Solar JV (Siemens), IOGEN (ethanol). Shell Solar, Shell Renewables | 20% of ECD (advanced batteries, fuels cells, solar) Venture capital firm promote JVs |
| Main fuel cell Activities | Ford partnership since 2000 | Exxon-GM and Toyota since 2000 | Daimler and Ballard since 1998. Shell Hydrogen | Texaco Energy Systems 1999 Chevron Texaco Technology Partners |

*Source*: Levy and Kolk, 2002, p. 287 and company reports

recently has ChevronTexaco become more 'European' in this respect. These initiatives again have spilled over into the resources dedicated to renewables investments. While all forms of alternatives to oil and gas are being investigated by firms such as BP and Royal Dutch Shell, it is their efforts in solar technologies and in fuel cell/hydrogen alternatives which are particularly striking.

## Investing in renewable technologies: two interpretations

In the introduction to this chapter, I discussed the concern of super majors' shareholders over the degree to which these companies were taking account of the developments in renewables technologies. Given that shareholder proxy proposals in this respect are often moved on the initiative of a set of environmental organisations who also happen to own shares in the companes concerned, it is only natural to ask whether the concern expressed in these resolutions is actually justified.

The degree to which the renewables glass is half empty or half full largely depends on the perspectives one has of oil industry R&D and innovation efforts. To illustrate this, I first advance what I consider the conventional view of the industry. Thereafter, I present a more radical view of super major renewables R&D efforts.

### Declining industry, declining R&D

The oil industry is often classified as a mature industry in decline. Such industries have been characterised by competition between standard products, a lack of innovative effort, and an aging bureaucratic organisation (Grant, 1995). Profitability in such industries, according to one authority, is a function of cost advantage, of slimmed down bureaucracies, of market leadership in specified areas, and of adjusting capacity to demand. Grant (1995, p. 299) essentially characterises the oil industry as such, an industry where 'strong competition' and the 'limited opportunities for establishing sustainable competitive advantage that creates impetus in marketing, product design, customer service, and organisation'.

The oil industry generally, and the four super majors in particular, appear at first glance to conform to the mature industry explanation. This can be seen in a low rate of R&D investment (in all areas of activity) combined with a high rate of fixed investment, as well as an aversion to innovation in radically new technologies, and to investment in non petroleum activities.

Firstly, it is indisputable that, given the last ten-year emphasis on the 'lean corporation', the R&D efforts of the oil majors have fallen off considerably. According to Olivier Appert, Chairman and CEO of the prestigious Institut Français du Pétrole, US majors have cut their R&D expenditures in half during the last decade. R&D expenditures by European oil firms have been cut only slightly less drastically. In both cases, companies are focussing on a relatively few technologies which confer competitive advantage (and improved shareholder returns). Service and supply companies have partially compensated for these cuts as these have raised their R&D expenditures by 60 percent during the same period, but over-all industry R&D expenditures have fallen by 30 percent (Tippee, 2004).

That there is a low rate of R&D investment and a high rate of fixed investment within the industry is amply demonstrated by Creusen and Minne (2000) in Table 10.2. As of the turn of the century the major firms later constituting the super majors generally invested considerably less than one percent of their annual sales in corporate R&D. At the same time, their investment intensity over-all can amount to as much as 13.7 percent of annual sales (both figures in terms of nominal data). This picture of low corporate R&D investment rates and high investment intensity in other areas has not materially changed since 1998.

What are the R&D priorities of the companies? Here too, the picture generally conforms with the proposition that most R&D efforts are conditioned by the vertical integration of the firm. By far the most significant R&D activities here are in the downstream sector of the industry. Looking at the pattern of European patents taken out for each link in the value chain. Creusen and Minne (2000, p. 32) noted that in terms of patenting among the oil companies surveyed,[7] only 5 percent involved exploration, 11 percent oil production, 30 percent refining, 45 percent petrochemicals, and 9 percent 'specialities and life sciences'. It should be noted in this context that marketing innovations cannot be patented. In 1999, it was estimated that the brands Shell and BP had a value of around $3 billion dollars (ibid).

**Table 10.2    Research and investment intensity: major oil companies, 1997–1998**

|                | Investment Intensity | | Research Intensity | |
|----------------|----------------------|----------|--------------------|---------|
| Oil Company    | 1997                 | 1998     | 1997               | 1998    |
|                | pct. of annual nominal turnover | | | |
| Exxon          | 5.39                 | 7.06     | 0.39               | 0.47    |
| Mobil Oil      | 6.36                 | 10.93    | 0.36               | 0.38    |
| Shell          | 9.55                 | 13.72    | 0.52               | 0.85    |
| BP             | 8.06                 | 10.69[a] | 0.32               | 0.60[a] |
| Amoco          | 9.20                 | [a]      | 0.42               | [a]     |
| Chevron        | 9.29                 | 12.7     | 0.43               | 0.61    |
| Texaco         | 7.77                 | 9.78     | 0.32               | 0.44    |

[a]1998 figures for Amoco included with BP (BP Amoco) in 1998
*Source*: Creusen and Minne, 2000, p. 42

Given this pattern of innovative activity, it should come as no surprise that many of the super major GHG initiatives illustrated in Table 10.1 involve downstream activities, most notably the GHG emissions monitoring and trading programs. BP originally led the pack, having introduced measurement and trading of their

---

7    In addition to the companies listed in Table 10.2, this group includes: Phillips, Elf, Total and Petrofina.

$CO_2$ emissions from 1997, external auditing from June 1999. Royal Dutch Shell began reporting its $CO_2$ emissions in 1998 and internal trading in January, 2000. ChevronTexaco began internal measurement of its $CO_2$ emissions in 2002, began submitting its figures to external audits the following year, and since 2004 has reportedly quietly committed itself to GHG measurement policies in advance of those of its competitors. ExxonMobil, currently conducting internal measurements of its $CO_2$ emissions, has not yet announced any further steps. Reaching quantitative GHG targets also differs among companies. BP's goal of reducing GHG emissions to 10 percent below 1990 levels by 2010, has been met eight years ahead of schedule and the initiative has essentially paid for itself in terms of greater efficiencies. Royal Dutch Shell is not too far behind BP. ChevronTexaco is in the beginning stages of its radical reforms. Information on the ExxonMobil internal monitoring program remains confidential.

Creusen and Minne also note that technological competition in the oil industry is characterised by strong overlaps with companies pursuing similar research, essentially improving similar industrial processes at the same time. They note:

> The potential duplication in research is wasteful from a social point of view, because knowledge spillovers are insufficiently exploited. The companies, however, do not consider the overlapping research as wasteful because they derive their competitive advantage mainly from their unique production processes (Creusen and Minne, 2000, p. 34).

Furthermore, oil company R&D in general has not enjoyed high rates of return (Creusen and Minne, 2000). A major reason for the fall off in the rate of oil MNE R&D noted earlier is that R&D has simply not proved as profitable as other oil company activities. A significant problem with renewables investment is that renewable alternatives, if not uneconomic, face potentially large coordination problems in their implementation and commercialisation. As such they are the worst short term investment in the typical oil company R&D investment portfolio, a portfolio pressed overall by management desire to keep a competitive edge in what is becoming an increasingly competitive industry.

*A dissenting view*

In contrast to the negative picture of the previous section, one can argue convincingly that the renewable picture is less bleak than might otherwise be thought.

Firstly, there exist several misconceptions about the petroleum industry commitment in terms of the arguments behind Table 10.2. A comparison of an oil company's annual fixed asset investments with the monies devoted to research in renewables, a favourite theme of green environmental groups, is misleading. Given the high R&D content of renewables investment, a better comparison would be over-all investment in renewables as a percentage of over-all corporate R&D. For example, in 2000, BP (then BP Amoco) committed itself to a $250 million investment in renewables R&D over five years. This was increased to $500 million over three years. Looking at BP Amoco's fixed investments for the year 1998, $68.3 billion, this may not seem much. Looking at BP Amoco's R&D investments for the same year, we find that these totaled some $410 million. The BP Amoco 2000 commitment to renewables R&D, spread out over three years, means their commitments would constitute roughly 40 percent of the 1998 BP Amoco R&D budget per year. Similarly, BP has committed some $100 millions per year for environmental research (there could be an overlap between the two figures).

The same might be said of the Royal Dutch Shell R&D investments. Its total R&D investments in 1997 was $665 million. Measured in this light, its commitment of $500 millions to renewables in the period 1997–2002 may be more significant than is generally thought. Added to this is the estimated $500 million to $1 billion committed for the period 2002 through 2007.

And while commitment from the two American companies has been perhaps less significant, it does exist. ChevronTexaco, prior to its policy change of 2004 had committed $80 million per annum in windpower and gasification technologies, and had acquired minority interests in a range of companies engaged in promising avenues of R&D exploration. Since 2004, it has promised to make a major investment in this field. ExxonMobil has spent $150 million on 'health, safety and environment' (although a further breakdown between expenditure categories is not available).

A second misconception lies in the degree that internally generated and financed research is seen as the most significant measure of oil company R&D. In the oil industry, as elsewhere, external R&D collaboration in the form of diverse hybrid organisational arrangements has become more and more significant. Thus, when Appert decries the halving of US majors' R&D investments, over-all but particularly in upstream R&D, it is worth noting that their upstream service and supply firms have increased their R&D investments by 60 percent. Upstream R&D developments continue, but they have been externalised from the vertically integrated firm. (A similar tendency may hold for future oil company renewables R&D as we will note later.)

Externalisation has been particularly significant in the upstream segment of the industry. The sudden fall in crude prices in the mid 1980 caused extensive soul searching within the industry. The results were the establishment of new forms of service firm agent/oil company principal relationships, often, as in the North Sea, with government encouragement. New forms of project information management, the use of concurrent engineering techniques, new partnering relationships, and, above all, radically changed project management methods, led to a very different dynamic in the offshore exploration and development segments of the industry. This enabled faster access to new technology, economies of scale in R&D, and readier oil major acquisition of know-how from without the oil company organisation. Thus, for example, it makes far more sense for a service firm such as Schlumberger, a leader in geophysical seismic technology, to specialise in seismic R&D where the results would be readily available to all oil companies, than for each of these latter to invest heavily in seismic R&D. In the latter scenario, not only would the oil companies perhaps duplicate each other's R&D programmes, but they could not have realised the specialisation or gains in economies of scale available to Schlumberger. Arguably, it is better for all concerned that Schlumberger invest some 5 percent of its turnover in seismic R&D and the resulting technology and knowledge be accessible to all oil companies through Schlumberger's operations as a oil company service firm.

## The problem of achieving complementarities

While the nature of existing corporate R&D in a vertically integrated mature industry may be a major problem in developing renewable technologies, perhaps a more serious set of constraints is the need to coordinate renewable technologies. To be interesting to oil companies these technologies should entail complementarities, so that the development of renewable technologies increases corporate marginal returns elsewhere. This problem becomes more difficult in that the integration of the various renewable complementary activities is highly costly, often too costly for the individual firm. In the following, we first identify the nature of the problem, essentially a coordination problem. We then review the organisational solutions to the problem, and then discuss their ramifications for two areas of super major activities: solar photovoltaic technology and fuel cells.

*Non-integrated complements: the problem*

The dilemma of non-integrated complements is perhaps first best explained by a hypothetical example which will then be generalised in game theoretical terms. Assume that in order to conform to some stringent environmental regulations imposed by the state of California for motor vehicles, the various automobile firms introduced their own solutions to the problem. One firm introduces vehicles fuelled by compressed natural gas (CNG). Another lauches super efficient diesel vehicles, a third firm, hybrid vehicles, a fourth, fuel cell powered units. Each of these innovative vehicles is dependent on its own infrastructure. If they cannot be serviced conveniently, customers will not buy them. Providing the necessary infrastructure could be the responsibility of the auto manufacturers. But this is likely beyond their resources. Assume that oil firms are to provide the infrastructure. In which infrastructure do they invest? And can they be sure that their investment will be justified over time? Should one vehicle type be withdrawn by its manufacturer, how will the infrastructure investment be recovered by the oil firm concerned? Yet, if there is no oil firm investment, introduction of the innovative vehicles will fail. While this example is overdrawn, variations of this game will likely be characteristic of the introduction of renewables, and is a major cause for corporate reluctance here.

This problem is easily generalised. Let us assume a simplified world where introduction of a renewables technology is dependent on three players: a firm, $i$, introducing the new technology, $t$, a second firm, $j$, manufacturing complementary components essential to the commercial success of $t$, and a third firm, $k$, which will consume the final product incorporating $t$. In each case, committing to the final marketable product is a function of the costs of commitment, $c$; these costs are different for the various players. For $i$ they are the opportunity costs of $i$ 's investment in $t$. For $j$ and $k$ they are essentially switching costs, as these firms change their orientation from $-t$ towards $t$. For the latter two players, the crucial variables are their reservation prices, R. For the three we have the following relationships:

For $i$:  $\Pi_i = p_{it} - c_{it} - p_{i\text{-}t}$ where $-t$ represents the existing technology

For $j$:  $\Pi_j = Rj - p_{it} - c_{jt}$ if $j$ accepts the new technology, or
$\phantom{\text{For } j:  \Pi_j = } Rj - p_{i\text{-}t}$ if $j$ remains committed to the existing technology from $i$

For $k$:  $\Pi_k = R_k - p_{jt} - c_{kt}$ if k accepts t, otherwise
$\phantom{\text{For } k:  \Pi_k = } R_k - p_{j\text{-}t}$

Given that each player will attempt to maximise her winnings under the constraint that the others will behave similarly, one has a three-person coordination game with commitments.

The outcomes of such games are highly dependent on the context in which they are played. Here, for any equilibrium solution, a critical variable is that the stakes for all three players are compatible with one another. There are several contexts where this is particularly important.

The first context would require that $i$'s new technology, $t$, is compatible with the preferences of player $j$, and that $j$'s resulting product fits the preferences of $k$. Assume that $i$ has developed a renewables widget which if incorporated in $j$'s product might appeal to consumer $k$. Working backwards, one can understand the complexity of the problem. Suppose that $k$ is convinced that there is little consumer demand for the new product, or that $k$ has found alternative solutions, for example, through use of tradable emissions quotas, or through implementing energy efficiency measures of her own. In each of these scenarios, $k$'s switching costs, $c_{k\text{-}t}$, increase with the result that the entire enterprise falls apart. (Note that a similar situation could well exist for $j$ as well.)

The second context where compatibility is important lies the division of the corporate returns for each player. Particularly if the commitments of $i$, $j$ and $k$ are incompatible at the outset, it would be rational for each player to adopt what is defined as a dominant strategy, that strategy by which a player, for example, $i$, takes account of all possible strategies of the other players, $j$ and $k$, and chooses his moves so that he maximises his pay-offs no matter what strategies the other players, $j$ and $k$, may adopt. If all the players respond by choosing their dominant strategies, the game results in a dominant strategy equilibrium, a variation of the two person prisoner's dilemma in which the payoffs to rational players are their second-best alternatives (Crawford, 1982).

A third context is one characterised by several sets of players and more than one technological innovation. To this point we have assumed individual firms in a three person game with one technological innovation, $t_i$.

If we assume that each player belongs to a larger set of players, $i \subset I$, $j \subset J$, and $k \subset K$, the game becomes far more complex. While one could argue that the existence of larger sets of players increases the number of alternatives for each of the players in this game, it complicates the signaling of commitments.

An additional factor could be that within each set $I$, $J$ and $K$ there could exist a contest as to which of several competing technologies, designs, or solutions will become standard for firms within that set. Here we assume that both $t_i$ and $t_{-i}$ belong to $T$ a much larger set of feasible technologies. The existence of multiple technologies can to some degree simplify the pairing of players, as these might pair according to their technological preferences. But multiple technologies can also increase difficulties. To return to our example, a consumer, $k$ of automobiles could be confronted by conventional gasoline automobiles, environmental diesel, hybrids, CNG driven automobiles, battery powered and (eventually) hydrogen powered vehicles. While consumer preferences will be defined in the market place, this places the oil industry at an disadvantage, particularly if the example is the American market where transportation accounts for over one half the total consumption of oil products.

While competition between technologies presents difficulties, these can be complicated by competition within the same technological architecture, in particular the establishment of industry standards. The emergence of a particular renewables standard, for example an inexpensive technological solution for storing liquid hydrogen, could be worth many billions for the firm with property rights to that standard. Thus agreement between $i$, $j$ and $k$ in our example could be further hindered by standards battles at one or more stages (see Besen and Farrell, 1994, for a discussion of standards 'wars').

*The problem of complements: organisational and investment consequences*

The discussion of coordinating complements to this point have been essentially focussed on the market coordination of complements. Yet, coordination of technologies need not be confined to markets. Table 10.3 illustrates the extremes. Horizontally, the locus of renewables innovation takes place either in-house within the single firm or among different firms, The vertical axis defines the nature of the possible resulting complementarities.

**Table 10.3    Coordinating complements in renewables technologies**

|  | Location of R&D/Innovation | |
|  | In-house | Among firms |
| --- | --- | --- |
| Intra firm complements | vertical/horizontal integration | market coordination (arms length) |
| Inter firm complements | merger solution | hybrid organisational solution |

To take in-house R&D first, an oil firm can concentrate solely on internal R&D, keeping such R&D strictly within the vertically integrated firm .This view of oil company R&D has been espoused by Armour and Teece (1980). Rather than achieving internal complements through internalising their own R&D and relying on the market for other technological inputs a characteristic of non vertically integrated firms, they argue, oil company technological innovation occurs between the different stages of the production process. When 'various stages of a production process bear technological similarities and complementarities, common ownership of R&D and production facilities will enhance technological innovation' (p. 47). According to this interpretation, it is the nature of the vertically coupled processes which determines innovative activity, a determination which, if true, would structurally exclude efforts in non-vertically integrated fields of research activity.[8] An alternative mode of achieving in-firm complementarities is through friendly or hostile take over or merger with other firms deemed to possess the necessary technological complements. (ExxonMobil's strategy in the early 1980s in fact was largely that of firm acquisition.)

Alternatively, an oil company can combine its R&D and innovative capacities with other firms to its achieve to achieve inter-firm complementarities. This can either be done through an arms length market relationship as in the previous section's discusson of coordination, or by a form of industrial organisation 'between market and hierarchy', what Powell (1987, p. 67) has labelled 'hybrid organisational arrangements'. This term refers to a multiplicity of inter-firm cooperative arrangements, strategic alliances, partnering, establishing joint ventures, equity partnerships, collaborative research agreements, the setting up of satellite organisations, and/or (within the firm itself) the setting up of semi-autonomous units to deal explicitly with these hybrid organisational arrangements.

What is of interest here is that the logic of developing renewable technologies, with a few exceptions, favours the creation of such hybrid organisational forms. Acquiring a renewables firm with a radically different technology, organisation, and strategy has proved a costly strategy for oil firms, particularly given the emphasis on lean organisation and shareholder returns currently demanded in corporate equity markets. On the other hand, creating a hybrid organisation with an existing firm, specialising in a particular renewables technology, enables potential complementarities without the costs of alternative arrangements.

*Coordination and complementarities: two examples*

Given the number of other players involved in the energy industry and their widely diverging interests, it is in the interests of all to focus on one or two green technologies. These should be characterised by one of the following characteristics which also act as constraints:

---

8    In fact oil companies have historically relied on a high degree of external R&D in the processing sectors.

- The technology must be modular, that is, without need for vertical integration, and capable of wide application, and/or
- The technologies involved must focus on an end-use, or fuel, for which a significant majority of the competing players are eligible to compete and where their diverging technological solutions have a chance of being complements in the sense this term is used in this chapter.

Photovoltaics and fuel cell technologies are candidates which potentially fulfill these requirements, photovoltaics because they are an essentially modular technology, fuel cell technology because even though it requires vertical integration, it is a technology on which multiple industries are focussing in terms of its long-term potential, and involves technologies with which oil firms are familiar.. Developing fuel cell technology favours hybrid organisational solutions as there are many potential partners, and the generation and treatment of the hydrogen on which fuel cells will depend is related to areas of oil corporation core competencies, a prime requirement of corporate diversification.

*The super majors: photovoltaics?*

In accordance with the problems of complements, solar photovoltaic power is seen to present few if any coordination problems, the future sale and installation of photovoltaics have been compared to the market for transistors in the 1960s and early 1970s an immense potential market where photovoltaics can be used for a wide range of energy uses. Much as in the case of the transistor then, future photovoltaics may easily be incorporated into final products and sold directly to the customer. BP Solar makes this point in its description of its Millennia photovoltaic modules, modules which use 'hundreds of times less energy to manufacture than conventional photovoltaics' (BP Solar, 2004).

Millennia modules are available in two voltage categories, the MV system designed for moderate- to high-voltage arrays and the LV systems designed primarily for systems using 12-volt batteries or for other applications requiring a multiple of the nominal 12-volt batteries. MV products are particularly applicable to residential, commercial, and industrial utility-interactive arrays. LV products are applicable to all traditional remote PV systems, particularly basic power systems for homes in developing nations (ibid).

Yet while photovoltaics may have a potential for future widespread application, it is unlikely that this application will first occur within the OECD countries, given the problems associated with their introduction discussed previously and consumer expectations of photovoltaic performance. The picture is perhaps significantly different in developing countries where the existing electrical generating and supply infrastructure is either insufficient to match growing demand or deficient in reliability. It could well be that much like how satellite connected cell telephone networks have enabled developing countries to skip costly wirebased telecom networks, photovoltaics here will enable developing countries to skip the immense costs of building new and upgrading old electrical generating capacity through the acquisition of new photovoltaic capacities.

*The super majors: fuel cell technology?*

Coordination problems for fuel cell technology are a different matter altogether. Here there are problems of hydrogen separation, transport, distribution, storage, and marketing in addition to the problems of developing economically viable fuel cell technologies, a set of major coordination problems. In this field, oil multinationals have an advantage as the most feasible fuel cell technologies today are based on supplies of either hydrogen or methanol. That oil multinationals are investing in hydrogen-based energy solutions is not illogical. The fuel is clean. It is readily available and can be extracted from a wide variety of resources (gasoline, natural gas, methanol, coal, biomass, propane, alcohol, water). Of particular interest to the industry, however, is that the production and utilisation of hydrogen is central to the refining process, particularly as regards the use of hydrogen to upgrade heavier crudes so these can be refined into premium products. Indeed intelligent refinery hydrogen management adds to refinery bottom line results. The production of hydrogen from fossil raw materials, moreover, accounts for 96 percent of the hydrogen produced today (48 percent from natural gas, 30 percent from crude, 18 percent from coal), the balance coming from water electrolysis (Office of Energy Efficiency and Renewable Energy, 2004). Then too, as we have noted earlier, oil MNEs R&D efforts tend to focus on the refining industry. As such, it is logical for these companies to realise possible synergies in this field.[9] While implementation of refinery-based hydrogen sources industry-wide will be costly, they best enable oil industry adjustment towards a hydrogen economy.

Yet, while it is quite likely that eventual synergies between a future hydrogen/ fuels cell economy and oil industry technological expertise are a major reason for oil MNE interest in hydrogen, there are coordination problems with the number of other players researching technological solutions to the problems involved in the separation, transportation and utilisation of hydrogen as a fuel. Thus hydrogen separation also has the interests of firms in the nuclear industry, the electrical utility industry, the coal industry, and the chemical industry, to name but the more obvious.

There are additionally problems with the transport and storage of hydrogen, since as a fuel it has a much lower ratio of gas volume to energy released than do petroleum products. Thus in volumetric terms, there are problems with its storage. For example, it is impractical to store sufficient compressed hydrogen in an automobile to power it 350 miles (567 kilometers), the current performance of American automobiles.

---

9   Currently, of the three major areas of investigation here – the improvement of the traditional production of natural gas (steam methane reforming) through adding an absorbent to the reformer separating $CO_2$ from the product stream; the development of a ceramic membrane reactor; and investigating the feasibility of biomass pyrolysis – oil industry attention is primarily directed at the first two.

While it can be liquefied, the required cryogenic temperature is $260^0$ C. which also creates practical engineering problems. Needless to say there also is research here, particularly in the areas of storing hydrogen in metal hydride allows, in carbon nanotubes, or in glassmicro-spheres. In each of these areas, multiple firms with multiple technological solutions have committed substantial resources to uncertain markets.

It is notable that all four super majors in Table 10.1 have begun coordinating work in fuel cell technologies, in some cases by joint venture and acquisition, in others, through partnerships, particularly with the automobile industry. While their expertise may lie in the production and treatment of hydrogen, these are insufficient grounds to tackle the multiple problems of developing fuel cell technologies. For example diversification into the development of fuel cells (or even hydrogen storage) is beyond the core competencies of the super majors. Hybrid organizational solutions may be the answer here. To return to California again, all four companies, including ExxonMobil, are cooperating with the automobile industry, and a series of corporations specialising in fuel cell technologies in the California Fuel Cell Partnership. This is a programmme aimed at introducing experimental hydrogen fueled fuel cell driven vehicles to the California highways, and tentatively testing the hydrogen infrastructure necessary for their support. The efforts of automobile manufacturers, firms developing fuel cell technologies, firms developing hydrogen separation and storage technologies, and firms, here largely the oil companies, specialising in hydrogen separation and in providing the necessary infra-structure support must be coordinated if the new technology is to be successful. The information generated in this hybrid organisation is vital to solving the set of coordination problems prerequisite to any future fuel cell powered vehicle commercial introduction.

### Renewables R&D and innovation: the rise of hybrid organisational arrangements

In the 1970s oil MNEs perceived that diversification into non-petroleum activities offered better, more secure returns. A wave of merger and take-over activities led to oil company acquisition of mining firms, agricultural interests, retailing and direct mailing activities, to name but a few (Energy Information Administration, 1994). (See Ghosh, 1985 and Heifat, 1989 for other analyses of this diversification.) The oil price crash of 1986 led to an abandonment of non-petroleum-related activities in the industry. This was prompted by a cash flow shortage, a curious phenomenon in that returns to the latter activities had been largely unaffected by the fall in crude oil prices. A major study of oil company divestiture at this time (Lamont, 1997), however, revealed that many of these non-petroleum activities had yielded below average profits and had, in fact been cross-subsidised by the firms concerned (p. 103). Attempts to derive synergies from these activities had failed, a failure which still affects industry preferences, here an aversion to diversifying into non-petroleum endeavours (Lynch, 1993).

What is interesting about oil major diversification into renewable technologies in this context is how different things are from the 1970s. A glance at Table 10.1 shows that today's super major seldom acquires another firm when it attempts to diversify. (There are of course some exceptions, such as BP's acquisition of Solarex.) Rather, the table illustrates a wide variety of hybrid organisational solutions in super major renewables investment policies. These include the following: research partnerships with universities and other public authorities in the US, the UK and China (BP), hydrocarbon trading relationships with electrical utilities (BP and Electricite de France), joint venture arrangements (Royal Dutch Shell/IOGEN/Siemens and ChevronTexaco/ECD), the establishment of venture capital firms to promote future JVs (ChevronTexaco), partnering arrangements (BP/Ford; ExxonMobil/GM/Toyota; Royal Dutch Shell/Ballard/Daimler Benz). And, as noted previously, all four super majors are cooperating in the California Fuel Cell Partnership.

An additional hybrid organisational innovation can be seen in attempts to dismantle the hierarchical vertical integrated relationships within the firms themselves, relationships which could function as barriers to renewables development. This phenomenon, 'vertical disaggregation' (Powell, p. 73), is a vertically integrated corporate response to the liabilities of large scale organisation. Smaller, more flexible entities within the oil major can better respond to rapidly developing technologies, new markets, and opportunities for specialised cooperation with other specialised firms. But of the three super majors utilizing hybrid organisational solutions to renewables, each has a different manner of integrating its renewables interest to the main organisation. Royal Dutch Shell, for example, has formed two operating companies within its organisation: Shell Renewables and Shell Hydrogen. The manager of each of these companies is responsible for their economic performance. BP, on the other hand, has placed BP Solar in its 'Natural Gas, Power, and Renewables Business Stream'. While, this may seem to be an upgrading of solar and renewables, BP is particularly committed to the expansion of its natural gas business, and this commitment may ultimately reduce resources to the other two activities.[10] ChevronTexaco, on the other hand, explicitly states that the purpose of its Chevron Technology Ventures is the establishment of hybrid organisational arrangements with unrelated outside firms. Chevron Technology Ventures is under a Vice President who simultaneously is the Chief Technical Officer of the firm with additional responsibilities for 'Energy Technologies', and 'Information Technologies'.

Notably absent from these hybrid organisational solutions is ExxonMobil, a company still sobered by its experiences in its failed 1970s diversification into renewables:

---

10 In BP's document 'Financial and Operating Information 1999-2003', for example, discussion of the natural gas, power, and renewables business stream is almost wholly dedicated to BPs natural gas and LNG prospects. Solar energy is mentioned in two sentences almost as an afterthought. Other renewables are not mentioned at all.

ExxonMobil had previously invested significant sums of money (in excess of $500 million) in commercial ventures involving renewable energy, particularly solar energy. Because they are not as reliable or affordable as conventional fossil fuels, renewables compete in niche applications and hardly at all in transportation fuels. In view of their technological limits and excess costs, which prevented widespread deployment, a business decision was taken many years ago to concentrate on our core energy and petrochemical businesses (ExxonMobil, 2001, p. 8).

## Conclusion: 'Why don't oil companies commit more to "renewables"?'

The rhetorical question posed in the title to this chapter raises a series of issues. Firstly, why should the super majors commit to 'renewable technologies'? Secondly, is such a commitment desirable, given the existence of other corporate objectives? Thirdly, given such a commitment, are super major strategies viable? And, finally, given the problems of coordination outlined here, are the hybrid organisational solutions undertaken by the industry a viable strategy?

Rather than focus on the oil industry stance towards the Kyoto GHG Accord, and its possible causes, we have emphasised the role of corporate governance in determining the stance of the oil industry towards the GHG problem generally and the issue of renewables in particular. It is our contention that the role of proxy resolutions in corporate AGMs has been much underrated. Here the issues are clear, and founded on owner self interest. In the US in particular the large institutional investors, in particular pension funds, are seriously concerned as to the long term future of any investment in oil firms listed on the New York exchanges. At the very least, shareholders wish to know how their companies are planning to cope with what is seen as a major environmental problem. There are also shareholders who are concerned about a lack of diversification away from purely petroleum based activities, who see long term commercial possibilities in such a diversification. In corporate governance terms, whether such a diversification is advisable becomes a matter of ownership preference. That there are owners and managers resisting GHG related proxy resolutions should not surprise. The management at ExxonMobil relying on its own internal GHG expertise is a prominent opponent of such proxy resolutions, and it is not alone. The AGMs of the smaller US independents such as Marathon, Apache and Andarko remain battlegrounds for proxy resolution adherents.[11] Furthermore, even where management has promised changes in policy, it is not clear whether promises will be substantially fulfilled. There can be little doubt that commitment to renewables (unlike the implementation of GHG emission reduction measures) involves short term losses in the tens or even hundreds of

---

11 In the 2004 proxy season, an identical resolution backed by a variety of financial interests asking for a company report as to how it was going to respond to GHG issues was supported by 37 percent of the shareholders present and voting in the Apache AGM, 28 percent in the Anarko AGM, and 27 percent in the Marathon AGM (CERES, April 28, 2004).

millions of dollars annually, as is the case with Royal Dutch Shell's operational companies, Shell Hydrogen and Shell Renewables.[12]

Given the nature of the oil industry, one might say that the commitments of BP, Royal Dutch Shell and ChevronTexaco to renewables technologies is impressive, given that (1) the industry is a mature industry, the firms comprising it are constantly restructuring, and cutting all unnecessary R&D expenditures, (2) much renewable technology does not lie within firm core competencies, and (3) the primary obligation for oil companies today can be said to find, produce and sell oil and oil products (see Chapter 11). Seen in this light, much environmental criticism of the industry would seem misplaced.

Arguably, what differentiates super major commitment to renewables from more mundane corporate diversification is the scale of the problems involved, the number of technological solutions possible, the long lead times involved before any of these technologies becomes commercially viable on the scale necessary for profitability, and, last but not least, the need for complementarities with other corporate activities as demonstrated in Table 10.3. To the degree that the technology involved is not modular, such differences highlight the problems of intra and inter-firm coordination. For example, at each stage of the hydrogen powered fuel cell economy – hydrogen separation and manufacture, hydrogen transportation, hydrogen storage, hydrogen distribution, fuel cell manufacture, fuel cell compatibility problems, fuel cell safety – there are multiple known technological solutions, sometimes numbering in the dozens. And here we are confining ourselves to solutions currently known to be possible, not presently unknown solutions.

In such a case, the oil industry itself realises that it has coordination problems. A common solution to these problems is often that of organising R&D and innovation investments within the frame of various types of hybrid organisations.

Will these hybrid organisations work? A possible indication might be that of looking at industrial hybrid solutions elsewhere, notably in the refining and the upstream segments of the industry. The refining sector has been increasingly characterised by corporate partnering as has been stressed elsewhere in this volume. One can argue that such solutions are not beyond the purview of oil company management competence. This may be less true of the upstream industry where experiences appear to have been more mixed.[13]

---

12 In 2003, these two industrial segments, together with another segment, Shell Consumer, ran losses of $207 million.

13 The oil majors may have utilised hybrid organisations to press rents from their upstream cooperating partners. The situation has become worse as concentration of the significant oil producers becomes higher. In 1980 the top five oil firms accounted for 14 percent of all hydrocarbons spending. In 2000, the five accounted for 30 percent. This consolidation has strengthened the bargaining power of the oil majors leading to desperation in the oil industry service and construction sector. Oil company practices here have included 'launching of imprecise tenders, acceptance of dumping or abnormally low prices, disregarding contract clauses, setting unrealistic objectives and refusal to assume the operator's responsibilities'

To be successful hybrid organisational relationships need the commitment of a large amount of resources, support from the partnering parties, and pressure to perform. High cost offshore oil or natural gas projects tend to fulfil all three of the above criteria. By definition, these are costly, demand resources, and are visible to the partnering parties. There is also considerable pressure for the hybrid arrangement to perform. A complex partnering arrangement among a large oil major operator and a set of offshore service firms has these characteristics. Furthermore many of these parties will have had a long term relationship with the oil company operator, and do not wish to damage it. For its part, the oil company operator will want to retain the advantages of flexibility, access to outside knowledge, and risk sharing in its hybrid arrangement. The hybrid relationship works because of its profitability and the pressure to perform. (In this respect, the offshore oil industry shares many facets with other high technology firms employing hybrid organisational arrangements.)

The problem with renewables and other GHG minimisation technologies is that they may not have these characteristics. They exist for the purpose of generating mutual knowledge. They have very long lead times. Nor are the economic returns from investment in such technologies sufficient to exert the same degree of pressure on the cooperating parties as in the case of a costly, but profitable, offshore project. Finally, and most importantly, perhaps with the exception of modular technologies, there are severe coordination problems. The renewables path is unmarked. Oil companies and other energy companies are willing to invest in renewable technologies. What remains is the dilemma of who is going to be the 'playmaker', the agent who will determine the nature of future industry standards, who will encourage or perhaps even co-finance the infrastructure necessary for success, and who will define the terms of future competition. Here, governments may begin to play a more active role than previously. In this regard, the recently launched multi-billion US dollar *Hydrogen Posture Plan* (United States Department of Energy, 2004) may be a sign of things to come.

## References

Armour, H.O., and D. J. Teece (1980), 'Vertical Integration and Technological Innovation', *The Review of Economics and Statistics*, **62** , pp.470-474.

Avati, H. (2003), 'Love Affair Gone Sour', Petroleum Economist, December, p. 1.

Besen, S.M., and J. Farrell (1994), 'Choosing How to Compete: Strategies and Tactics in Standardization', *Journal of Economic Perspectives*, **8**(2) Spring, pp. 117-131.

BP Solar (2004), 'Photovoltaic Modulers: Millenia', http://www.wisdomlight.com.np/millennia.htm. Accessed June 21, 2004.

Carleton, W.T., J.M. Nelson and M.S. Weisbach (1998), 'The Influence of Institutions on Corporate Governance through Private Negotiations: Evidence from TIAA-

---

(Avati, 2003, p.1). Such a record does not encourage hopes for similar hybrid organisational arrangements in the renewables field.

CREF', *The Journal of Finance*, **53**(4) August, pp 1335-1362.

CERES (2004), 'Global Warming Resolutions at US Oil Companies Bring Policy Commitments from Leaders and Record High Votes at Laggards', http://www.ceres.org/news/
news_item.php?nid=56. Accessed November 30, 2004.

Corporate Library (2004), 'Shareholder Proposals', http://www.thecorporatelibrary.com. Accessed October 12, 2004.

Crawford, V.P. (1982), 'Disagreement in Bargaining', *Econometrica*, **50**(3) May, pp. 607-637.

Creusen, H. and B. Minne (2000), *Falling R&D but Stable Investments by Oil Companies: Why?* Research Memorandum no. 164, The Hague: CPB Netherlands Bureau for Economic Policy Analysis, April.

Duncan, A. and A. Sauer (2002), *Changing Oil: Emerging Environmental Risks and Shareholder Value in the Oil and Gas Industry*, Washington, D.C: World Resource Institute.

Energy Information Administration (1994), *Performance Profile of Major Energy Producers, 1993*, Washington D.C.: U.S. Department of Energy, available at http://www.eia..doe.gov/emeu/frs/pphype.html. Accessed August 1, 2004.

ExxonMobil (2001), 'Global Climate Change', April.

Ghosh, A. (1985), *Competition and Diversification in the United States Petroleum Industry*, Westport, Conn: Greenwood Press, Quorum Books.

Gow, D. (2003), 'BP Bosses Stay Safe and not Sorry as Protests Mark Meeting', *The Guardian*, April 25.

Grant, R.M. (1995), *Contemporary Strategic Analysis: Concepts, Techniques, Applications*, 2nd edition, Oxford: Blackwell Publishers.

Heifat, C.F. (1989), 'Investment Choices in the Petroleum Industry', *Journal of Economic Behavior and Organization*, **11**(2), pp. 253-283.

Kolk, A. and D. Levy (2001), 'Winds of Change: Corporate Strategy, Climate Change and Oil Multinationals', *European Management Journal*, **19**(5), pp. 501-509.

Lamont, O. (1997), 'Cash Flow and Investment: Evidence from Internal Capital Markets', *The Journal of Finance*, **52**, 1 March, pp. 83-109.

Levy, D.L. and A. Kolk (2002), 'Strategic Responses to Global Climate Change: Conflicting Pressures on Multinationals in the Oil Industry', *Business and Politics*, **4**(3), pp. 275-300.

_____ and S. Rothenberg (1999), 'Corporate Strategy and Climate Change in the Global Automobile Industry', Working Paper E-99-13 Global Environmental Assessment Project, Belfer Center for Science and International Affairs, John F. Kennedy School of Government, Harvard University, October, 28pp.

Lynch, M.C. (1993), 'Shoulder against Shoulder: The Evolution of Oil Industry Strategy', *Journal of Energy and Development*, **91**(1), pp.15-56.

Macalister, T. (2000), 'BP Bows to Solar Power Pressure,' *The Guardian*, May 10.

Mansley, M. (2002), 'Risking Shareholder Value? ExxonMobil and Climate Change: An Investigation of Unnecessary Risks and Missed Opportunities', Claros Consulting: Claros Discussion Paper, May, http://www.ragm.com/exxon/

RiskValueReport.pdf. Accessed September 30, 2004.

Markides, C. and P. J. Williamson (1996), 'Corporate Diversification and Organizational Structure', *Academy of Management Journal*, **39**, pp. 340-367.

Merewether, E.A. (2003), 'Alternatives Sources of Energy – An Introduction to Fuel Cells,' *USGS Survey Bulletin # 2179*, 7

Milliam, K. (2004), 'Investors Ask for Climate Factors', *Explorer* (American Association of Petroleum Geologists) http://www.aapg.org/explorer/2004/04apr/dal_climate.2.cfm. Accessed November 2, 2004.

Office of Energy Efficiency and Renewable Energy: Hydrogen Fuels Cells (2004-2005), 'Hydrogen Production and Delivery'http://www.eere.energy.gov/hydrogenandfuelcells/production/basics.html. Accessed September 14, 2004.

Powell, W.W. (1987), 'Hybrid Organizational Arrangements: New Form or Transitional?', *California Management Review*, **30**(1), pp. 67-99.

Prahalad, C. K. and P.J. Williamson (1996), 'Corporate Diversification and Organisational Structure', *Academy of Management Journal*, 39, pp. 485-502.

Prahalad, C.K. and R.A. Bettis (1986), 'The Dominant Logic: A New Linkage Between Diversity and Performance', *Strategic Management Journal*, **7**, pp. 485-501.

Rowlands, I.H. (2000), 'Beauty and the Beast? BP's and Exxon's Positions on Global Climate Change', *Environment and Planning*, **18** (2) pp. 339-354.

Simpert, J.L. and I. M. Duhaime (1997), 'In the Eyes of the Beholder: Conceptualizations of Relatedness Held by Managers of Large Diversified Firms', *Strategic Management Journal*, **18**(2), pp. 111-125.

Skjaerseth, J.B. and T. Skodvin (2001), 'Climate Change and the Oil Industry: Common Problems, Different Strategies', *Global Environmental Politics*, **1** (4), pp. 43-64.

_____ (2002), 'The Oil Industry and Climate Policy: Corporate Sources of International Envronmental Regime Effectiveness', paper presented at the 43th Annual ISA Convention, New Orleans, Louisiana, 23-27 March, 32pp.

Tippee, B. (2004), 'Point of View: IFP Chief Says Industry's Key Challenges are Fossil-energy Supply, Climate Change', *Oil and Gas Journal Online* at http://ogi.pennent.com/articles/EdPro_Article_Display.cfm?&Section=Articles&Subsection=Display&ARTICLE_ID=204247&PUBLICATION_ID=7&%20amp.VERSION_NUM=9. Accessed August 2, 2004.

United States Department of Energy (2004), *Hydrogen Posture Plan: An Integrated Research, Development, and Demonstration Plan* (April).

# PART 3
## Conclusion

## Chapter 11

# Conclusion – The Limits of the Firm: Configuration and Change?

### Jerome Davis

'If you can't forecast accurately, then forecast often' (H.L. Longwell, 2002, p. 100).

### Configuration and change

At the commencement of this volume, the dependence of the global economy on oil and oil products was likened to that of a set of riparian states to a major river system flowing through their territories, the river system being both a blessing and a curse. Nation states might set about minimizing its negative features. Individuals could pattern their behaviour around spring floods and summer drought. Upstream riparian states could undertake initiatives which disadvantage those further downstream. In this conclusion we come full circle to the beginning. Much as in our introductory riparian analogy, the oil and gas system remains vital to economic growth and progress. But how, we must ask, has the system changed? How has external change impacted the system? More importantly, how has the role of the oil multinational furthered this change and in turn been changed by it?

Each of the contributors to this volume has addressed an aspect of these questions. For convenience sake, these contributions can be subdivided into two major overlapping categories: the ongoing reconfiguration of the industry, prompted by the nature of the industry itself and by the nature of the demands placed on it by external actors, and the current challenges confronting the industry and their implications for future oil industry strategy. In the following, we will review the reconfiguration issues raised in this volume. Then we will proceed to a discussion of the future challenges confronting the industry.

### The oil MNE: ongoing reconfiguration? An MNE perspective

The widely accepted approach to multinational business activities has been that of Dunning's 'eclectic' model (alternatively named the OLI model) in which MNE profit maximization is seen as a function of O, ownership, L, location, and I, integration (Dunning, 1988, 1980; see also Buckley and Casson, 1976; Caves, 1996).

What is of interest here is combining these approaches into something useful in analysing oil MNE activities. This is in effect what Grossman and Helpman's arguments may facilitate, as expressed in a series of three NBER papers (2002a, 2002b and 2002c). What follows is derivative of their insights. We consider two of the Dunning variables, ownership and integration, in terms of transaction costs and principal agent relationships (see Grossman and Hart, 1980, for an early example of this approach). We assume that both with regard to outsourcing activities and keeping these in-house, transaction costs are incurred. The goal of management is to minimize these costs through a combination of externalization and internalization.

This leads to the problem expressed in Figure 11.1 below. The goal is to maximize revenues, $\Pi$, relative to managerial effort, $E$. $I$-$I'$ represents the indifference curve between those activities where the return on managerial effort is best confined to the firm $\Pi/E(F)$, or is better outsourced $\Pi/E(OS)$. $F$-$F'$ represents firm effort with respect to these two alternatives. As can be seen from the figure, some activities where the return/effort relationship is lowest are best confined to the firm ($A$-$B$ looking along the indifference curve). Between $B$ and $C$ (also along the indifference curve), there occur a set of activities where the returns on effort through

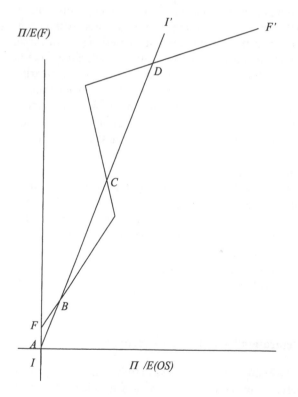

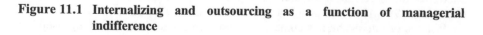

**Figure 11.1   Internalizing   and   outsourcing   as   a   function   of   managerial indifference**

internal contracting and management are less than those obtained through outsourcing these activities to outside contractors. These tend to be relatively low priority areas where the returns to firm management are not that high to begin with. The outsourcing involved is relatively straightforward.

But above this point the returns to management effort gain through integration within the firm ($C$ to $D$). Management in this case will attempt to retain these activities within the firm. It is here where the advantages of vertical and/or horizontal integration are best achieved.

What of the points above $D$? Clearly in terms of return on managerial effort these represent activities where the corporation would dearly love to enter. It is prevented from doing so due to two factors: either lack of resources or the problem of logistics (the latter being very important to an integrated oil company). Here, it is better for the firm to contract with other firms to provide the services or capital goods provided. It can always attempt to 'capture' some of the profits accruing its outsourcing partner through some sort of profit sharing arrangement.

Intuitively, the relationships illustrated in Figure 11.1 appear to fit reality within the oil industry.

Let us begin with oil industry outsourcing. There are two types of outsourcing here. The low level outsourcing of tasks well within the reach of the company is one of these. Here, in the upstream offshore industry the leasing of supply boats, the provision of drill pipe and so on, as Kvaløy has described in his contribution, are unlikely to be integrated within the firm (the interval $B,C$ on the corporate indifference cure in Figure 11.1). The technology is well known and profit margins for the successful supplying firm very low.

At the other end of the spectrum, the reverse is the case (above $D$ on $I,I'$). The outsourced activities are highly profitable in terms of return on management effort. This is for one of three reasons: (1) the firms involved highly skilled and/or employing advanced technology are earning significant rents and their acquisition costs exceed the resources of the integrated firm; (2) the nature of firm activities is so specialized that its acquisition is impractical; (it is here that the highly technical upstream service firms described by Wiig might be found; the specialized renewables technology firms discussed in Chapter 10 may also fall into this category) and (3) the firms have a specific locational/sunk cost advantage which makes them difficult to acquire (an attractive foreign market which for logistical reasons lies outside the purview of firm activities is an example of this location problem).

Staying with the upstream industry, Stabell's contribution investigates how firm exploration activities fit a Porter derived model, and how these might be reconfigured through his insights.

Moving into downstream activities, Davis investigates the limits of firm integration into refining and distribution activities in Chapter 3. These tend to cluster around point $C$ on $I,I'$ in Figure 11.1. When profits in refining and distribution are attractive, oil MNEs are liable to acquire refining assets, only to sell them off when profit rates fall, in order to focus on other activities yielding higher returns.

What of the activities lying above point $D$ in Figure 11.1, those activities which are highly profitable, but are beyond the means of firm acquisition? Osmundsen, Mohn, Emhjellen and Helgeland investigate the advantages conferred on corporate reconfiguration by the recent wave of corporate mergers. These are essentially three in nature, the retention of the more profitable activities of the two merged firms (and sale of the rest), organizational synergies, and last (but not least) the pursuit of resource intensive, highly profitable, but costly activities previously beyond the resources of the two individual firms, activities such as investment in giant fields in Russia, offshore Africa, and, last but not least, in the Caspian area.

There are two dynamic aspects, one of which Figure 11.1 does not convey, the other, an aspect, perhaps inadequately treated in this book. Firstly, Figure 11.1 is static. In fact, firms are constantly managing their $F$-$F'$ boundaries, depending on shifts in transport costs, crude prices, technology and competition. It is the management of these $F$-$F'$ boundaries which we argue have affected refining operations which can be effectively 'outsourced' or divested entirely (the range of activities between $B$ and $C$ in Figure 11.1) or upstream activities (activities above $D$). Secondly, and perhaps more importantly, the theoretical roots of the figure lie in the principal-agent problem, the ability of a principle to coordinate and monitor a host of diverse agents all engaged in the diverse activities characteristic of vertically integrated multinational enterprises. This has led to oil company abandonment of geographically based organizational structures in favour of globally organized business units, 'increasingly based in subsidiary locations' (Levy and Kolk, 2002, p. 293), a topic not covered in this volume.

Other aspects of the reconfiguration of the oil industry focus on the external impact of such a reconfiguration. The contribution by Osmundsen, Emhjellen and Halleraker discusses the problems of scale lying behind the oil multinational investment decision making process, an analysis with implications for those countries with relatively small resource endowments. Noreng explores the European dimension of the restructuring wave, pointing out that national policies may impact on management decision making when it comes to corporate reconfigurations. And two chapters by Davis cover the issues of resource depletion and super major greenhouse gas investment strategies and the problems of coordination.

## The oil MNE: future challenges

There are not a few predictions as to how the international oil industry is evolving. Generally there seems to be consensus as to the following (see, for example, Simmons and Company, 2001):

- While there are corporate advantages to size, the mega-sized oil companies of today can pose problems, particularly as resources are diverted from vital investment areas towards more and more consolidation. (Here industry concern is focussed on exploration and development, not on investment in renewables.)

- There is a significant chance that demand for oil will outrun supply even at higher prices (particularly in the period after 2008).
- The industry needs new 'financial drivers' to increase its rates of exploration and production.
- These predictions are not uncommon, and have been made in many other contexts. While definitive answers to these predictions are beyond this book, the individual contributions may nevertheless shed some light and add to our appreciation.

*The costs of consolidation?*

A major theme of this volume has been the ongoing consolidation within the oil industry generally, the super majors in particular. This drive to consolidation was perhaps best reflected in Osmundsen, Mohn, Emhjellen and Helgeland (Chapter 2), and their analysis of super major *ex post* merger profitability, but is also a topic covered by the chapters on the refining industry (Davis in Chapter 3), on European restructuring (Noreng in Chapter 8), and on the status of renewable technologies in super major investment portfolios (Chapter 10).

While undoubtedly there have been both private and welfare economic gains from this consolidation process, there could well be associated political and economic costs as well.

These latter in large part may be due to the overall changes with have taken place in the oil industry since the heyday of 'big oil' when the Seven Sisters controlled upwards of 80 percent of all crude production in the world. Table 11.1 contrasts the worldwide crude and NGL production shares of the major companies in the year 2000. As can be seen from the table, the super majors produced no more than 11.6 percent of world crude and NGLs, a far cry from the figures of the late 1960s.

What is the significance of this downturn? There are two factors of interest here. Firstly, the crude production plans of the Seven Sisters earlier were virtually synonymous with the matching of OECD demand. If crude supply outran demand, it was implicitly assumed that the Seven Sisters were responsible. When, as was indeed the case in the early 1960s, demand outran supplies or vice versa the Seven Sisters were often blamed. (In the first oil crisis in 1973–74, blame took the form of criticizing the Seven Sisters orchestrating the crisis so as to obtain 'monopoly profits'.) This was not the case in the early 1970s. It is even less so today. From a consuming nation viewpoint the super majors cannot of themselves solve any future shortfall in crude and NGL supplies. To assume otherwise is to delude one self, much as was the case in the early 1970s, when OPEC had taken over the role of supplier of crude to the world.

**Table 11.1    Global crude oil and NGL production shares in 2000 – major producing companies**

| Companies | Share of Worldwide Production (pct) |
|---|---|
| Saudi Arabian Oil | 10.6 |
| National Iranian Oil | 4.9 |
| Petroleos Mexicanos | 4.8 |
| Petroleos de Venezuela | 4.4 |
| Iraq National Oil | 3.5 |
| *ExxonMobil* | *3.4* |
| *Royal Dutch Shell* | *3.1* |
| Nigerian National Petroleum | 2.7 |
| *Chevron/Texaco* | *2.6* |
| Abu Dhabi National Oil | 2.6 |
| *BP/Amoco* | *2.5* |
| Kuwait Petroleum | 2.2 |
| Lukoil | 2.1 |
| **Total** | **48.0** |

*Source*: L. Spancake (2002). Super major shares are in italics

A second factor of importance is that even including the major OPEC state-owned producers, the total share of major oil company producers is no more than 48 percent of the world total, world production of crude is far more dispersed today than it was 35 years ago. Of particular significance is that the Middle Eastern state owned company share, that of the companies producing the lowest cost crude, is no more than 23 percent. Yet, barring unforeseen events, these are the sources of future crude supplies.

Policies followed by OPEC producers have tended directly or indirectly not to be helpful in this regard. On the one hand, the super majors and other companies have been granted access to Middle Eastern resources only under such restrictive conditions as to discourage investment in the Persian Gulf areas: on the other, many OPEC governments, intent on capturing rents from their national oil companies, have tended to restrain these from the increased investments required for the matching of future supply and demand.

*A capacity shortfall?*

Super major mergers, it has been argued elsewhere, are the result of two drivers, a need for higher expected returns on exploration investments, a need to replace those reserves produced annually with new reserves or, even better, to increase future oil company reserves net of annual production. Increasingly oil and gas projects are being evaluated on a portfolio basis, in particular through real options analysis. Such projects are frequently risky and as the sums involved in the projects are huge. An offshore African project, for example, can cost upwards of a billion dollars or more. The super majors are increasingly entering consortia with each other to develop them, a logical consequence of attempting to maximize long run shareholder value while reducing portfolio risk (US Energy Information Administration, 2003b, p. 65). This tendency towards gigantism is often fallaciously confused with the arguments that future supplies of crude and NGLs are about to run out (see Davis, Chapter 9). Here it is important to distinguish between a shorter-term production (or for that matter, refining[1]) capacity shortfall, and any possible approaching depletion of worldwide reserves. The two phenomena should be seen independently of one another. In this context, we look at the problems of production capacity. Our argument is that future supplies do exist, but an industry inability to keep up with demand may result in a capacity crisis.

*A trend towards gigantism?*

The 'flight' of the large majors: ExxonMobil, Shell, ChevronTexaco, BP-Amoco and others from the North Sea has been noted previously in this volume (Chapter 8). That there is evidence that this flight also involves North America is demonstrated in Table 11.2. This table contrasts the pre-merger total US crude production figures for ExxonMobil, BP, ChevronTexaco with post merger production figures. The drop in figures is remarkable, particularly for BP. (BP's production drops from a total of 600 million bbls for 1994, the total for BP, Arco and Amoco, to 224 million bbls in 2001). The fall in US production is also reflected in losses of 'market share' for these firms. From a share of 18.6 percent of total US crude production in 1994, BP Amoco Arco's share fell to 8.7 percent in 2001. Figures for the other two are somewhat less dramatic from 10.2 percent to 7.5 percent (ExxonMobil) and 9.8 to 8 percent (ChevronTexaco). A similar drop-off in interests has been registered for the North Sea oil province.

---

1   It should be noted in this context that more and more of the crude coming onto world markets today is of the 'sour' variety. A major future refining task therefore is to upgrade existing facilities so as to match sour crude changing market demand. Failing this, it could well be that a refining inability to deliver higher grade products may be a cause of a future supply crisis.

**Table 11.2    Pre- and post-merger production (US): ExxonMobil, BP Amoco and ChevronTexaco**

|  | 1994 | 2002 |
|---|---|---|
|  | --------------million bbls/year ----------- | |
| Exxon | 216 } | |
| Mobil | 114 } | 210 |
|  |  |  |
| BP | 251 | |
| Amoco | 107 } | 243 |
| Arco | 242 } | |
|  |  |  |
| Chevron | 158 } | |
| Texaco | 158 } | 224 |

*Source*: US Energy Information Administration, 2003, p. 62

For it is on the discovery and development of giant oil fields that the world oil economy depends. Table 11.3 illustrates the problem nicely. Fourteen fields producing in excess of 500 000 bbls/day alone account for 20 percent of crude produced today. Another 41 fields producing between 200 000 and 500 000 bbls/day account for a further 15 percent. If we include all those fields currently producing 100 000 bbls/day the over-all total worldwide is only 116 fields which alone account for 47 percent of the total crude produced and this number is only about 2.7 percent the total number of producing fields! In short, the world of oil can be characterized in terms of a few giants and many midgets.

**Table 11.3    Giant fields and the others: size is important**

| Field Size | Number of Fields | Average Production | Percent of World Total |
|---|---|---|---|
| --- bbl/day-- | | --- bbl/day--- | ---- pct.---- |
| >500 000 | 14 | 993 000 | 20 |
| 300-500 000 | 12 | 342 000 | 6 |
| 200-300 000 | 29 | 221 000 | 9 |
| 100-200 000 | 61 | 130 000 | 12 |
| <100 000 | 4000 | +9 000 | 53 |

*Source*: Simmons, 2003

**Table 11.4**    **Giant fields/mega projects coming on stream (over 500 million bbls reserves)**

| Year | Number of fields | Total production |
|------|------------------|------------------|
| 2003 | 9 | 1.2 million bbls/day |
| 2004 | 11 | 2 million bbls/day |
| 2005 | 18 | 3 million bbls/day |
| 2006 | 11 | 2 million bbls/day |
| 2007 | 3 | 0.320-0.470 million bbls/day |
| 2008 | 3 | 1.270 million bbls/day* |

\* Of which 900 000 bbls/day from Kashagan (Caspian-Kazakhistan).
*Source*: Skrebowski in the *Petroleum Review*, January 2004, pp. 18-19

If the future of oil is determined by the so called 'mega projects', there may be problems on the horizon. The number of giant fields discovered and coming into production seems to be peaking and will shortly be falling (for the short term at least). Table 11.4, a tabulation of the giant fields due to come into production between 2003 and 2008, illustrates this problem. There is a significant falling off of projected giants coming on stream in the years 2007 and 2008. This trend is reinforced by the discoveries of the last several years. Success here has been disheartening. In the year 2000 there were six oil/gas giants found, seven giant gas/condensate find and three gas finds; in 2001, two oil/gas finds, four gas condensate finds, and two gas finds; and in 2002 just two oil/gas finds and one gas find. Given the fact that on average six years elapses between discovery and production, the trend does not bode well for 2007 and 2008, particularly in that world demand is scheduled to rise from 78 million bbls/day in 2001 to around 84 million bbls/day in 2008 and production from existing sources is declining by around one million bbls/day per year. There are 21 other giant discoveries which could be used to 'plug the gap', but only three of these involve Western MNEs in operator roles.

Furthermore, many of the giant fields in Saudi Arabia and elsewhere currently in production are aging. For many of these fields, production is declining or is set to go into decline. For others, continued production will involve higher costs than previously. Matthew R. Simmons, in a detailed study of Saudi Arabian reserves, has advanced the thesis that these reserves quite likely contain considerably less than the amount generally anticipated today. Five Saudi super giant fields discovered between 1940 and 1965 produce 90 percent of all Saudi Arabian oil. Characteristic of these great fields was that they produced primarily from one geological oil bearing sedimentary layer which had excellent permeability and porosity characteristics and enjoyed a water drive from an underground aquifer. There are about 85 other oil fields in Saudi Arabia, but many of these are small and there is little to indicate that these will be as productive as the five super giants. Signs are that many have problems with porosity, permeability, or lack of water drive or all three. Producing from these fields may be a good deal more costly than is currently thought (Simmons, 2003). Even secondary recovery from the larger fields may be difficult. [2]

*Is non-conventional crude the answer?*

An alternative to finding and developing conventional oil resources has long been the development of non-conventional crude, here predominantly the Canadian Albertan tar sands and Venezuelan Orinoco heavy crude mentioned in Chapter 9. Will developments here counter any short term future shortfall?

**Table 11.5    Unconventional crude oil resources: Orinoco bitumen and Canadian 'tar sands'**

|  | Reserves | | Production | | Total Projected Investment |
|---|---|---|---|---|---|
|  | Total in Place | Re-cover-able | 2004 | 2015 | To 2015 |
|  | -------- billion. bbls------ | | ----mio. bbls/year--- | | ---$ bio-- |
| Orinoco | 1300 | 270 | 177[a] | 241[a] | 12[a] |
| Western Canada | 1600 | 175 | 365 | 730 | 60 |
| Totals | 2900 | 445 | 542 | 971 | 72 |

[a]Zuata, Hamaca and Cerro Negro areas

*Sources*: Talwani, 2002, pp.19-22; National Energy Board of Canada, 2004, pp. xii-xiv

Table 11.5 illustrates the short term perspective and gives a thumbnail view of the issues involved here. Currently recoverable reserves are enormous, Orinoco bitumen alone promising as much (or even more) as Saudi Arabia. Investments in unconventional crude resources are also significant. By 2015, seventy billion dollars will have been invested in these projects. Yet the total amount of refinable crude predicted produced by that time will be relatively modest, in the range of 2.66 million barrels of oil per day, 970 million barrels per year. To place these figures in context, given a per annum 2 percent increase in global crude consumption, by the year 2010, global crude demand will be in the range of 30 billion bbls/year. In relation to current commitments, Orinoco and Canadian unconventional oil will at best cover 3.23 percent of world demand by then, and, given necessary project lead times, it is difficult to see how this forecast production can be further increased in the next six years.

---

2    For example it is estimated that it will take the Haradh project some 500 000 bbls/day of water injection to recover 300 000 bbls/day of crude – and the project is enormous: 224 producing wells with horizontal completions, 103 water injection wells, a salt water treatment plant and 250 kms of pipeline to convey the water to the injection wells. Nor have advanced oil technologies necessarily helped in the area, as experiences with the Omani giant Yibal have shown (ibid).

What is at issue here? It is important to remember in this context that the some two million barrels a day shortfall is a drop in the ocean when it comes to global oil consumption which currently stands at some 83 million barrels a day. What might make this shortfall critical is that while oil consumption in set to continue to increase (as Asian, particularly China's, economies continue to develop and expand), production from newly found giant fields may be unable to cover demand by the year 2007 should current trends hold. ExxonMobil's Longwell states the problem succinctly:

> [W]hile demand increases, existing production declines. To put a number on it, we expect that by 2010 about half the daily volume needed to meet projected demand is not in production today and that is the challenge...(Longwell, 2002).

## New 'financial drivers'?

According to the recently published International Energy Agency (IEA), *World Energy Outlook 2004* (2004), some four trillion dollars of upstream investment will be needed to keep up with current global demand for oil and gas for the next 25 years. The figures for matching increased future demand, upstream and downstream are even more impressive. Total investments in oil and gas are forecast to amount to more than $6 trillion to 2030, or around 38 percent of all global energy investment to 2030. Other estimates of the need for additional investments are hardly more optimistic. Discussing the need to meet forecasted demand for 2010, ExxonMobil's Longwell in an interview with *World Energy* mentioned a figure as high as one trillion US dollars over the next eight years, or roughly $125 billion per annum, a figure 'substantially more than industry is spending today' (Longwell, 2002, p. 101).

Nor are the incremental reserve increases on upstream investment particularly encouraging. Simmons has put it succinctly for the entire industry. Citing Andersen's 2001 report on global exploration and production trends, he notes that in 1996, 144 companies invested US$65.5 billion to produce 24.8 million barrels of oil equivalent (BOE). In the year 2000 capital expenditures totalled US$107.8 billion, and production was no more than 26.9 million BOE (Simmons, 2001).

How is the demand for future capital investment to be satisfied? In part, capital will be attracted to the oil industry due to market forces. Future 'shortages' of crude oil or of refined oil products will undoubtedly attract investment. Much here depends on the willingness of OPEC governments and their SOEs to ante up the sums necessary.

The IEA sees an increased supporting role of government in this regard:

> Governments will play a vital role in creating the preconditions for energy investment. Increasingly, this will involve adopting the policies and setting the conditions for private investment, relegating to the past direct state-financed investment or ownership. This will involve greater attention to overall policy, legal and regulatory frameworks, identifying changing risks and ways to lower barriers to investment. In many parts of the world, there

is still a long way to go to ensure that basic instruments of good governance, both in the energy sector and more generally, are reinforced, applied and respected (International Energy Agency, 2004).

It will be interesting to see if the Agency's strictures are followed in the future, particularly since the oil and gas industry today as yesterday has been an area of state assertion of its ownership prerogatives.

## Conclusion

To conclude, the contribution of this book lies in its analysis of the consolidation of the oil industry, as exemplified by the super majors, and how this consolidation impacts on the range of issues discussed in the individual chapters and in this conclusion.

To return to the riverine analogy of our introduction, the presence of water or its absence has long been a major political issue to riparian states, dependent on a major river for their water supplies. In the oil world too, there must be concern as to how the evolving world of oil is renewing emphasis on finding political solutions to problems of supply, capacity, investment, and cost.

A good example of an increased reliance on political skills was referred to earlier in this chapter, in the discussion of the importance of giant fields, of which there is at least a short-term shortage. This is illustrated in Table 11.4 which shows the mega projects coming on stream in the next eight years. Six of the 55 projects listed are Caspian projects (Karachaganak, phase 2, 200 000 bbls/day in 2003; Azeri-Chiraz-Gunashli, 1 000 000 bbls/day in 2005: Kashagan phase 1, 450 000bbls/day, and the Tengiz expansion, 250-450 000 bbls/day in 2006; Kashagan phase 2, 900 000 bbls/day in 2008). Impressively these six projects alone account for almost 51 percent of the total anticipated production. Looking beyond 2008, the only reasonably certain giant projects worldwide listed for the years 2009 and 2010 are Karagachanak, phases 3 and 4 (daily production unspecified) in 2009 and Kashagan, phase 3 (1 200 000 bbls/day) in 2010 (*Petroleum Review*, January, 2004, p. 20). There are few geographic areas characterized by more political uncertainty, remoteness and uncertainty than the Caspian, where the clashing interests of Western Europeans, Americans, Russians and Iranians are combined with a high degree of regional instability, ethnic and religious conflict, and autocratic regimes.

While Western consuming states are becoming more dependent on geographically remote, politically unstable regions for supplies of crude, they are confronting an increased challenge from a growth in worldwide demand, prompted by such economically rapidly developing nation states as India, China and the ASEAN nations. In the last several years, China alone has accounted for 40 percent of the overall growth in world demand for crude and oil products. In 2003 the Chinese economy surpassed the Japanese in its consumption of oil products, and this increasing trend is expected to continue.

Governments of countries such as China cannot be expected to sit passively by while oil consumers in the industrialized countries gobble up all the major promising petroliferous prospects. The Chinese National Petroleum Company has acquired concessions in Sudan, Iran, Iraq, Kazakhstan, Venezuela, Peru and Azerbaijan. The Chinese are also contributing heavily to the development of Saudi natural gas reserves, and are establishing friendly relations with the Kingdom.

With economic development the demand for oil grows and with it come new entrants to compete for the available resources. Simultaneously, the search for oil resources is becoming more politically uncertain than ever before in history. What Daniel Yergin, in his Pulitzer Prize-winning industry classic has termed 'the epic quest for oil, money and power' (Yergin, 1991) is entering into a new phase where the stakes are higher and the outcomes are more uncertain. Yet whatever the outcome, the four super majors will continue to form change and, in turn, be formed by it.

## References

Avati, H. (2003), 'Love Affair Gone Sour', *Petroleum Economist*, December, p. 1.

Buckley, P. and M. Casson, (1976), *The Future of the Multinational Enterprise*, London: Macmillan.

Caves, P. (1971/6), 'International Corporations: The Industrial Economics of Foreign Investment, *Economica*, **56**, pp. 279 -293.

_____ (1996), *Multinational Enterprise and Economic Analysis*, Cambridge: Cambridge University Press.

Dunning J. (1980), 'Towards an Eclectic Theory of International Production', *Journal of International Business Studies*, **11**, pp. 48 -72.

_____ (1988), 'The Eclectic Paradigm of International Production', *Journal of International Business Studies*, **19**, pp.1-31.

Grossman, S. and E. Helpman(2002a), 'Outsourcing in the Global Economy', *NBER Working Paper No. 8728*, Cambridge, Massachusetts: National Bureau of Economic Research, February.

_____ (2002b), 'Outsourcing versus FDI in Industry Equilibrium', *NBER Working Paper No. 9300*, Cambridge, Massachusetts: National Bureau of Economic Research, April.

_____ (2002c), 'Managerial Incentives and the International Organization of Production', *NBER Working Paper No. 9403*, Cambridge, Massachusetts: National Bureau of Economic Research, December.

International Energy Agency (2004), *World Energy Outlook 2004*, Paris: International Energy Agency.

Levy, D.L. and A. Kolk (2002), 'Strategic Responses to Global Climate Changes: Conflicting Pressures on Multinationals in the Oil Industry', *Business and Politics* 4(3), pp. 275-300.

Longwell, H.J. (2002), 'The Future of the Oil and Gas Industry: Past Approaches, New Challenges', *World Energy*, **5**(3), pp. 100-104.

National Energy Board of Canada (2004), *Canada's Oil Sands: Opportunities and*

*Challenges to 2015; An Energy Market Assessment*, Ottawa: NEB, May.

Sever, M. (2004), 'Booking and Rebooking Oil Reserves', *Geotimes* (September) 4pp. available at http://www.geotimes.org/sept04/resources.html.

Simmons, M.R. (2001), 'Financial Drivers and Oil Industry Restructuring: What is in the Cards?' ppt presentation to the Oslo Industry Evaluation Roundtable, Simmons & Co International, August 17, 2001.

_____ (2003), 'The Saudi Arabian Oil Miracle', Power Point Presentation at the 'Conference: Future of Global Oil Supply-Saudi Arabia', Washington D.C: Simmons & Company International for the Center for Strategic and International Studies, February 24, http://www.csis.org/energy/

Skrebowski, C. (2004), 'E&P Review: Oil Field Mega Projects 2004', *Petroleum Review*, January, pp. 18-21.

Spancake, L. (2002), 'Figure 2. Worldwide Crude Oil and Natural Gas Liquids Production Shares of Companies with More Than 2 Percent of Worldwide Production, 2000', available at http://www.eia.doe/gov/emeu/finance/mergers/fig2.htm.

Talwani, M. (2002), 'The Orinoco Heavy Oil Belt in Venezuela (Or Heavy Oil to the Rescue?)', Energy Study: *Latin America* (The James A. Baker III Institute of Public Policy of Rice University, April), 34pp, available at http://www.rice.edu/energy/latinamerica.html.

United States Energy Information Administration (2000), 'U.S. Independent Oil and Gas Producers, 1993-1998: Survivors and Nonsurvivors', April, available at http://www.eia. doe.gov/emeu/finance/sptopics/Aapg2/sld001.htm.

_____ (2003), *Performance Profiles of Major Energy Producers 2001*, Washington, D.C.

Yergin, D. (1991), *Prize: The Epic Quest for Oil, Money and Power*, New York: Simon and Schuster.

# Index

Note: Italic page numbers indicate figures & tables. Numbers in brackets preceded by *n* refer to footnotes.